FAMILY
ETHICS

Moral Traditions Series
James F. Keenan, SJ, Series Editor

FAMILY
ETHICS

PRACTICES
FOR
CHRISTIANS

JULIE HANLON RUBIO

GEORGETOWN UNIVERSITY PRESS / WASHINGTON, D.C.

Library of Congress Cataloging-in-Publication Data

Rubio, Julie Hanlon.
 Family ethics : practices for Christians / Julie Hanlon Rubio.
 p. cm.
 Includes bibliographical references and index.
 ISBN 978-1-58901-639-2 (pbk. : alk. paper)
 1. Family—Religious life. 2. Family—Religious aspects—Catholic Church.
3. Christian ethics—Catholic authors. I. Title.
 BX2351.R83 2010
 241'.63—dc22

                    2009024526

∞This book is printed on acid-free paper meeting the requirements of the American National Standard for Permanence in Paper for Printed Library Materials.

15 14 13 12 11 10   9 8 7 6 5 4 3 2
First printing

Printed in the United States of America

For Martin

Contents

Acknowledgments

I started out to write a history of American Catholic thinking on marriage and family, but it slowly became clear to me that I really wanted to write a book on family ethics to answer questions that refused to go away. I changed course and began the work I think I have been meaning to write since I first began to study theology.

Along the way, many people have helped me think through and prepare this book. Series editor Jim Keenan and Georgetown University Press director Richard Brown were incredibly supportive of my ideas from the beginning, and the many editors who have worked on the text have saved me from countless errors.

Colleagues in professional organizations and journal boards generously provided feedback on papers and articles that turned into chapters as the book evolved. Even more important, people such as Flossie Bourg, David McCarthy, Bill Mattison, Jana Bennett, Tobias Winright, John Berkman, and David Cloutier have engaged me in many long conversations about discipleship and family life. I am also mindful of colleagues whose writing on marriage and family paved the way for my work: Michael Lawler, William Roberts, Margaret Farley, Patricia Beattie Jung, Barbara Andolsen, Lisa Sowle Cahill, and Christine Firer Hinze. Without them there would be no Christian family ethics.

At Saint Louis University I have had the support of several wonderful research assistants—Heidi Bess Bergeron, C. Annie Chen, Sarah Sparks, and C. Michael Shea. The university also granted me sabbatical leave and a Mellon summer research grant in 2006 that allowed me to write the first several chapters of the book uninterrupted. Discussions with students in my courses—Sexual Ethics, Social Justice, and Marriage and Family Ethics— helped to develop my thinking on the idea of practices and made me more realistic in my outlook on them. The Puleo family gave me the opportunity to go to Nicaragua with four of my students in the summer of 2007 to experience both incredible poverty and overwhelming hospitality and to think again about the ethical import of American family life. My many students who have made much more radical choices than I have inspired me to keep searching for ways to bring social justice concerns into the lives of ordinary Christian families.

Work with the Karen House Catholic Worker community in St. Louis never failed to get me thinking about the deficiencies of middle-class life in the suburbs where I live. The discussion group my husband and I formed at our parish five years ago has been an ongoing source of support as we balanced practices of resistance with the ordinary travails of family life. We are blessed to have Richard Baugh and Elizabeth George, Mike and Maureen Hoock, and Kathleen Gallagher and Jim Buckley as our good friends and companions on the journey.

It is always my own family that offers me the most inspiration and the most spirited challenges. Dominic, Tom, and Stephen tolerated my enthusiasm for new practices and were generous with their love when I had a deadline to meet or just needed to laugh. My husband, Marty, always listened, even when he surely wished we could simply be married for a change, instead of talking about it. He has been my friend for twenty-five years and my husband for seventeen. With deep gratitude for his love for me, his work as a teacher, and his care for our three boys, I dedicate this book to him.

Why Be Concerned with the Ordinary?

My thirteen-year-old son tells me he does not understand why I spend my time writing, teaching, and talking about ordinary things. For him, the more important questions are the extraordinary ones: What does it mean to have faith? What happens when you die? Is the Bible true? Is there human life on other planets? How did the world begin? In his confirmation classes at church and in conversations with friends of different faiths, my son ponders these questions.

He is not alone in his fascination with big questions. Popular religious discussions often revolve around enduring controversies both theological and moral. At Saint Louis University, my colleagues and I tell students that if they want to "ask the big questions," they should major in theology.[1] Undergraduate theology courses are far easier to fill and construct if one focuses on enduring theological questions such as the meaning of existence or hard cases in moral life. Books on such subjects are more easily conceived and published because of the obvious importance of the subject matter.

Even academic moral theologians tend to be more invested in moral issues such as euthanasia, abortion, and war than in the ordinary struggles of daily life. Moral theology had its beginning as a pastoral theology recorded in manuals designed to aid confessors in giving appropriate penances.[2] The sins that dominated were ordinary: sexual immorality, deception of friends and family, work in compromising occupations, and failure in keeping commitments.[3] However, the academic discipline of moral theology came to focus first on technical analyses of sexual sins and later, especially in the post–Vatican II era, on significant problems in medical and social ethics.[4] Ordinary dilemmas that appeared in the moral manuals no longer interested those devoted to the study of moral theology. Academics wanted to distance themselves from the parochialism of pastoral cases and give more attention to pressing ethical issues in public life.[5] Ordinary dilemmas such as those taken up by the manualists became the concern of those doing pastoral work and writing in pastoral journals.

Moral theology as it is taught today focuses not only on extraordinary issues but also on extraordinary people and their exemplary lives. Courses in social justice uphold heroes such as Dorothy Day or Oscar Romero, who sacrificed ordinary home life and career paths, along with material comforts, and, in Romero's case, life itself, for the sake of a greater cause. These persons are presented as role models for students seeking to live authentic Christian lives. Even if their professors dare not hope that their students will become saints or martyrs, they do hope to inspire change by telling stories of extraordinary commitment. The more mundane dilemmas of ordinary Christians are rarely discussed.

In his influential book *Heroes, Saints, and Ordinary Morality*, Andrew Flescher defends this focus on the extraordinary and goes further by defining morality as the struggle to be truly virtuous rather than living an ordinary life.[6] He suggests that readers should not dismiss the moral significance of figures like Dorothy Day by naming them as saints or heroes. Rather, "we ought to read about heroes and saints because of their potential to serve as mentors for those interested in living a virtuous life."[7] Hearing these stories will help ordinary people grow in virtue, and as they grow, their understanding of what is required of them will likewise increase.[8] More people will strive to live heroically, because they are no longer limited by the low expectations of the ordinary.

Though there are good reasons for Christians to read about the saints and martyrs, encouraging believers to follow the lead of extraordinary persons sidesteps some of the complexity of living a moral life. Flescher contends that, when we fail to take heroes and saints seriously enough, we fail in virtue.[9] Certainly he is correct to call attention to a widespread lukewarm commitment to living well. However, while a lack of virtue affects the ability to see the will of God and do it, other important concerns may hold people back from living heroic lives: uncertainties regarding, for instance, how family commitments ought to reshape responsibility for social justice, how the effects of simple living compare to engagement in the economy and sharing one's wealth, and whether participation in party politics might be more helpful to those in need than engagement in civil disobedience, to name but a few. Modern prophets such as Day inspire, but without the social analysis to consider particular choices, Christians are still left without moral guidance for all of the ordinary dilemmas that constitute their daily lives.

A sound moral theology that aspires to aid the discernment of ordinary Christians requires more realism, in the best sense of the term. Currently there is a tension in social ethics between those who focus on personal pursuit of perfection and those who engage in more realistic, public ethics. In a recent article Kristin Heyer draws attention to the divide in social ethics between the reformist model (represented by J. Bryan Hehir) and the radical model (represented by Michael Baxter).[10] While Hehir concentrates on applying principles of Catholic social teaching to policy debates, Baxter emphasizes the need to sustain the church as a contrast society formed by the works of mercy.[11] Baxter charges that mainstream American Catholic social ethics is marked by an unwillingness to allow theological discussion of ultimate ends—especially those upheld in the liturgy—to influence ethical analysis. As a result, faith is privatized.[12] He suggests that Christians ought to begin their resistance to American culture by spending time with family, reading the Bible, attending liturgy, and keeping the Sabbath.[13] Baxter argues that real political change must include work at the ground level, because Catholics are called "to live heroic lives patterned after the example of Christ and the saints," while Hehir recommends Catholic participation in public policy debates on economics, war, and other social issues of the day.[14]

A balanced ethical approach for ordinary believers would draw from both the reformist and the radical models. Radical social ethics is attractive because its clear invitation to discipleship seems more connected to the life of Jesus of Nazareth than the realist, natural law analysis of the reformists. In addition, it calls attention to how lay Christians live their everyday lives. Yet a major problem with ethics of this kind is that it often ignores families in order to focus on saints and heroes who are single and childless. Andrew Flescher's recent discussion, for instance, assumes that what makes a person a hero or saint happens outside the family.[15] He says, "Being humanely responsible is acknowledging that we do not have the luxury of retreating into our private lives where we can bask in the comfort of moral neutrality and stasis."[16] Those who live in families with children or others in need of care know that private life is rarely a luxurious retreat from responsibility or moral quandary. Potential for moral excellence and moral failure lies in the home as well as outside it. Both radical and reformist models tend to ignore this reality, but radical social ethics has at its core an impulse to examine every aspect of life in light of the gospel that can be harnessed by those who would like to give attention to ordinary ethical dilemmas. From the reformists we can adopt close analysis that takes account of the contingencies of real life in a fallen world. This combination offers a way to approach ordinary moral problems with enough rigor to yield useful answers and enough humility to avoid leaving ordinary people with saints and heroes as their only models.[17]

Some contemporary theologians of the family have begun to do just this, practicing what might be called the ethics of ordinary life. Florence Caffrey Bourg's book *Where Two or Three Are Gathered: Christian Families as Domestic Churches* is a wonderful example of a practical theology of the family.[18] Beginning with ecclesiology, she mines the Christian tradition for an understanding of families as domestic churches and then attempts to retrieve and flesh out the concept for contemporary Christians, providing both a vision and an account of how the vision is practiced in virtues nurtured in the home. The centerpiece of the book is her moving story of how she came to see her care for a sick child on one Holy Thursday as service to Christ. This new vision was not the result of a blinding light, she claims. Rather, "this incident illustrates the respective roles of the Church at large, the domestic church, sacramental liturgy, and ordinary activity as cooperative causes— with divine intervention—in the gradual formation of explicitly Christian sacramental vision."[19] Both her formation in the church and her experience as a parent led her to the point where she could see her action in the light of her Christian commitment: "If I hadn't heard that Gospel and participated in the Holy Thursday liturgy in years past, I wouldn't have had the necessary reference point to understand what it meant to wash the vomit off my son's feet. But if I hadn't washed the vomit off my son's feet, I wouldn't have had the necessary reference point to appreciate all those Holy Thursday Eucharists I had participated in before."[20] Ecclesial formation and specific domestic practices of care both contribute to her socially conscious understanding of domestic church. She provides not just a vision but a thick description of a family trying to live out that vision.

Bourg's final chapter calls attention to the problem that arises when a great idea in social ethics (Cardinal Bernadin's consistent ethic of life) is disconnected from specific contexts (primarily the family and neighborhood) where it must take shape.[21] Perceptively, she sees that Catholic social teaching cannot continue to operate simply at the level of policy. Rather, theologians must look to how and where values and practices are cultivated, and that means paying attention to the home. Bourg composes a list of practical questions to facilitate the cultivation of the consistent ethic of life: "What will we (not) buy the kids for their birthdays? Whom will we invite (or neglect to invite) to our home? How low on the food chain were our meals today? Is our babysitter being paid a living wage? Should I refrain from gossip as a habit of violence? Are the punishments I use with my kids mostly violent and retributive, or crafted to promote reconciliation and responsibility?" and so on.[22] Bourg has started to craft an extremely helpful ethical vision, yet important ethical questions such as the ones she puts before her readers are only just beginning to be asked.

David Matzko McCarthy's advocacy of the "open home" in his book *Sex and Love in the Home* can be seen in a similar light. He comes at the ethics of ordinary life by analyzing family practices that sustain a community. He contrasts the independent, upper-middle-class, "closed," suburban home where goods and services are purchased rather than exchanged with the open home where "ordinary practices of local interdependence are the substance of a complex system of interchange and a rich community life."[23] McCarthy explains that when people offer hospitality to other families' children, labor on a home improvement project, extra baked goods, or produce from a garden, they are engaging in an informal, asymmetrical network of gift exchange that, unlike the money economy, creates interdependent relationships.[24] Keeping up these practices is essential, in his view, for building community and maintaining a Christian home that is more than a private haven.

McCarthy's focus on the home is controversial in the context of Christian ethics. In opposition to major thinkers in the academy, McCarthy contends that the connected love of family and friends is more central to Christian life than the disinterested love of agape.[25] In contrast to those who in recent years have spoken of the family's mission to work for social justice in the world, McCarthy focuses on what families can do by staying home. He realizes that focusing on mundane practices such as snow shoveling and giving away clothes may concern those who would call our attention to grave social injustices that are so prevalent and so destructive. Yet, in the very particular descriptions of daily life that make up his contrast between the open and closed homes, he draws his readers' attention to the profound ways in which practices we assume to be mundane form a pattern of living, shape both adults and children into certain kinds of people, and constitute our most fundamental and enduring contribution to the world. The emphasis on everyday ethics in the works by both McCarthy and Bourg is a welcome change from a Christian ethics of the extraordinary.

Still, there is work to be done. McCarthy and Bourg provide visions capable of inspiring readers to adopt new practices, and they give powerful examples that are accessible to ordinary Christians. A healthy consciousness of the limits of individual families thankfully prevents either from counseling perfection. The next step is providing a more robust analysis of everyday family practices more akin to ethical treatments of sex, divorce, war, and economic justice that can aid moral discernment.

Yet, one might ask, if moral discernment is the goal, why is it necessary to turn to the family? Wouldn't it be more helpful to simply discuss the ethics of ordinary life without assuming a family context? After all, fewer than 25 percent of Americans have traditional families with two parents and children under eighteen, and less than half live in any kind of a family with children living at home. Still, with the exception of those who live alone or in nonfamily households (about one quarter), the vast majority do live in some sort of family, whether single-parent, blended, newly married, or empty-nesting.[26] Even intentional communities, whether religious or not, can be seen analogously as families. Jana Bennett uses the term "household" to include all of these groupings, as well as singles who are often left out of theological discussions.[27] I prefer an inclusive definition of family because families of some sort are the place where the majority of people encounter their most ordinary and pressing ethical dilemmas. Without a family context, an ethics of everyday life may remain marginal to many believers. I know that, as a teacher of Christian ethics, year after year I see students who are inspired by heroes and saints but remain at a complete loss as to how to integrate their examples into the family life to which they look forward. At the very least, this is a place to begin a substantive analysis of ethical practices, though I welcome readers who live outside family groupings to join in the conversation. Singles in the church remain a source of inspiration for a rigorous theology of the family, and along with Christian families they face decisions about the practices that shape their lives and the world around them.

Some may be concerned that more systematic ethical analysis in which I aim to engage may force abandonment of the strengths of the new theology of the family: its emphasis on the theological foundations of ethics and attention to character and virtue development. However, with care it is possible to retain these strengths and delve more deeply into ethical analysis. Virtue theory moves naturally from reflection on character to consideration of practices that shape persons in significant ways. Some admit that it can include casuistry of a certain kind.[28] Analysis of practices seems a necessary part of a wholistic ethics of ordinary life, yet not infrequently virtue ethicists have been reluctant to provide detailed reflection on practices.[29]

Avoiding this analysis leaves us with inadequate ethical models. For instance, James and Kathleen McGinnis, the founders of the Parenting for Peace and Justice network, are often used as exemplars when theologians want to talk about applied family ethics.[30] In their pastoral writing, the McGinnises speak of their desire to hold onto their social justice commitments while raising their three children. Their choices to live relatively simply, practice nonviolence, resist sex-role stereotyping, and involve their children in social action are seen as models of applied Catholic social teaching and the theology of the domestic church. While most would find their program hard to maintain, the McGinnis family is celebrated for efforts "to act for justice without sacrificing our children and to build family community without isolating ourselves from the world."[31]

Yet could the McGinnises' choices hold up to the rigors of academic ethics analysis? Some practices are relatively uncontroversial (recycling, exposing children to different cultures, avoiding physical punishment), while others (taking children to antiwar protests, buying mostly used clothing, offering hospitality to those without shelter) are far more complex. A few theologians have criticized the McGinnises' program as overly ambitious.[32] Others leave the ideal in place and imply that those with determination will strive to realize it, but do not argue for its validity in relation to other possible choices.[33] On the whole, writing like this is not taken as seriously as other forays into applied ethics, because the leaps from principle to practice are too quick, and difficult questions are avoided. It functions as inspiration rather than argument.[34]

The Catholic Worker model presents a similar difficulty. Dorothy Day becomes more a part of the Catholic social tradition every day, because her story presents a compelling, effective way of teaching social ethics. Her own unconventional family life receives significant attention, for she gave up being a partner and was an unusual mother and grandmother, in that she shared her living space, time, and possessions with the very poor.[35] Students who are exposed to her often pick up on the problem—her lifestyle is attractive, and they could go and live it now (and some do, joining intentional communities), but what about later, when they start families? Few seek family life like Day's, and not simply because they are insufficiently committed. Rather, they see other goods that would be lost if they embraced a life like hers. In the meantime most academic social ethicists present Day as a radical alternative without seriously analyzing her practices.[36] Many probably adopt some practices of simple living and political engagement but would allow that a more rigorous social analysis might lead in directions other than the ones Day chose. Her example remains challenging as personal witness but not as moral standard, because while it was clear to Day that one can draw a straight line from the Sermon on the Mount and the Last Judgment to a life of voluntary poverty, war resistance, and direct service to the poor, it is not so clear to the majority of Christians.[37]

Promoting radical practices without going through the kind of nuanced reflection that reformist social ethics embraces is insufficient. As Heyer notes, "prudential discernment" is needed in order to make good judgments, especially in the case of everyday dilemmas, which tend to be "more mundane and perhaps less straightforward than the cases of religious liberty or Nazi Germany."[38] While ethicists could demur that prudential discernment is the responsibility of individual Christians or pastoral theologians, it is not clear that the dilemmas of family life are any less serious or worthy of serious ethical consideration than the social and medical issues that remain subjects of intense concern.

This book is devoted to serious ethical analysis of the ordinary dilemmas most Christians face in their families or households. In the first part I draw on resources from the Catholic tradition: in chapter 1, the best of Catholic sacramental and liturgical theology on marriage, and in chapter 2, Catholic social teaching. I hope to show that both traditions speak to the ethical and social significance of marriage and family. In chapter 3 I pause to answer a crucial concern of critics of theology of the family: the limitations of a theology of ideals. I argue that the strength of the tradition is its ability to account for and hold together both grace and sin. It is from this vantage point that I begin ethical consideration of family practices. The second part offers five practical applications: eating, tithing, making love, serving, and praying. In these chapters Christian theological concerns are brought to bear on ordinary actions, social analysis is utilized to aid consideration of what is lacking in Christian family life, and hard questions are asked about the ethical significance of specific practices.

Throughout the book five claims are central: First, that mainstream American family life is problematic both for families and for the common good. Second, that the Christian tradition serves as a valuable resource for Christians seeking a better vision of what families are for and a direction in which families ought to go.[39] Third, that distinctive disciplines or practices are necessary if families are to resist the culture and live their faith. Fourth, that discerning what kinds of practices to adopt is complex and requires serious attention to social science and moral casuistry. And, finally, that family practices are directed not only to communion within the family but to solidarity with the poor and social change. Attention to the ordinary dilemmas of families is warranted because the lives of persons, families, and communities can be transformed through Christian practices in the home.

While acknowledging their fundamental importance to Christian ethics, I will leave others to discuss the great heroes, saints, and public policy issues. This book is meant as a contribution to the large body of discernment the church so desperately needs on the mundane dilemmas of everyday life—a life most Christians live out in families of one sort or another. As I hope my son will one day come to see, ordinary dilemmas are but smaller parts of the larger question of how to respond in faith to the God who gives us life.

Notes

1. Saint Louis University Department of Theological Studies, *Ask the Big Questions*, departmental publication for theology majors and minors.
2. See John Mahoney, *The Making of Moral Theology: A Study of the Roman Catholic Tradition* (Oxford: Clarendon Press, 1987), 1–17.

3. Mahoney comments on the focus on individuals, especially individual sexual sin, in *Making of Moral Theology,* 32–34. Charles E. Curran and Richard A. McCormick include a chapter from John A. McHugh's *The Casuist* in their book *Readings in Moral Theology No. 11: The Historical Development of Moral Theology in the United States* (Mahwah, NJ: Paulist, 1999), 115–19, which provides memorable cases of the cab driver who takes men to brothels and the priest who accepts questionable stipends for mass intentions, illustrating the concerns of the manualist tradition, and McCormick's own essay "Moral Theology, 1940–1989: An Overview," 47, in the same volume provides a few more illustrations (including the problems of needing sustenance while fasting and attending masked balls), while characterizing the moral theology of the manuals as both sin centered and "realistic, compassionate, open and charitable."
4. See McCormick, "Moral Theology, 1940–1989."
5. Of course, theologians working on these issues were concerned with the effects of bad arguments and teachings on the real lives of Christian believers. I am not arguing that moral theologians were unconcerned with ordinary people. I am contending that the ordinary moral issues of daily life were left to those in the pastoral field.
6. Andrew Flescher, *Heroes, Saints, and Ordinary Morality* (Washington, DC: Georgetown University Press, 2003).
7. Ibid., 8.
8. Ibid., 239.
9. Flescher claims, "To fail consistently in one's life to go above and beyond the call of duty is to betray certain shortcomings of character for which one can be morally blamed." Ibid., 10. The key is to keep moral angst alive and keep striving for moral excellence. Ibid., 25.
10. Kristin Heyer, "Bridging the Divide in Contemporary U.S. Catholic Social Ethics," *Theological Studies* 66.2 (2005): 401–40.
11. Ibid., 410–11.
12. Ibid., 413.
13. Ibid., 415. Baxter maintains that these practices can help Americans see the right way to resist evils such as war, which is why ethicists ought to direct their attention less toward policy reform and more toward pastoral encouragement. In Heyer, "Bridging the Divide," 415n65.
14. Ibid., 421.
15. Flescher, *Heroes, Saints, and Ordinary Morality,* 24–25.
16. Ibid., 309.
17. I do not mean to diminish the importance of efforts to draw upon the saints as inspirational models, as in James Keating and David M. McCarthy, "Moral Theology with the Saints," *Modern Theology* 19.2 (2003): 203–17; and Christopher Steck, "Saintly Voyeurism: A Methodological Necessity for the Christian Ethicist?" in *New Wine, New Wineskins: A Next Generation Reflects on Key Issues in Catholic Moral Theology,* ed. William C. Mattison III (South Bend, IN: University of Notre Dame Press, 2005), 25–44. I do want to suggest that rigorous analysis must follow.

18. Florence Caffrey Bourg, *Where Two or Three Are Gathered: Christian Families as Domestic Churches* (South Bend, IN: University of Notre Dame Press, 2004), 133.
19. Ibid.
20. Ibid., 133–34.
21. Ibid., 155.
22. Ibid., 149.
23. David Matzko McCarthy, *Sex and Love in the Home*, new ed. (London: SCM Press, 2004), 86.
24. Ibid., 93–94.
25. Ibid., 127–51.
26. See U.S. Census Bureau, "America's Families and Living Arrangements: 2003," www.census.gov/prod/2004pubs/p20-553.pdf (accessed January 15, 2007). Sixty-eight percent of households in 2008 were family households, 5.6 percent were nonfamily households, and 26.4 percent were single-person households. Of course, many single persons will eventually marry or remarry.
27. Jana Maguerite Bennett, *Water Is Thicker Than Blood* (Oxford: Oxford University Press, 2008), 3–31.
28. See Stanley Hauerwas, "Casuistry as Narrative Art," in *The Peaceable Kingdom: A Primer in Christian Ethics* (Notre Dame, IN: University of Notre Dame Press, 1983), 116–34; and James F. Keenan and Thomas A. Shannon, "Contexts of Casuistry: Historical and Contemporary," in *The Context of Casuistry*, ed. James F. Keenan and Thomas A. Shannon (Washington, DC: Georgetown University Press, 1995), 221–31.
29. Hauerwas, *Peaceable Kingdom*, is notable in this regard, as there is very little comment on the sorts of practices that train Christians in the ways of peace.
30. See, for instance, James McGinnis and Kathleen McGinnis, "Family as Domestic Church," in *One Hundred Years of Catholic Social Teaching*, ed. John A. Coleman (New York: Orbis, 1991), 120–34, and "Building Families of Faith and Outreach," in *Using a Family Perspective in Catholic Social Justice and Family Ministries*, ed. Patricia Voydanoff and Thomas M. Martin (Lewiston, NY: Edwin Mellen Press, 1994), 167–201.
31. James McGinnis and Kathleen McGinnis, *Parenting for Peace and Justice: Ten Years Later* (Maryknoll, NY: Orbis, 1990), 2.
32. See McCarthy, *Sex and Love in the Home*, 109–11.
33. Bourg, *Where Two or Three Are Gathered*, 138–41.
34. The work of Jim and Kathy McGinnis has been an incredible inspiration to me. I do not mean to criticize but to call theologians to go further.
35. See Katherine M. Yohe, "Dorothy Day: Love for One's Daughter and Love for the Poor," *Horizons* 31, no. 2 (2004): 272–301.
36. See, e.g., McCarthy, *Sex and Love in the Home*, 137.
37. Eileen Egan once said that "much of theology consists in getting around the Sermon on the Mount. Well, Dorothy and Peter didn't get around the Sermon on the Mount. They accepted it straight on." Quoted in Rosemary Riegle, *Dorothy Day: Portraits of Those Who Knew Her* (Maryknoll, NY: Orbis, 2003), 137.

38. Heyer, "Bridging the Divide," 436. See also Florence Caffrey Bourg's review of Andrew Flescher's *Heroes, Saints and Ordinary Morality*, in which she suggests that Flescher gives very little sustained attention to ordinary morality or analysis of where sacrifice is most needed. Bourg, Review of *Heroes, Saints and Ordinary Morality*, *Theological Studies* 66, no. 3 (2005): 693–94.

39. I will draw upon resources in the tradition that I see as central and prophetic (e.g., a rich vision of marriage oriented to the common good). Of course, the tradition is also flawed, but I will focus on its best elements. It is my hope that my family ethic will be useful to the wide diversity of Christian families seeking a good life inside and outside the home.

Part I / Resources from the Catholic Tradition

CHAPTER ONE

A Catholic Theological Understanding of Marriage

This book aims to develop a Christian ethic of the family that is both personally and socially conscious. It offers ethical analysis of moral issues that arise in the lives of ordinary Christians, most of whom live in some sort of family, and suggests ways that some everyday choices may promote or impede social goods such as justice, participation, and equality. Some who are sympathetic to the social justice part of this book may worry that the ordinary moral dilemmas of families are marginal to social ethics. Catholic theology of the family in particular, it is thought, has been concerned largely with the relationship between husband and wife and their procreative project to the neglect of larger, more important social issues. Thus, it is argued, those who would call Christians to discipleship in the world would do well to move beyond the family, that is, beyond the ordinary concerns of life in the home.

However, I argue in this chapter that family life is often the place where Christians experience the unity of the personal and the social. The household is a unique locus of personal choices of social significance. This is usually where the ethics of ordinary life is played out, where daily decisions that impact the shape and progress of the world are made. Catholic theology allows us to see this reality more clearly, for it is marked by an understanding of the family as both personal and social. This chapter examines the unity of personal and social dimensions of the family in the marriage liturgy, scripture, and sacramental theology and contrasts this understanding with the more private, romantic, individualistic view of American middle-class culture. The richly personal and social Christian vision of the family will provide a crucial part of the theological foundation for the ethical analysis of practices that is taken up in the second half of the book.

Cultural Understandings of Marriage

In American popular culture, portrayals of marriage are rare. In fact, anyone who listens carefully to prominent cultural narratives about marriage might be forgiven for asking, "Why get married?"[1] While it is true that a multimillion dollar wedding industry continues to thrive, that many girls grow up dreaming about their perfect day, and that most Americans still want to live happily ever after, very few stories about "the ever after" are actually told.[2]

The most popular stories fall into a few predictable genres. There are the fairy tales such as *Cinderella, Snow White, Sleeping Beauty, Beauty and the Beast,* or *Pretty Woman* that narrate the meeting of two lovers and point to the happily ever after but almost never portray it. There are also numerous boy-meets-girl, boy-loses-girl, boy-and-girl-make-up-and-plan-to or actually-do-get-married movies (*Love Story, When Harry Met Sally, Titanic, My Big Fat Greek Wedding, Wedding Crashers*). These are stories about love's beginnings—but then what? Note that in several examples someone dies before the couple can actually experience much, if anything, of marriage. The great love stories once people are married are about their affairs (*Casablanca, The English Patient, An Affair to Remember*). During this last set of movies, despite the nearly universal condemnation of infidelity, the audience roots for the lovers, because their passionate relationship always seems more real than the passionless marriages the lovers leave behind. True, there are comedies about family life such as *Parenthood, The Parent Trap,* or *Cheaper by the Dozen,* but these films exaggerate so much in an effort to get laughs and heartwarming endings that they fail to get to the reality of familial relationships. Occasionally the audience is allowed a glimpse of married couples when they are older, as in *When Harry Met Sally*, but they rarely get to see what happened between the romance of youth and the sweet embrace of old age. It seems that it is enough to know that at the beginning and the end the couple are soul mates: They are made for each other.[3]

These narratives remain compelling—even to those who easily dismiss them as unrealistic—because they seem to present an answer to the widespread problem of loneliness in a fragmented world. The unity of family, friends, and neighborhood that prevailed throughout much of the early twentieth century has given way to compartmentalization. The lives of most are split into many different segments, making the sustaining of personal bonds difficult. Catholic life in particular used to be centered around the neighborhood parish, where children went to school, families walked to Mass, and relatives and friends met for worship, prayer, and socializing.[4] Ties between parishioners were multilayered, overlapping, and regularly reinforced through frequent interaction. However, most families today are involved in multiple communities connected to one or two jobs, a neighborhood (or more when parents are separated or divorced), multiple children's schools, a parish, interest groups formed around sports or other activities, friendships, and extended family networks that increasingly span the nation or even the world. For Catholics, like most Americans, this leads to a sense of fragmentation or, in popular language, of being "pulled in too many different directions" or "spread too thin." As many have noted, the dissolution of the Catholic subculture is associated with lower levels of identification of young adults with the church as institution or community.[5] However, sometimes overlooked is the reality that social ties are also thinner. Marriage seems to be the only tie with potential for thickness, and this is why romantic narratives of various types continue to dominate popular culture and shape views of marriage.[6] In the midst of social fragmentation, romantic marriage is valued as the one relationship that can provide what is lacking, diminishing the necessity and importance of the rest of the fragmented world. Romance is supposed to sustain and fill those who have lost a larger sense of connectedness to church, neighborhood, and community.

This is a seductive story, and a powerful one, but it does not tell the whole truth about marriage. The tragedy of marital breakdown clearly shows that all marriages do not have a "happily ever after." Though there has been some leveling off of the divorce rate in the last decade, a little less than half of all marriages still end in divorce, more than half of all second marriages break up, and about half of all children spend some of their childhood in single-parent homes.[7] Moreover, since the early 1990s, it has become clear that divorce can cause as many problems as it solves. Social science researchers are mostly in agreement that children affected by divorce are worse off, on average, than their peers in intact families.[8] Children of divorce are more likely to get pregnant before marriage, drop out of school, experience relationship problems, and get divorced.[9] Men and women who leave difficult marriages are not guaranteed happiness either, and some studies find that they are less well off, on average, than those who stay married.[10] In the case of marriages that are violent or high-conflict (about one-third of all marriages), civil divorce may be the best option. Still, the wide-ranging effects of divorce on individuals and society as a whole are difficult to underestimate, and the prevalence of divorce engenders less certainty about people's ability to make and sustain commitments. Given this reality, romantic views of marriage fail to convince. People know from experience that it does not always work out this way, as much as they continue to hope that their marriages will turn out differently.

Even when romantic marriage does succeed at providing emotional satisfaction for spouses and children, it may still be less than it could be. A marriage that is simply private is limited in that it does not have anything more than itself to sustain it. Turned in upon itself, it has nowhere to go.[11] Perhaps this is why there are so few cultural portrayals of marriage. It is not that the project of loving another person through time is uninteresting; there is great adventure in maintaining love through the inevitable difficulties and changes that both spouses will experience.[12] But there is more pain and growth in the reality than the dominant cultural narratives allow, and much more to say about the ways in which married couples who love each other deeply are able to reach beyond the home and give themselves to others.

The Catholic tradition offers a way of seeing marriage that speaks more profoundly of both its reality and its potential. Within the Catholic narrative, marriages are not simply romantic relationships of two people finding mutual fulfillment in completion. Rather, marriage is situated within family, community, and church. Families are not isolated havens, but small, sacramental, grace-filled communities connected to and engaged in a larger world. Marriage is a sacrament, the Catholic tradition says, in love and pain, strength and weakness, intimate partnership and work for the common good. Marriage is also a covenantal relationship, sustained by public promises and capable of communicating to others the value of long-lasting love and fidelity. The Christian narrative offers an alternative vision more attuned to the human experience marked by strength and brokenness and better able to help spouses move beyond fragmentation and keep commitments to each other as well as to others in their community.

The difference between this understanding of marriage as a personal and social reality and the popular cultural view is striking. For example, the 2004 movie *The Notebook* caught the imagination of many high-school- and college-aged viewers who found its old-fashioned portrayal of romance inspiring. The film moves back and forth between past and present. An elderly man reads a love story to an elderly woman who struggles with Alzheimer's disease. As he reads, it becomes clear that the story he tells is their story. They were love-struck teens who wanted to marry after a summer romance but were kept apart for years by the girl's controlling mother. Their romance is striking because it is quaint, exuberant, and intense. The romantic story of the couple's courtship and the realistic portrayal of the difficulties of Alzheimer's they experienced at the end were attractive to many. Still, one is left to wonder, "What happened in between?" A viewer could be forgiven for looking into the faces of the young actors and the older actors, trying unsuccessfully to see the connection between them. One might even distrust the movie: "Could the old couple really be an older version of the boy and the girl? Could they really have changed that much? What was their life like? How did they grow so old? Were they passionate to the end, until she forgot who he was?" Despite the boy's prediction in the beginning that marriage would be hard, that they would have to work at it every day, the audience never sees that work portrayed in the movie. They see only the beginning and the end, a stretched-out Romeo and Juliet, with no middle, no life, no marriage. This, it seems, is the story of marriage in American culture—it is about two people, irresistibly drawn to each other, in spite of their families and apart from their communities, from beginning to end.

The middle is not portrayed because it is an unimportant part of the romantic story.[13] As David McCarthy has perceptively written, marriage or the home has become a terribly boring place to be. In American culture, passionate desire is very valuable, and when people stop desiring (when they are satisfied), they think something is wrong.[14] Married couples who are worried that they are not desirous enough are told by relationship experts to get away for a weekend, to make their room look and feel more like a hotel, or otherwise re-create the tension and suspense of their dating days, so that they will feel more romantic. Marriage seems guaranteed to deaden relationships by providing them with stability, routine, place, and responsibility. Though this is supposedly what people seek (why else would they keep returning to those romances with happy endings?), there is something unsettling about home, something not worth writing about. Satisfied with romantic beginnings, we lack narratives of marriage in its reality and its fullness.

The Christian tradition, in contrast, has tried to talk seriously about marriage not simply as a romance but as a union of two called to live in love, sustained through their relationships with children, neighbors, church, and community. In the rest of this chapter, I want to flesh out my claim that the Christian tradition does well to speak of marriage as a sacrament with personal and social dimensions and to suggest that this vision is more real, more daring, and even more screenworthy than the one popular culture has portrayed over and over again.

Liturgy: The Personal and Social Dimensions of Christian Marriage

I turn to the liturgy to understand Catholic thinking about marriage in part because liturgy is a key resource for contemporary Christian moral thought. According to Stanley Hauerwas, a key proponent of the move to connect ethics and liturgy, "The liturgy offers ethics a series of ordered practices that shape the character and assumptions of Christians and suggest habits and models that inform every aspect of corporate life."[15] Rituals say a great deal about what Christians believe, affect the kind of persons they are, and influence how they live. Moral character is intimately connected to worship, for, as Virgil Michel maintains, "The liturgy is essentially the Christian life prayed."[16]

Even more significant for the purposes of this book is the idea that the liturgy is the Christian life prayed together. In an insightful analysis of the liturgy as the starting point for Christian ethics, Therese Lysaught writes, "To worship is to make a public statement. It is a public act. . . . Here Christians are 'called out' of the world. We assemble together as 'church,' as body of Christ, as citizens of the kingdom of God."[17] As a body, suggests Lysaught, we hear "God's story" and "begin to see the world, see 'reality,' in a new way."[18] In the ritual actions of the liturgy, we practice living more consciously as disciples of Christ, not as individuals, but as a community: "We train our bodies to live as he lived—to pass peace, to keep silence and listen attentively to God, to give abundantly of our gifts. We are formed in the habit of being receptive to God's action in the world. We come to know the fullest vision of 'the good life,' or God's life with us."[19] All liturgy is communal action and communal formation.

A turn to the marriage liturgy is, then, essential to Christian family ethics, for the story told at Christian weddings is the most well-read of all theologies of marriage and the most widely shared experience with potential to shape Christian understandings of marriage that might challenge the narratives of popular culture.

Marriage has evolved significantly over the course of church history from a largely private matter to a public and ecclesial relationship, and this evolution can be seen in the development of the wedding ritual. In the first few hundred years of the church's existence, marriage was a civil affair involving betrothal, a contract between families, and a ritual transfer of the bride from her father's house to the home of the groom.[20] Christians simply followed the local wedding customs, and most bishops and theologians had little to say about marriage.[21] From the fourth century on, a bishop or priest would sometimes offer a blessing on the marriage at the feast that followed the wedding, in the wedding chamber, or at a mass after the wedding, but the blessing was not essential at first.[22] Over time, the nuptial blessing became more and more central, especially for weddings of clergy. Gradually the ceremony moved inside the churches, and the secular ritual was transformed into an ecclesial ceremony, with a great deal of local variation.[23] By the twelfth century, as the public character of marriage became more accepted, there was usually an official ritual involving the exchange of consent and a nuptial blessing.[24] Finally, at the Council of Trent, in 1563, the church declared that all Christians who wished to have a valid and sacramental marriage must marry in the presence of a priest and two witnesses.[25] The core of the marriage liturgy remained essentially the same for hundreds of years, though specifics varied according to local contexts.

The rite used today is the product of new guidelines for the marriage liturgy issued in 1969 emphasizing covenant rather than contract imagery and the active roles played by spouses as ministers of the marriage sacrament.[26] In 1990, a second edition of the 1969 guidelines was approved by John Paul II, and this time new developments in liturgical theology were included.[27] The prevalence of the term "people of God" in Vatican II documents, especially *Gaudium et spes,* and the reinvigoration of the role of the assembly in *Sacrosanctum concilium* affected the way all liturgies were celebrated. Yet the congregation's participation in the weekly Mass was slow to cross over into the marriage liturgy. The American bishops and liturgical theologians pointed out that marriage in particular demanded a focus on participation of the congregation and recommended appropriate changes in liturgical practice to highlight the important role of the assembly.[28] A new, more social understanding of the marriage liturgy began to emerge.

The new official guidelines for Catholic weddings encourage couples to greet their family and friends at the door of the church, suggest that they process in together with their parents and other liturgical ministers, and encourage them to ask the assembly to sing and join the celebrant in blessing them.[29] The ministry of hospitality exercised by the couple invites guests to become an assembly, the inclusive procession highlights the familial and ecclesial nature of marriage, and encouraging participation brings forward the community's role in the marriage beginning in its midst. Theological claims about the social nature of marriage are further concretized in suggestions that weddings should take place at the local parish of the couple and include parishioners and in the challenge to involve parish ministers in wedding planning.[30]

The social character of the wedding so central to the new guidelines is evident throughout the ceremony. Opening prayers at the very beginning of the rite introduce the public character of the wedding, as they refer to the bride and groom coming together in the church so that God can seal their love in the presence of the church's minister and community and express the hope that their lives will bear witness to their love for everyone around them.[31] The vows they will take, witnessed and blessed by a community, are not only personal promises but public claims.

Guidelines strongly recommending that the marriage rite take place within a mass are also significant. In the Eucharist, the church community reenacts the Last Supper and thus actualizes or creates itself as the community of disciples of Jesus Christ. Thus marriage, also a sacrament of unity, belongs in the context of the Eucharist.[32] The marriage liturgy includes the whole body of the assembly in its ritual because the sacrament of two of its members is also the sacrament of all of its members. Marriage is a deepening and extending of the original unity, as the words of the ritual make clear. The presider prays, "Lord, in your love you have given us this Eucharist to unite us with one another and with you. As you have made (this couple) one in this sacrament of marriage and in the sharing of the one bread and the one cup, so now make them one in love for each other."[33] The placement of the rite of marriage right before the Eucharist reinforces the connection between marriage and the cross and implicates the couple in Christ's mission to the church.

Guidelines that call for a collection for the poor emphasize the idea that a marriage that is blessed by the church community is given the task of being a living example of Christian community.[34] In their love, and in their participation in communal and ecclesial life, the married couple actualizes in a very human way what the church is called to be. Their relationship is not, according to Catholic theology, simply about creating a world that only two can share but rather is about building a small community at service to a larger one.

It is this image that all Catholics are called to embrace. The new marriage liturgy offers a ritual expression of the church's developing social theology of marriage. However, most parish priests do not insist on the new practices, and those that do often find that couples resist their attempts to remake weddings in accord with new theological understanding. Although Hauerwas asserts that "the practices that shape human lives are seldom points of conflict; on the contrary, they are the very things that people take for granted," in reality, conflicts over marriage liturgies are not uncommon or insignificant.[35] According to David McCarthy, underneath disagreements over the use of secular music and readings is a failure of ordinary Catholics to understand and accept the idea that Christian marriage is "taking on a way of life in a community of faith."[36] As McCarthy notes, couples want a church wedding without participation in the parish. Their concerns are romantic: "Colorful vestments, flowing veil, morning coats, and perhaps a horse-drawn carriage. All these will make perfect sense, while the words of Scripture and the Eucharistic prayer will present annoying but tolerable puzzles."[37]

The communal nature of marriage can be better understood and appropriated when the human need for community is remembered. McCarthy writes that marriage within the church "is a witness of faith. This great joy is ours because we are not alone; we are part of a people, a body, and a countersociety that sets itself to the task of living in light of God's self-giving love. In this regard, it is important to live out the union of marriage within the habits of the Eucharist and the continuing life of the Church. The promises of self-giving love are not our private possessions, but shared in the worship and works of the Church."[38] Human promises are fragile but taken up by God and supported by the faith of the community.[39] In this context, community is not an externally imposed burden but a source of support and context for Christian living.

The abstract ideal of the marriage sacrament signifying the love between Christ and the church is also clarified by turning to the liturgy. Reflecting on the coming together of a couple in a wedding, two theologians assert, "Marriage is a statement against the isolationism of the world. This union is to empower people to live more fully, to connect and act together."[40] When linked to a specific couple with a history who have found each other and decided to bind their futures together, knowing the difficulties they will inevitably face, the idea of marriage as prophetic symbol begins to make sense.[41]

A strong married couple can be a symbol of hope to the community because they care for each other and remain together even when it would be easier not to. "To a world craving reconciliation and community," their continual striving for a better, deeper relationship can be an inspiration.[42] Their willingness to know and be known, to keep striving for more intimacy, can give those around them hope for true human unity.[43] Their empathy for each other despite their differences could give others hope for social reconciliation among those divided by race or class.[44] If they can overcome their differences, what more can be overcome? The hope for unity is especially present in the wedding liturgy as the assembly witnesses the vows of the couple and is given the opportunity to take in the commitment of the couple and recall their own commitment vows as well as those among their family and friends. The social function of the wedding liturgy provides a glimpse of the social importance of marriage itself.

The liturgy thus interpreted is cracked open so that it tells the story of marriage anew, clarifying its communal significance. It is a rich resource affirming the personal and social dimensions of married life. Though for many, weddings speak only of the beginning of lifelong romance, when properly celebrated and understood they can tell a story about marriage as an intimate union directed to the good of many.

Scripture and the Social Import of Family Life

The social significance of marriage can be seen not only in the wedding liturgy but also in scriptural wisdom relating to marriage and family, though the Catholic tradition has not always emphasized this message. Traditional theological treatments of family and scripture often centered on a few standard texts. The Genesis creation narratives were used to establish God's plan for human beings to marry, gender relations within marriage, and the call to fertility. Often the story of Hosea and Gomer was brought in to give evidence of God's enduring love in the face of obstacles and provide a model for Christian marriage. Jesus's affirmation of lifelong marriage was brought forward (Matt. 19:3–9), and Ephesians 5:21–33 was drawn upon to establish the sacramentality of marriage and the need for Christlike sacrifice on the part of the husband and holy submission on the part of the wife.[45] More modern discussions found greater equality in Genesis and Ephesians and emphasized the biblical idea that marriage is the primary metaphor for God's covenantal relationship with human beings.[46]

Newer scholars have begun to look at New Testament texts that were rarely considered in earlier theological treatments of marriage—the radical sayings of Jesus and Paul. Turning to these "hard sayings"—those teachings of Jesus that seem to ask the impossible of his disciples—involves recognizing that the Christian tradition is not at all of one mind when it comes to marriage and family. Rather, celibacy is upheld as a privileged way of life with God, even as images of the holy family dominate Catholic life and much popular theological writing. A desire to reconcile the hard sayings that underlie the case for celibacy with the lofty visions behind the tradition of the holy family is a mark of contemporary family ethics.

Despite traditional theological claims to the contrary, family values are hardly prevalent in the New Testament. Jesus himself locates his vocation outside of his family. This can clearly be seen when, in response to his family's attempt to interfere with his preaching, he identifies those who do God's will as his true family (Mark 3:31–35). This passage can be misread as denial of the moral value of family life or too easily explained away as a lesson about priorities. In fact, biblical scholar Halvor Moxnes claims that, while Mary has come to protect the family honor by taking Jesus home, Jesus rejects it in order to fulfill his mission.[47] Jesus names the community of believers as his true family and finds his public vocation in and through this community.[48] Here and in other hard sayings, Jesus poses troubling questions about the compatibility of discipleship with family duties.

Yet Jesus also looks back to the Genesis creation narrative in order to uphold the sanctity of the marriage covenant (Mark 10:6). This indicates that his concern is not with marriage itself but rather with the idolatry of family that can stand in the way of the broader mission that is integral to disciple-ship. Thus, while affirming the goodness of marriage, he challenges his hearers by calling them to "hate" their families (Luke 14:26) and by asking them to leave their families behind for his sake and their own (Mark 10:29–30). As Lisa Sowle Cahill notes, while these sayings may seem baf-fling, they become clear when viewed in the context of Jesus's public min-istry to the marginalized, for "loyalty to one's own group and dedication to the status of that group over all others and at the expense of whoever stands in the way are incompatible with a life of mercy, service, and compassion for the neighbor in need or for the social outcast and the poor."[49] If Jesus preaches that devotion to family can be dangerous to the person who wants to live a holy life marked by compassion, the implication is that his disci-ples who marry and become parents must resist the temptation to make care for kin their only mission in life.

The earliest Christians evidently tried to recenter their lives around mis-sion rather than kin. As a result, they were sometimes called "homewreck-ers" by critics who questioned their willingness to let faith conflict with duty to family.[50] On the one hand, both in Roman and in Jewish contexts, Chris-tians stunned others with their refusal to honor cultural norms prioritizing the family.[51] On the other hand, New Testament affirmations of marriage (such as Eph. 5:21–33) indicate that some Christians tried to reconcile their faith with their highest estimations of ordinary family life. This strain of Christian thinking developed over time into a strong theology of marriage as sacrament. Yet the dominant strain of early Christian thinking appears to have been suspicion of the value of family life when compared to the value of single-hearted discipleship.[52]

When considering the sort of marriage required by Christian faith, scrip-tural passages "which seem to recommend avoiding marriage altogether," including Matthew 22:30 ("For in the resurrection they neither marry nor are given in marriage, but are like angels in heaven") and 1 Corinthians 7:38 ("So that he who married his betrothed does well; and he who refrains from marriage will do better") must also be considered.[53] Patristics scholar John O'Keefe explains that believers in Paul's time expected Jesus to return any day and cared little about the maintenance of social institutions such as marriage, while Jesus envisioned a kingdom of God that similarly lacked the structures of life taken for granted today.[54] Early Christians often turned to ascetic practices in imitation of Christ and because they "believed that through their practices of physical renunciation they could begin to live now in anticipation of the way we will live after the resurrection."[55] Embracing a lifestyle of renunciation was key to discipleship, regardless of one's state in life. The early Christians saw celibacy as the most obvious way of doing this, but married life offers abundant opportunities for renunciation for the sake of others as well.[56]

The significance of celibacy in the Christian tradition cannot be overlooked. In a recent review of books on Christian marriage, Chris Roberts notes the high view of marriage in all three and asks, "What about celibacy?"[57] Not content to relegate the ambivalence of the early church with regard to marriage and celibacy to the ancient past, he is puzzled by scholars who "cite the authority and potency of patristic Christianity without drawing significant lessons from that era's teachings on virginity" and "give such light attention to scriptures that are skeptical of marriage."[58] As Roberts notes, some focus on biblical texts more favorable to marriage while others confront the more troubling passages but contend that Jesus worried about patriarchy and clan, not family ties. According to Roberts, though few take seriously the idea that such ties were "transformed and subordinated to the higher demands of house church and kingdom," the pressing social obligations of discipleship cannot be denied.[59]

Recent New Testament scholarship confirms this claim. Susan Calef examines the significance of the fact that Jesus "abandoned his household and its work and called others to do the same," concluding that he "pits discipleship against family loyalty" and "dismisses the priority of the duty to kin."[60] Still, Jesus supports families by healing sick family members, by affirming teachings against divorce and adultery, and by entrusting his widowed mother to his beloved disciple at the cross.[61] In addition, in his parables, Jesus uses the language and imagery of the household to subvert the reality of exploitation in Palestinian society, indicating that compassion in families is not problematic but worthy of imitation.[62] Modern Christians seeking to make sense of both sides of Jesus's view on family should, according to Calef, acknowledge that "radical reprioritization" is required. Being a Christian family means becoming part of the larger family of the church, prayer, charity and justice, critical reflection on use of possessions, works of mercy, and hospitality. All of these difficult practices are made possible by the knowledge that, because of Jesus, families are not limited by the options chosen by the many. Rather, they know "it could be otherwise."[63]

New Testament scholars agree that Jesus redefines family, linking it primarily to obedience to God rather than to blood ties, but also acknowledge that he and his followers depend on families in their itinerant ministry. "It is through the houses of his supporters that Jesus extends his mission and in them that he meets with his disciples, his family."[64] Reconciling the two strains of the early Christian tradition, we find a strong valuing of marriage rooted not in kin but in faith and a challenge to bring family outside of its own concerns to embrace a larger mission using its unique strengths.

Whereas earlier generations of theologians may have limited their scriptural analysis of marriage to a few positive texts in order to mount a strong defense of family and support its private obligations, recent scholarship reads the scripture more broadly and understands the family as directed to love, charity, and justice. Through deeper exploration of the marriage liturgy and New Testament texts on marriage, contemporary Catholic theology on marriage has moved from a focus on personal and sexual issues to an understanding of the social implications of familial practices in the home and a call for more social action on the part of families outside the home. Marriage and social justice are no longer separate; an ethics that stops at the bedroom door is no longer adequate. Retrieval of the tradition (especially its liturgy and scripture) has made possible a family ethics that is about much more.

Marriage as Sacrament: Beyond Relationship to Communion

The social significance of marriage that is central in liturgy and scripture is also central to traditional sacramental understanding of marriage, but recent developments in sacramental theology have allowed for a deeper appreciation of this dimension of married life. The contemporary Christian tradition tries to speak of the sacrament of marriage, which is not simply a ceremony but a sharing of lives. The tradition parts company with the culture both in this unromantic focus and in its insistence that a couple's relationship is fundamentally open—to children, extended family, neighborhood, community, nation, and world. Karl Rahner speaks of this particularly Catholic vision of marriage when he says, "Marriage is not the act in which two individuals come together to form a 'we,' a relationship in which they set themselves apart from the 'all' and close themselves against this. Rather it is the act in which a 'we' is constituted which opens itself lovingly precisely to the ALL. This aspect of the basic essence of such love 'appears' already in the very fact that those united by married love themselves already come from a community. In their love they do not abandon this—indeed they must not abandon it."[65] Rahner's eloquent words bring forward the communal context of sacramental marriage that begins with two persons coming from two families to the Christian community for blessing of a union that will not be directed inward, but outward.

More recently, John Paul II, who gives serious attention to relationships between spouses, also speaks movingly of the open nature of sacramental marriage. The spousal communion of which he speaks is total but not at all insular. "By virtue of the sacramentality of their marriage, spouses are bound to one another in the most profoundly indissoluble manner. Their belonging to each other is the very real representation, by means of the sacramental sign, of the very relationship of Christ with the church."[66] Their relationship is not just for their own good; it is rather a participation in the cross and a sign to others of Christ's self-giving love. Children are the first and most tangible sign of the sacramental self-giving of a couple—"a living and inseparable synthesis of their being a father and a mother."[67] The pope's celebration of children as a sign of spousal giving recalls the words of St. John Chrysostom, who wrote that with their children husband and wife constitute a three-in-one flesh unity.[68] Chrysostom compares the bodily union of marriage to the union of Christ and the church.[69] In both cases, they are one family, one sacrament. This image of husbands and wives poured out in children stands in contrast to the cultural focus on the couple. It is not that the marital relationship is downplayed in Catholic teaching. Rather, within a sacramental understanding of the marriage, the claim is that marriage points beyond itself, or better, includes more than itself within its bonds.

In the sacramental celebration of Eucharist, after receiving communion the congregation is sent forth to serve. Similarly, the communion of married love is not complete unless it flows outward. The couple's commitment to be a "fundamental school of social living" flows out of their love for each other.[70] "Service of life" is an ethical command, but it is also an essential part of the sacramental nature of marriage. God's grace is present through a woman and man's love for each other, in their love for their children, and in their efforts to make their home a place where people strive to become more and more open to others.

A family's work to transform the world around them through charity and justice is also fundamental to sacramental marriage. For John Paul II, "Far from being closed in on itself, the family is by nature and vocation open to other families and to society," and thus "it cannot stop short at procreation and education."[71] Anticipating the criticism that such work is not at all what sacramental marriage is about, John Paul II insists that, "by taking up the human reality of the love between husband and wife in all its implications, the sacrament gives Christian couples and parents a power and a commitment to live their vocation as lay people and therefore to seek the kingdom of God by engaging in temporal affairs and by ordering them according to the plan of God."[72] The sacramental nature of their relationship invests couples with the strength to be open to the needs of others and participate in their own way in the transformation of the world; indeed, it obliges them to be and do so. Their marital covenant is not simply about fidelity to each other; it is also about keeping faith with the needy in their midst. In reaching out to others, their love is strengthened, and their ability to serve as a sacramental sign of God's love is renewed.

The genius of Catholic teaching on the family is its refusal to limit families by telling them to simply focus on themselves. Christian families, from this perspective, are to grow in self-giving love within and outside the bonds of kinship. This constitutes a distinctive way of being family in which communion and solidarity are connected. As Pope John Paul II puts it in *Ecclesia in America*, "The awareness of communion with Christ and with our brothers and sisters . . . leads to the service of our neighbors in all their needs, material and spiritual, since the face of Christ shines forth in every human being."[73] Such a way of life means a fuller realization of sacramental marriage and a diminished sense of the fragmentation that so plagues modern families, for in this vision, familial communion calls forth connection to others.

The social dimension of the sacramental vision of marriage is something married persons are supposed to embrace and actively live out as a vocation. Families then have the potential to become a transforming social force. This call is a manifestation of the modern Catholic understanding of lay vocation in the world. Married love *is* discipleship, an "active choice of mutual giving and receiving."[74] It is defined by what it does. As Thomas Kelly says, "Sacramental love never simply stays at home. . . . [A]n intrinsically sacramental marriage will model and extend self-gift as a way of being, both inside and outside the family."[75] Sacramental marriage, rather than being a retreat from the world, ought to be a vital source of solidarity.

Though some might worry that a family committed to solidarity would necessarily find its internal communion diminished, the Catholic tradition holds these two important goods together. Because human beings are inherently social, a person who is a person for others becomes more fully herself by being in relationships with other people. Similarly, a marriage that is open to others strengthens the bonds between the two spouses. As they serve others, they become "more married." They become the community of disciples that the sacrament of marriage calls them to be.

Conclusion: Family as Primary Christian Community

I have tried to argue in this chapter that the Catholic vision of marriage as a personal-social reality stands in contrast with the more common private, romantic narrative. In popular culture, marriage is valued for its potential to provide the love, care, and connection that is lacking in most other spheres of life. The Catholic tradition does not deny the value of personal love—in fact, it celebrates its depth—but it sees loving marriage as an inherently social reality. The wedding liturgy situates the uniting of the spouses in the Eucharist; asks couples to invite their friends, family, and fellow parishioners to participate in the Mass; and calls on the congregation to bless and support the marriage. Scripture is not filled with romantic descriptions of marriage. Instead, the Hebrew Bible offers an analogy between marriage and the covenant between Yahweh and Israel, emphasizing the way in which marriage serves as an icon of God's love for humanity. The New Testament affirms marriage but warns of idolatrous family-focused love that never opens beyond itself. Contemporary sacramental theology locates grace in the life of two people who are committed to each other and to a way of life that is centered on service to others.

This view of marriage integrates the personal and the social, showing that what at first may seem to be the most private of relationships is in fact inescapably social. It follows that all the personal choices embedded in married life have social implications. Far from mundane, these choices are among our most significant. Thus consideration of marriage and of the ethical choices families make allows for an ethical analysis of the demands of

Christian discipleship. The home is the locus of most ordinary, yet personally and socially significant, practices of the Christian moral life.

Notes

1. The 2007 movie, *Why Did I Get Married?*, directed by Tyler Perry, which explores the challenges of married life in documentary style, is a stark exception. See www.whydidigetmarriedthemovie.com.
2. Despite the prevalence of cohabitation, the overwhelming majority of Americans continue to marry, although the rate has dropped slightly. See David Popenoe, "The State of Our Unions 2007," http://marriage.rutgers.edu/Publications/SOOU/TEXTSOOU2007.htm (accessed May 1, 2007). Still, cohabitation remains, for the most part, a prelude to marriage or breakup. See Michael G. Lawler, "Cohabitation and Marriage in the Catholic Church: A Proposal," in *Marriage and the Catholic Church: Disputed Questions* (Collegeville, MN: Liturgical Press, 2002), 166–68.
3. For a related critique of the soul mate idea, see David P. Gushee, *Getting Marriage Right: Realistic Counsel for Saving and Strengthening Relationships* (Grand Rapids, MI: Baker Books, 2004), 105–25.
4. See William L. Portier, "Here Come the Evangelical Catholics," *Communio* 31 (Spring 2004): 45–46.
5. Ibid., 50–52.
6. Ninety-four percent of young adults agree that one should marry a soul mate. See Barbara Dafoe Whitehead, "Predictors of Success and Failure in Marriage," www.dibblefund.org/Articles/Predictors-Of-Success-And-Failure-In-Marriage.pdf (accessed September 15, 2008).
7. For a more in-depth analysis of the social scientific claims made in this paragraph, see my, "Three in One Flesh: A Christian Reappraisal of Divorce in Light of Recent Studies," *Journal of the Society of Christian Ethics* 23, no. 1 (2003): 47–70.
8. See Paul Amato, "Children of Divorce in the 1990s: An Update of the Amato and Keith (1991) Meta-Analysis," *Journal of Family Psychology* 15, no. 3 (2001): 355–70; Judith S. Wallerstein, Julia M. Lewis, and Sandra Blakeslee, *The Unexpected Legacy of Divorce: A Twenty-five Year Landmark Study* (New York: Hyperion, 2000).
9. See Sara McLanahan and Gary Sandefur, *Growing Up with a Single Parent* (Cambridge, MA: Harvard University Press, 1993).
10. See Norval Glenn, "Values, Attitudes, and American Marriage," in *Promises to Keep: Decline and Renewal of Marriage in America*, ed. David Popenoe, Jean Elshtain, and David Blankenhorn (Lanham, MD: Rowman & Littlefield, 1996), 17–31.
11. For an example, see Sandra Tsing Loh, "Let's Call the Whole Thing Off," *Atlantic* (July–August 2009), www.theatlantic.com/doc/200907/divorce (accessed August 15, 2009).

12. Richard Gaillardetz makes this point very well in *A Daring Promise: A Spirituality of Christian Marriage* (New York: Crossroad, 2002).

13. The book-sequel to the movie *The Notebook, The Wedding*, has not been made into a movie, in spite of the success of the first installment. Even this book does not give much detail on the married life of the two united in the first film. See Nicholas Sparks, *The Wedding* (New York: Warner Books, 2003).

14. McCarthy, *Sex and Love in the Home*, 34–42.

15. Stanley Hauerwas and Samuel Wells, "Christian Ethics as Informed Prayer," in *The Blackwell Companion to Christian Ethics*, ed. Stanley Hauerwas and Samuel Well (Malden, MA: Blackwell, 2004), 7.

16. Virgil Michel, *The Liturgy of the Church: According to the Roman Rite* (New York: Macmillan, 1987), 16.

17. M. Therese Lysaught, "Love and Liturgy," in *Gathered for the Journey: Moral Theology in Catholic Perspective*, ed. M. Therese Lysaught and David Matzko McCarthy (Grand Rapids, MI: Eerdmans, 2007), 31.

18. Ibid., 31, 32.

19. Ibid., 36.

20. Kenneth W. Stevenson, *To Join Together: The Rite of Marriage* (New York: Pueblo, 1987), 18.

21. Joseph Martos, *Doors to the Sacred* (Garden City, NY: Doubleday, 1981), 409. There are exceptions, of course, in figures such as John Chrysostom and Clement of Alexandria, but overall the early church fathers had much more to say about virginity than marriage.

22. Jean Evenou, "Marriage," in *The Church at Prayer: An Introduction to the Liturgy*, new ed., ed. Aime Georges Martimort (Collegeville, MD: Liturgical Press, 1988), 189–90. Blessings in the East often involved the crowning of bride and groom, while in the West, veiling of the bride was more common. See also Stevenson, *To Join Together*, 22–23.

23. Martos, *Doors to the Sacred*, 425.

24. Evenou, "Marriage," 199. Stevenson notes that as consent became more central, betrothal waned in importance. Stevenson, *To Join Together*, 52.

25. Evenou, "Marriage," 200. Marriages celebrated before the council were considered valid as long as both husband and wife had given their consent. Local service books included additional ecclesial and domestic rites. Stevenson, *To Join Together*, 102.

26. Martos, *Doors to the Sacred*, 446. The guidelines also allow for more choices in scriptural texts and prayers. Stevenson notes that the nuptial blessing was rewritten so as to address both bride and groom. Stevenson, *To Join Together*, 125.

27. The 1990 version has not yet been translated into English because translation of the Mass has received more attention and because controversies about correct translation continue. Paul Covino, e-mail message to author, November 20, 2007.

28. Liturgical theologians have working translations from the Latin that make possible their commentary. See Paul Covino, ed., *Celebrating Marriage: Preparing the Marriage Liturgy; A Workbook for Engaged Couples* (Washington, DC: Pastoral Press, 1994); and United Conference of Catholic Bishops, *Order of Celebrating*

Marriage 28 (Washington, DC: International Commission on English in the Liturgy, 1996).

29. Paul Covino, "Christian Marriage: Sacramentality and Ritual Forms," in *Bodies of Worship: Explorations in Theory and Practice,* ed. Bruce T. Morrill (Collegeville, MD: Liturgical Press, 1999), 111–16. Though both the 1969 rite and the 1990 guidelines recommend that the bride and groom be met at the door of the church by the priest and process in together with him and the ministers of the liturgy (and parents and witnesses if desired), the traditional Western procession in which the bride walks with her father to meets groom at the front of the church continues to be common practice.

30. See Austin Fleming, *Parish Weddings* (Chicago: Liturgy Training, 1987).

31. James L. Empereur and Christopher G. Kiesling, *The Liturgy That Does Justice* (Collegeville, MD: Liturgical Press, 1990), 198.

32. Hauerwas and Wells write, "Gathering to eat together gives the Church its identity because it gives God's people a definitive practice . . . [they] become what they eat—the body of Christ." Hauerwas and Wells, "Christian Ethics as Informed Prayer," 20.

33. United Conference of Catholic Bishops, *Marriage in Christ* (Collegeville, MN: Liturgical Press, 1991), 24.

34. Covino, "Christian Marriage," 116.

35. Hauerwas and Wells, "Christian Ethics as Informed Prayer," 35.

36. David Matzko McCarthy, "Becoming One Flesh: Marriage, Remarriage, and Sex," in *The Blackwell Companion to Christian Ethics,* ed. Stanley Hauerwas and Samuel Wells (Malden, MA: Blackwell, 2004), 279.

37. Ibid., 283.

38. Ibid.

39. On this theme, see also Jo McGowan, "Marriage versus Living Together," in *Perspectives on Marriage: A Reader,* 2nd ed., ed. Kieran Scott and Michael Warren (New York: Oxford University Press, 2001), 83–87.

40. Empereur and Kiesling, *Liturgy That Does Justice,* 183.

41. Michael G. Lawler, "Marriage in the Bible," in *Perspectives on Marriage: A Reader,* 2nd ed., ed. Kieran Scott and Michael Warren (New York: Oxford University Press, 2001), 11–12.

42. Empereur and Kiesling, *Liturgy That Does Justice,* 185.

43. Ibid., 186.

44. Ibid., 187.

45. See Pius XI, *Casti connubii,* no. 5 (New York: Paulist, 1939). See also Theodore Mackin, *The Marital Sacrament* (New York: Paulist, 1989), 24–36, 59–78.

46. See Lawler, "Marriage in the Bible," 7–16.

47. Halvor Moxnes, introduction to *Constructing Early Christian Families,* ed. Halvor Moxnes (New York: Routledge, 1997), 28.

48. See Julie Hanlon Rubio, *A Christian Theology of Marriage* (New York: Paulist, 2003), 46–60. Recently, Moxnes names Jesus's challenge to the household as his primary challenge, noting that he relocates people from family to the body of believers. Halvor Moxnes, *Putting Jesus in His Place: A Radical Vision of Household and Kingdom* (Louisville, KY: Westminster John Knox Press, 2003), 15, 53.

49. Lisa Sowle Cahill, *Family: A Christian Social Perspective* (Minneapolis, MN: Fortress, 2000), 29.

50. Andrew Jacobs, "A Family Affair: Marriage, Class, and Ethics in the Apocryphal Acts of the Apostles," *Journal of Early Christian Studies* 7, no. 1 (1999): 106.

51. See Rubio, *Christian Theology of Marriage and Family*, 52–54.

52. See Peter Brown, *Body and Society* (New York: Columbia University Press, 1988), 36. Taking this seriously, I have argued, means not abandoning family or the work of discipleship but maintaining a dual vocation to family and the larger community. See Julie Hanlon Rubio, "The Dual Vocation of Christian Parents," *Theological Studies* 63 (December 2002): 786–812.

53. John O'Keefe, "Marriage Is Good, Celibacy Is Better," in *Marriage in the Catholic Tradition: Scripture, Tradition, and Experience*, ed. Todd A. Salzman, Thomas M. Kelly, and John J. O'Keefe (New York: Crossroad, 2004), 78.

54. Ibid., 79.

55. Ibid., 82.

56. See also William C. Mattison III, "'When they rise from the dead, they neither marry nor are given to marriage': Marriage and Sexuality, Eschatology, and the Nuptial Meaning of the Body in Pope John Paul II's Theology of the Body," in *Sexuality and the U.S. Catholic Church: Crisis and Renewal*, ed. Lisa Sowle Cahill (New York: Herder & Herder, 2006), 32–51.

57. These books include Bourg, *Where Two or Three Are Gathered*; Don S. Browning, *Marriage and Modernization: How Globalization Threatens Marriage and What to Do about It* (Grand Rapids, MI: Eerdmans, 2003); and Gushee, *Getting Marriage Right*.

58. Chris Roberts, book review in *Journal of the Society of Christian Ethics* 25, no. 2 (2005): 220–25.

59. Ibid.

60. Susan A. Calef, "The Radicalism of Jesus the Prophet," in *Marriage in the Catholic Tradition: Scripture, Tradition, and Experience*, ed. Todd A. Salzman, Thomas M. Kelly, and John J. O'Keefe (New York: Crossroad, 2004), 56–57.

61. Ibid., 57 and n266.

62. According to Moxnes, Jesus revives "household sharing and village solidarity," which had been lost with the rise of large estates and wage labor. Moxnes, introduction, 25.

63. Calef, "Radicalism of Jesus the Prophet," 63–64.

64. John Painter, "When Is a House Not Home? Mark 3.13–35," *New Testament Studies* 45, no. 4 (1999): 513.

65. Karl Rahner, *Theological Investigations*, vol. 10 (New York: Herder & Herder, 1973), 207.

66. John Paul II, *Familiaris consortio* (Washington, DC: United States Conference of Catholic Bishops, 1981), no. 13.

67. Ibid., no. 14.

68. John Chrysostom, "Homily on Ephesians," in *Marriage in the Early Church*, ed. and trans. David G. Hunter (Minneapolis, MN: Fortress, 1992), 83.

69. Ibid.

70. *Familiaris consortio*, no. 37.

71. Ibid., nos. 42, 44.

72. Ibid., no. 47.

73. John Paul II, *Ecclesia in America* (Washington, DC: United States Catholic Conference, 1999), no. 52.

74. Thomas M. Kelly, "Sacramentality and Social Mission: A New Way to Imagine Marriage," in *Marriage in the Catholic Tradition: Scripture, Tradition, and Experience*, ed. Todd A. Salzman, Thomas M. Kelly, and John J. O'Keefe (New York: Crossroad, 2004), 149.

75. Ibid., 152.

CHAPTER TWO

Between the Personal and the Political

Families as Agents of Social Change

In chapter 1, I furthered my case that the moral dilemmas of ordinary family life deserve more sustained analysis in social ethics by arguing that, in scripture, the liturgy, and sacramental theology, marriage is viewed as socially significant and families are charged with social responsibilities. However, many readers may be skeptical that a concentrated approach to family life is a viable way to approach social justice. One might justifiably ask, "Why not focus on larger social forces that shape daily life? Are not these forces more worthy of rigorous ethical treatment than everyday choices? Does not the tradition of Catholic social teaching, in particular, focus its attention on political choices relating to justice, solidarity, and the option for the poor rather than on the daily lives of families?"

Catholic social teaching (hereafter CST) is, in fact, often viewed as only tangentially related to families. Courses and books on CST usually include sections on the economy, war and peace, human rights, and perhaps the environment, racism, or sexism, but typically they do not devote much time to social ethics issues pertaining to families, and only rarely do they include principles designed to facilitate reflection on the kinds of actions families ought to take. In his recent book, *Catholic Social Teaching, 1891–Present: A Historical, Theological, and Ethical Analysis,* Charles Curran provides justification for this emphasis with his assertion that family issues "lie outside the scope of Catholic Social Teaching, which is primarily focused on changing institutions and structures" rather than changing hearts.[1]

Other authors may not be as explicit, but most seem to share Curran's assumption about the marginal place of family in CST. In a recent book Thomas Massaro and Thomas Shannon contrast the countercultural model of radical Catholic thought, which though strong in "moral clarity" is weak in its reliance on "simplistic analysis and cultural disengagement" with the mainstream model they favor.[2] The caution and humility of the mainstream model admired by the authors is accompanied by a focus on policies and social structures rather than community, individual, or familial practices. Others explicitly argue in favor of this approach, claiming that, while commitments to home and parish are fundamental, Catholic social teaching should move all Catholics to engage in politics at some level.[3] While they acknowledge that striving to become better persons in private life is important, these authors insist that social reform is the more significant task for Catholics who take their social teaching seriously.

Analysts of the Catholic social tradition who encourage Catholics to see the necessity of political reform are not misguided; in many cases, it is the best way to address social inequity. Moreover, it is difficult to dispute Curran's characterization of policy as the major concern of Catholic social encyclicals. Plainly, as Massaro and Shannon see it, there is much to recommend in the measured analysis that most social documents apply to political issues, and, as I pointed out in the introduction to this book, it is very difficult to apply the witness of radical Christians to the lives of ordinary people. The mainstream tradition of Catholic social ethics has applied most of its energy to issues pertaining to governments and businesses rather than families or individuals, for good reasons, and Catholic social ethicists do well to direct Catholics to pay more attention to this crucial dimension of public life.

However, reflection on the ethical contributions that families make to communities and cultures is also a crucial piece of the Catholic tradition deserving of attention. Without minimizing the importance of political change, CST has always insisted on the moral and social significance of what people do in their private lives.[4] This distinctive perspective is, I would argue, both an unrecognized strength and an underdeveloped strain waiting to be brought to full potential. From the earliest of the social encyclicals, there is a recognition that social change cannot be brought about by laws and rulers alone. A society cannot be judged solely on its policies and structures. Rather, what families do is crucially important, and their health is an important indicator of a society's success in encouraging human flourishing. A full analysis of the Catholic social tradition requires attention to family life, for one cannot make sense of Catholic prescriptions for social healing if one bypasses what is said about this smallest of Christian communities.

In this chapter I claim that family is a fundamental part of the Catholic social tradition's vision of social reform. I show this through an analysis of the earliest papal social documents (1891–1931), the early social writings of the American bishops (1919–60), and a selection of contemporary social documents (1965–99). In each section I give some attention to Christian social movements that stand as alternative paths to social justice. In the conclusion, I review contemporary debates on CST and make the case for a social ethic that takes family life seriously without advocating social withdrawal or giving up on political change.

Early Documents and Movements: 1891–1931

Leo XIII wrote *Rerum novarum* (*RN*) in response to the growing social crisis brought about by industrialization, and his prescriptions for change, like those of contemporary movements, were directed to governments, communities, and families. Most European movements for social change at this time advocated some government action, but they also pursued a reconstruction of the social order through the institution of small groups organized around different professions that would bring workers and owners together.[5] Social Catholics in Europe were distressed about the new industrial capitalist system they saw as "a lifeless mechanism, disorganized, lacking an inner harmony and held together by a coercive external power."[6] Some wanted a return to medieval structures of society, while others accepted modern economic systems but sought to "restore medieval spirit" via a corporatist model organized around groupings by craft called, interestingly enough, "families."[7] Marvin Krier Mich notes that these groups were correct in their assessment that "the free enterprise system, based on the notion of competition and strife, had transformed the natural human need to associate for the sake of the common good into a selfish search for power for the sake of individual gain" and in their judgment that "society had lost its organic unity and was disorganized, anonymous, and impersonal."[8] Out of this concern came proposals for state regulation of industry and governance from below by smaller organizations with moral motivations. The goal was nothing less than restoring humanity to society by reinvigorating local community with help from above and below.

RN follows this pattern in calling for government enforcement of a just wage, legalized unions, and a safety net for the poor but also devotes a great deal of attention to family, community, and religion. Leo did not adopt a utopian model. He accepted that suffering would dominate life for the majority but offered a social solution involving intermediary associations.[9] Although these sections of the document are not always well remembered in subsequent commentaries, they are nonetheless crucial to Leo XIII's social ethic.[10]

Some critics of the first social encyclical praise Leo XIII for making a radical critique of the economic order and putting the church on the side of the poor but believe that he did not do enough to challenge the political order that sustained the economic conditions favoring the rich. They judge the document insufficiently politically radical. Donal Dorr writes that though "the encyclical was a strong challenge to the status quo," Leo's unwillingness to face the need for political change "imposed severe limits to the extent to which he could carry through that change."[11] He "called for a change of attitude by the rich and the acceptance of practices and laws that would protect the poor. But if such changes 'from the top' were not introduced, the pope had no very effective way in which he could promote fundamental changes in society."[12] The problem for Dorr is that Leo, in his naïveté, failed to recognize that the economic problems that so rightly concerned him would never change without serious political reform.

But Leo XIII may have had an alternative vision of social change. Fearing or not trusting in revolution, he grounded his hope in religion and individuals embedded in families. This need not be viewed as a naïve or arrogant nonanswer. That the church eventually comes to embrace legitimate struggle for political change on the part of the disenfranchised can only be viewed as a positive development, but one can recognize this and also see that revolution is often slow in coming and sometimes fails to come at all.

And still people are poor or struggling. What has the church to say to them, or to those who remain rich or middle class and alienated?

Politics is not the only route to change; individuals with the freedom to shape their lives can also change society from the ground up. A belief in this sort of change is behind Leo's defense of the right of human beings gifted with reason to labor, provide for themselves, and plan for the future.[13] His defense of the person and the family as prior to the state leads him both to disapprove interference by the state with the right of a worker to provide for his family and to affirm a positive duty of the state to aid families.[14] His first priority is ensuring that workers can do what they are obligated by faith and nature to do without interference from the state. As socialism seems to threaten workers' ability to carry out their duties, he concentrates his attention on tearing it down.[15] In addition, the church's influence is necessary to solve social problems, for it "uses its efforts not only to enlighten the mind, but to direct by its precepts the life and conduct of men."[16]

While modern readers must question Leo's confidence that social inequality is natural and his claim that "humanity must remain as it is," we ought to pay attention to his consistent return to religion and the home as fundamental to the amelioration of the social problem.[17] Clearly, the pope does not reject political solutions; his defense of a limited state government and advocacy of workers' rights and unions are evidence of his political will. However, equally important is his insistence that the meaning of this life is unclear without an understanding of the world to come. This is the foundation of his claim that Christian faith allows people to see that money and possessions have only relative worth and thus are to be used well and shared.[18] Furthermore, according to Leo, it is by Christian faith that people come to know that "poverty is no disgrace," that "the true excellence of man lies in his moral qualities," that the virtue is not concentrated in the rich but rather is "the common inheritance of all," and that "God himself seems to incline more to those who suffer evil."[19] Though the pope does not name the family as the sole locus of these lessons in virtue, his quarrel with socialism is rooted in a concern for the family as the crucible wherein Christian faith should provide a guide for right living.

Most contemporary theologians respond to early CST statements about religion by criticizing their presumption rather than affirming the enduring significance of religion as a cultural force. For instance, Mich notes that in *Grave de communi* the pope said that the social problem is not simply economic but primarily moral and religious, but he characterizes the conclusion that the church is necessary to solving the social problem as ecclesial arrogance.[20] Thomas Shannon agrees that for Leo, "while the social issues are important, even more important are the role of religion and the cultivation of piety among both employers and the employed," but he does not see this insight as a significant contribution.[21] No doubt Leo says too much when he claims that the church has all the moral answers to the social problem, but we cannot afford to overlook the important claim that there is more to solving the social problem than working for political change.[22]

Without denying that Leo is too accepting of poverty and suffering, it is possible to appreciate his teachings on the importance of moral vision. His elevation of the spiritual over the material, his rejection of the superiority of those who are rich, and his insistence on the dignity of those who are poor are still prophetic. He offers not just political solutions but religious teachings to be appropriated in community. For him, the church's most important role is "call[ing] men to virtue and form[ing] them to its practice," teaching both rich and poor to appreciate what they have rather than lusting after more.[23] Thus we should recall both his assertion that governments should guarantee workers a just wage and his claim that employers have a duty to protect the spiritual and religious well-being of their workers.[24] We should remember that his argument for a just wage is based on the idea that labor is personal and necessary, so wages must be adequate to provide for a decent life, a life that has both material and spiritual dimensions. These claims suggest the need for economic reform and reinvigoration of the personal and spiritual dimensions of the workplace.

Leo's treatment of the "private" moral life of families and communities is significant as well. Just as the employer is to recognize the human and religious needs of his worker, the worker is to labor well and live frugally, avoiding envy, so that his wages will meet his needs.[25] If Leo lacks the political savvy to judge how much coercion will be necessary to help governments act justly, he does understand the need for families to "study economy" and virtue, for labor groups to form their members in faith and morals as well as advocate for common needs, and for all persons to practice charity, whatever their station in life.[26]

The church and smaller communities such as families are central to Leo's argument, for, as he sees it, only they have the power to change hearts and encourage virtue. He believes that free persons who form families, labor to provide for themselves, join with others in local organizations and churches, and practice virtuous living will form more humane communities. Leo's choice to place his trust not in politics alone but also in intermediary groups gives early CST a depth that many political programs lack and provides a social ethic that speaks to Christians of their obligations in public life, in local communities, and at home.[27]

Pius XI's *Quadragesimo anno* (*QA*) follows in the tradition of *RN* but has a more developed corporatist vision that involves groups drawing workers together by trade or profession to develop their own ethic and promote the common good of their members.[28] These groups were an answer to antagonistic organizations of labor and management, an essential ingredient of the social harmony that Pius XI hoped to promote. Far from relying solely on the political order, the pope asserts that "social justice and social charity" should direct society from below and reminds readers of the state's limited role in safeguarding, but not enforcing, this order.[29] Faith is crucial to change because the "longed-for social reconstruction must be preceded by a profound renewal of the Christian spirit, from which so many of those engaged in economic activity have in many places unhappily departed. Otherwise, all our endeavors will be futile, and our social edifice will be built, not upon a rock, but upon shifting sands."[30]

Most commentators on *QA* question the enduring significance of Pius XI's proposals for social reconstruction, emphasizing instead his reaffirmation of the just wage and his pleas for social justice. O'Brien and Shannon judge the project of reconstructing the social order to be a failure.[31] Curran asserts that later popes "abandoned this concept without ever explicitly disagreeing with the proposal."[32] Yet, while the focus on guilds has been abandoned, the concept of small, often faith-based, intermediary groups between individuals and governments that form culture and contribute to social change remains central to CST. In fact, as Mich points out, in the 1930s, the pope's unrealistic sounding plan found its realization in lay movements. Reform took place from below through groups such as the Catholic Worker, Friendship Houses, and the Grail.[33] Moreover, as John Coleman asserts, "no one theme has so consistently been remarked on by commentators on the papal encyclicals as their insistence on a pluralism of societal authority and the right—derivative from the very sociality of human nature—of individuals to form associations intermediate between the state and individuals. The most usually cited exemplifications of this right to intermediate associations is the right to form labor unions, but the latest formulations of the grounding principle for this right, 'justice as participation,' really envisions a rich associative life in civil society."[34]

Coleman's point is key—for as important as the right to form unions is, it is but a piece of a much larger vision of social life that begins with families. Thus while early CST is no doubt dominated by reflections on social systems, it also concerns a change of heart, the virtue of individual lives, and the viability of associations shaped by faith and directed to the common good of society. Most commentators underemphasize this communal dimension of CST while affirming its historical significance. But if middle associations including families are crucial to the early Catholic social thought, what they do should be a matter of continuing concern. Most social ethicists do acknowledge the general importance of a "multi-associational society in which the common good includes everyone," the virtue of limited government to ensure a rich society, and the need for "a spiritually motivated and virtuous laity to engage in renovating culture and institutions according to the values and image of Christ's kingdom."[35] However, the vast majority of social ethicists' attention goes to advocating principles, policies, and structural change, not to reflecting on the responsibilities and possibilities of middle associations. Early CST challenges to develop virtue and create a more humane culture through associations are rarely taken up, which means that Christian social ethics is limited in its approach to social change.

Early American Episcopal Documents and Catholic Action Groups: 1919–65

The concern with the practices of intermediary groups evident in the foundation papal documents of CST is perhaps more prominent in the American Catholic Church of the early twentieth century. Some commentators point out that the immigrant church was first concerned with its own survival and a quest for acceptance. Only gradually did it come to challenge American social norms and political structures. This development is generally viewed as progressive, as an inwardly focused church anxious about its identity in a new land eventually feels comfortable enough to leave parochial issues behind so that it can become a serious dialogue partner in the political realm.

However, there is in early documents and movements much traditional Catholic wisdom about how a society might cope with social upheaval and suffering. One finds not only important calls for legal protection for workers but also an insistence on the centrality of faith in people's lives and a concern with what they do in families and religious groups. While the documentary history of papal CST shows increasing openness to national and even international political intervention along with concern for middle associations, in the early American context the focus on alternative avenues of social change is even more pronounced. This can be seen in official episcopal documents, the writings of Catholic sociologists, the actions of the Bureau of Family Life, and family-based movements.

In order to understand the contributions of the bishops' conference of the early twentieth century, it is necessary to look briefly at the documents of the nineteenth century and distinguish enduring contributions from more time-limited messages. Modern readers will notice the parochialism evident in the concentration on defending the legitimacy and rights of the church in America and keeping Catholics safe from the dangers of secular, mixed society. These issues are no longer major concerns. However, there are several themes that bear further consideration. First, good Catholic education is seen as a crucial remedy to the social problem and is distinguished from secular education primarily by its goal, which is not providing the keys to social success but forming persons of faith and virtue who will work hard and find happiness in whatever work they do because they are "not only clever but good."[36]

Second, family practices are taken quite seriously. The Third Plenary Council of Baltimore (1884), for instance, addresses its attempt to remedy the social problem primarily to Christian parents and asks them to cultivate homes in which marriage is honored, divorce is altogether avoided, morning and evening prayers are made together, good spiritual reading materials are provided, scripture is read regularly, the Sabbath is respected, and the virtues (especially charity) are taught and practiced.[37] The attention to everyday practices is striking in a social document directed at remedying social ills.

Third, the bishops place most of the rest of the burden of remedying the social problem on lay groups such as the Sacred Heart of Jesus, the Blessed Sacrament, the Blessed Virgin, Young Men's Catholic Association, St. Vincent de Paul, and various incarnations of Catholic Action.[38] These groups are charged with helping Catholics avoid secular dangers and accomplish good. More so than modern episcopal letters, these documents see social issues being solved through home, school, and intermediary organizations.

By 1919, when the National Catholic War Council (the first incarnation of the National Council of Catholic Bishops) issued its Program of Social Reconstruction, church leaders felt more comfortable advocating engagement in the political process in order to secure a living wage, social insurance, and basic rights for workers.[39] Still, the bishops concluded their proposal with an affirmation of the "Christian view of work and wealth" as the key to the social problem.[40] That vision of the human person with a basic dignity and an end that transcends this world was, they thought, the best they had to offer. When the bishops write again in the depths of the Great Depression, they mourn the suffering of the many and seek its true roots. While they acknowledge economic and political causes of the crisis, they remain convinced that "economic dictatorship," which leads to greed and an instrumentalizing of the person, is the real culprit.[41] The remedy is "restoring Christ" to a society that has forgotten him by reintroducing the idea of the dignity of the person, which would lead those with great wealth and power to create systems more in keeping with that dignity.[42]

To that end, they have much more to say about charity and morality than law. They give more attention to Catholic study groups, vocational groups, schools, and presses than workers' rights, though they do not neglect the latter.[43] Rather, in their social analysis they insist, "We must keep in mind what Leo XIII and Pius XI taught, 'that the social question is not merely an economic one, but that it is, first of all, a moral and religious question.'"[44]

Similarly, the National Catholic Welfare Conference, writing in 1940, identified three aspects of the remedy for the social order: the laws and regulations of the state, the work of mediating institutions, and moral reform.[45] They offer principles of sound government ("a via media" between liberalism and socialism) but say, "We need justice without doubt or equivocation, but we also need charity if we are to put lives in harmony with God's plan and promote that spirit of benevolence which will lift the burdens not only from the backs but also from the souls of men."[46] From the earliest days in America, the Catholic bishops saw the need not only for political reform but also for changes in the ways in which ordinary Catholics lived—in their family life, their communities, and their workplaces. Their vision of social ethics has personal, familial, and communal dimensions.

Catholic scholars who wrote on the family agreed with the bishops' analysis of the social problem. The key figures from the 1930s to the 1950s were sociologists Paul Furfey, E. Schmiedeler, John Kane, and John Thomas, who wrote what might be considered an early version of Catholic family ethics. None looked kindly on the mainstream American family of the early twentieth century. These professors mounted "the most severe critique of American society of any group in the American Catholic community."[47] Rejecting the neutral, objective perspective their fellow sociologists expected them to adopt, they were instead advocates for the Catholic tradition against what they saw as American cultural decline. They criticized growing acceptance of divorce, declining attention to children, increasing emphasis on individual happiness rather than on the value of marriage as an institution, and the intrusive role of agencies outside the family.[48]

To a modern reader, the rhetoric of these "moral alarmists" appears excessive, even quaint, given the depth of current problems. However, underneath this alarmism was a core consensus that the social crisis required attention to what families were doing, that a primary goal of marriage was the procreation and education of children, and that the ultimate goal of child rearing was "not worldly success of the child, but the child's eternal salvation."[49] Like the bishops, these sociologists were convinced of the social import of family, education, and the workplace.

Schmiedeler's *An Introductory Study of the Family* was the basic textbook for courses on the family in Catholic colleges for twenty-five years. He juxtaposed the individualism and rationalism of the Industrial Age with the medieval society in which families found a unity of purpose in a life lived for the good of others, and one benefiting both family and society.[50] He believed that parental education and training in the habits of self-denial and discipline was the only way out of the crisis.[51] Though many found his medieval, agrarian romanticism unrealistic, his work was valued for its insight into what had gone wrong in American society.

However, not all Catholic social scientists were wedded to the return of a family-centered agricultural society. John Thomas, author of *The American Catholic Family*, believed that it was no longer possible to convert the culture. Rather, Catholics should live as a distinct minority. The key problem was how to maintain countercultural ideals, and he saw families as the only vehicle that could provide the education, motivation, and solidarity necessary to maintain ideals.[52] While others might see such focus on vision as unrealistic, Thomas believed in the power of ideals, for "people tend to live as they think."[53] While not inattentive to social problems (he was founding editor of the journal *Social Order*), he placed most of his hopes on personal and familial change. He and Schmiedeler were proponents of "supernatural sociology," responding to the social problems of their time with a plea for a return to countercultural Catholic ideals and communal ways of living.[54]

The U.S. bishops addressed the social problems of the 1930s and 1940s through the Bureau of Family Life, a component of the National Catholic Welfare Conference. The goal of the bureau was to "encourage the building of successful Christian marriages and wholesome Catholic homes."[55] The bureau worked toward the goal at different times through parent education, critique of the economic order, national programs to raise consciousness on the corrosive effects of the success ethic (a new issue for the growing Catholic middle class), and encouragement of family prayer and devotion. Eventually, according to historian Jeffrey Burns, their efforts failed, due to a highly bureaucratic approach and a failure to trust lay organizations.[56] Nevertheless, the existence of the bureau for more than twenty years, under the U.S. bishops' Department of Social Welfare, suggests a key awareness at the episcopal level of the link between families and the social order.[57]

However, one cannot understand the full force of this consciousness in Catholic thought without attention to the movements that linked family and social reform on the ground. Two of the most significant were Integrity and the Christian Family Movement. Integrity lasted from 1946 to 1956 under the leadership of Ed Willock and Carol Jackson, who were convinced that "family renewal lay at the heart of social reconstruction."[58] Their mission was to promote family personalism.[59] Personalism began to catch on in the 1930s, as many were attracted to the demanding concepts of personal sacrifice and action for greater good, but it was not until after World War II that movements like Integrity began to apply it to families. Instead of asking what would happen if people as individuals became better, Ed Willock and Integrity wanted to know how society would change if families became better.[60] They took the standard Catholic position that the family was the primary unit of social change and said that, for social change to really occur, families would have to strive for perfection.[61] Insisting that it was a movement not for perfect people but for "perfecting people," Integrity tried to be both radical and inclusive. It attracted many working- and middle-class Catholics, some of whom tried rural communal living because large households in the city were becoming impossible to sustain.[62]

Calling marriage a "means to sanctity," Integrity believed that good families were "the basic unit of the spiritual and social revolution."[63] Criticized as unrealistic and simplistic, those inside the movement can still be celebrated, according to Burns, for "encourag[ing] couples to reach beyond the prevailing mediocrity of modern America."[64] Even today their writings challenge middle-class assumptions that have become commonplace in American Catholic life. Founder Ed Willock writes in a "Postscript on Poverty and Marriage" of a holy poverty in marriage that differs from the poverty of monks, in that it is "detachment from all things except those specific things that are required to maintain this family in the frugal comfort that encourages virtue."[65] Illustrations of nonnecessities include a car, a college education, new Easter clothes, and a washing machine. His stories of a simple life with his wife and seven children, and of a profoundly countercultural community of families marked by a mutual charity, are compelling. The unassuming but inspiring witness of these radical Christians make the short life of Integrity all the more disappointing.

The Christian Family Movement (CFM; founded in 1949 and still active today) was far less perfectionist, but it shared Integrity's assumptions about the role of families in changing the social order. Members believed that "if better family life was to be attained, the environment had to be changed."[66] CFM envisioned its small groups of six couples who met every two weeks as action groups rather than study groups.[67] The meetings followed a standard format: prayer, fifteen minutes of scripture reading and reflection, fifteen minutes of reflection on the liturgy, and forty-five minutes of social inquiry organized around the see-judge-act method of Catholic Action groups. The social inquiry prepared couples to commit to an action before the meeting's end. At the following meeting, members reported on their actions and so held each other accountable. CFM's membership consisted mainly of lay, urban, middle-class, white couples who were part of the new Catholic middle class.[68] They were motivated to engage in social action because of theological beliefs that marriage was a "social sacrament that implicated husbands and wives in the broader social order" and because they saw the economic order penetrating their homes and knew they could not escape it.[69] Rather than reaching back to a romanticized vision of the past,

CFM encouraged couples to bring Christ to the world in which they lived in a myriad of ways, small and large.[70]

With the Second Vatican Council came a unique opportunity for CFM to use its organization (which included forty thousand couples in the early 1960s) to influence the church and thereby significantly change the environment of Catholic families. Pat and Patty Crowley were part of the papal birth control commission and contributed surveys of thousands of CFM couples who told of their difficulties following church teaching against artificial birth control. Although Paul VI ultimately decided not to heed their cautious call for change, CFM became a voice for many Catholic couples in countries across the world and no doubt influenced the shift to personalist understandings of sexuality that became more common after the writing of *Humanae vitae*.[71]

The American Catholic Church in the first half of the twentieth century approached the social order in part through the family. The teachings of the bishops, official ecclesial organizations, and lay movements were all directed to advancing social change via lifestyle change. None eschewed politics altogether. Rather, they held a strong belief that political advocacy could not be the only strategy the church embraced. All also sought to change society from the ground up.

Contemporary Reflections: Changing Hearts and Structures

If it is clear that early American Catholic social ethics, like the earliest of papal social encyclicals, was marked by a concern for culture and middle associations such as families, one may nonetheless protest that modern Catholic social ethics is far more committed to political reform. No one who is interested in social change should deny or even downplay the gradual, growing willingness in CST to confront unjust structures and advocate political solutions. This is clearly one of the great strengths of the social tradition, and those who fail to acknowledge this reality risk misrepresenting the tradition.[72] However, it is also important to see that documents usually mined for their references to politics also contain challenging insights on the practices of smaller groups and their potential to affect social change.

I focus in this section mainly on the writings of John Paul II, but it would be remiss to ignore what is perhaps the foundational document for the politically focused reading of CST, *Gaudium et spes* (*GS*). The import of the structure of this well-read document can sometimes be overlooked. David Hollenbach's recent commentary, for example, first analyzes part 1 of the document, focusing on human dignity, the social responsibilities of persons, and the new relationship between church and world, wherein the church explains its biblically based perspectives but agrees to participate in a pluralistic dialogue.[73] Next he discusses justice, human rights, and war, skipping over the first two sections of the second part concerning family and culture.[74] Hollenbach offers important insight into the political aspects of *GS*. However, one might also draw attention to how the council's understanding of human dignity and social responsibility is advanced through a systematic treatment of ever larger groupings, beginning with families.[75] The structure is not accidental but brings together key pieces of the CST heritage, linking the meaning of human life revealed in Christ to the dignity of individuals marked by sin and grace, to family life that is a "school for deeper humanity," to culture, and then to national economic policy and international problems. Reading this fundamentally important document without attention to family and culture neglects the role of middle associations and exacerbates a problematic tendency in modern Christian ethics to bypass the large ethical sphere between marriage and politics.

The social teachings of John Paul II give substantial attention to this middle sphere. The late pope affirms the importance of lay responsibility for the world and suggests that bringing Christ to the world is not simply a matter of political activism, but rather something that should affect every aspect of life. John Paul II's personalism marks all of his theological writing, including his social teachings. Instead of abstract principles, he offers a personal call to responsibility. While most commentators count *Laborem exercens, Sollicitudo rei socialis,* and *Centesimus annus* as John Paul II's social teachings, I would include *Familiaris consortio* and *Ecclesia in America,* for each of these documents also deals with the personal responsibilities of Christians in the world. When read through a personalist lens, the pope's social teachings clearly leave a significant space for families and other community groups. In the following sections I highlight four key themes: work as vocation, personal responsibility for social change, the social mission of the family, and the transformation of culture.

Work as Vocation

Work is a particular concern of Pope John Paul II. Unlike earlier popes, who saw work as toil for the majority, from his vantage point near the end of the twentieth century, John Paul II was able to construct a spirituality of work that serves as a crucial piece of his theology.[76] He writes in *Laborem exercens* that "work is a fundamental dimension of man's existence on earth."[77] Work is not personal and necessary simply because it is something that a person does in order to eat. According to the pope, work is commanded by God in Genesis 1:28, and therefore it must be fundamental to the meaning of human existence. Because the subject of work is the human person, the work a person does must "serve to realize his humanity, to fulfill his calling to be a person that is his by reason of his very humanity."[78] A person's work is her vocation, one way in which she becomes the person she is called to be. Work is both an obligation and a right of all persons.[79]

The key ethical implication to be drawn from John Paul II's theology of work is that all persons have a calling that must be answered, an invitation to share in the shaping and molding of the world. Work is a right, not simply because all persons are due the basic necessities of life, but because all persons have something important to do in this world by which they will realize their very selves. The work that persons do is a fundamental part of their moral life. As the fathers of Vatican II wrote, Christians must not separate faith and life.[80] What people do with their days is a fundamental part of who they are. In his spirituality of work, the pope endows the work lives of ordinary people with dignity and challenges them to bring their true selves to work while recognizing the humanity of those with whom they labor. His spirituality of work is a profound contribution to the reinvigoration of culture.

Dorothy Day's insistence that work is prayer is in accordance with the pope's vision, as is the Catholic Worker movement in general. Day values work that truly meets the needs of human beings. In her book *Loaves and Fishes,* Day speaks about the quiet commitment of a woman named Marie who sweeps the floor of the Catholic Worker house each night and sees her work as a prayer.[81] The sweeping of the floor allows life to go on in a shelter for some of the most disadvantaged in the city. It is important to Day that she sweeps *this* floor. Day herself struggled until she found meaningful work that was in accord with her faith. Writing itself was not enough; she wanted to be a part of a Christian community committed to the poor. In this context, writing, cooking, and sweeping the floor are important work. Day's example is a reminder that all Christians are called to find work that constitutes prayer for them and to engage it as prayer.[82] In his theology of work, the pope opens up this possibility when he affirms that work is fundamental to the flourishing of human beings. In so doing, he calls attention to the social import of an area of life many see as unrelated to faith or social justice. In addition, he implicitly calls into question the commonly held view that any job that allows one to support a family constitutes good work. He calls Christians to see work inside and outside of the home as both personal and social.

Personal Responsibility for Social Change

In *Sollicitudo rei socialis* (*SRS*), the pope focuses directly on political and economic issues that undermine human dignity. He is particularly concerned with the inequities that divide the world and the failure to achieve authentic human development, but his personalist concerns ensure that this is not simply a political document. As Richard Gaillardetz comments, "The emphasis in the writing of John Paul II was placed more on the cultivation of Christian personalism that speaks to the sinfulness of the human heart as the root cause of social injustice."[83] Thus the pope lays out the problem: Poor countries are hampered by their lack of resources, and rich countries are hampered by materialistic desires that ensure that "dissatisfaction reigns."[84] He calls all citizens to take individual responsibility for authentic human development that is concerned with the whole human person. He speaks of the option for the poor not simply as a priority for political decision making but as something that "affects the life of each Christian inasmuch as he or she seeks to imitate the life of Christ, but it applies equally to our social responsibilities and hence to our manner of living, and to the logical decisions to be made concerning the ownership and use of goods."[85] The example that follows, "private property is in fact under a social mortgage," begins to show how solidarity could function as a norm for middle associations, especially families. In John Paul II's personalist social teachings, meeting "social responsibilities" means examining daily practices. Because what he offers is a moral theology rather than a political ideology, even when it sounds more political, as in *SRS*, it applies first of all to communities.[86]

The pope's personalist approach to social change continues in *Centesimus annus*, his most significant social encyclical that interprets one hundred years of CST. In it, he puts forward a distinctive understanding of the importance of the middle realm between individual and government. Notably, he recalls that *Rerum novarum* was a defense not only of governmental action but also of families and other intermediary groups.[87] Although there is a great deal of debate about how far the pope goes in blessing capitalism, his treatment is fairly traditional both in what it affirms (the market) and in what it decries (consumerism, alienation, and competition that undermine human dignity). There is a new, modern respect for economic freedom and enterprise coupled with understandings of business ("a community of persons who in various ways are endeavoring to satisfy their basic needs, and who form a particular group at the service of the whole society") and family ("a community of work and solidarity") that are profoundly countercultural.[88] A desire to balance subsidiarity (by focusing on individual hearts and communities) and solidarity (which is for John Paul II what friendship was for Leo XIII and what social charity was for Pius XI) animates the document.[89]

A personalist understanding of solidarity as moral empathy constitutes John Paul II's distinctive approach to combating social injustice. Daniel Finn writes that self-gift is as relevant to this document as it is to John Paul's writings on sexuality; it grounds the call to individual conversion.[90] There is also a deep concern for the "subjectivity" or character of society that implicates communities and inspires a desire to "help entire peoples," not just one's nearest neighbors.[91] Social responsibility means examining everyday choices and joining together with others to work for larger social change, and in doing this, communities are themselves transformed.

The Social Mission of the Family

Personal responsibility for social change translates into a social mission for the family in the family ethics of John Paul II. CST views the family not simply as a private haven but as a community with a mission that goes beyond itself. In *Familiaris consortio* (*FC*), Pope John Paul II defines the family as "a community of life and love" that has four major tasks. Each of these tasks has public dimensions. The first is the most obviously familial but the least obviously public. The family must "guard, reveal and communicate love."[92] John Paul II distinguishes himself from earlier popes by the inspired way in which he describes married love and demands that it rise to the heights for which it is destined. His personalist language represents an attempt to take seriously the importance that modern men and women give to spousal relationships. However, he insists that the love among family members is primary because it is the foundation for the rest of what the family does.

Second to love comes the task of "serving life." According to the pope, this means that parents have a responsibility to serve life by nurturing their own children and by bringing life to the world.[93] Having children is only the first step. Education is an important responsibility, and it includes the task of instilling in children "the essential values of human life," especially the idea that possessions do not make human beings what they are, and the responsibility to adopt a simple lifestyle.[94] The pope also affirms that when mothers and fathers teach their children about the gospel, "they become fully parents, in that they are begetters not only of bodily life but also of the life that through the Spirit's renewal flows from the cross and resurrection of Christ."[95] This seems to indicate that passing on the Christian faith is even more important than the admittedly awesome process of passing on life. Here, as in the gospel itself, the spiritual and public duty is placed above (but in relation to) the private duty. This emphasis on the spiritual is made clear when the pope claims that families have a "spiritual fecundity" through which they share with others the self-giving love they nurture within.[96] Families are called to respond especially to all of God's children with compassion.

The third task to which the pope calls families further indicates that families are not simply oriented toward their own good. Families are called to participate in the development of society, for "far from being closed in on itself, the family is by its nature and vocation open to other families and to society and undertakes its social role."[97] This means that families "cannot stop short at procreation and education"; they have distinct and fundamental social and political duties.[98] Specifically, the pope asks families, first, to practice hospitality, opening their table and their home to those who are not as fortunate as they are; second, to become politically involved, assisting in the transformation of society; and third, to practice a preferential option for the poor, manifesting a "special concern for the hungry, the poor, the old, the sick, drug victims and those with no family."[99] All of this is part of the social mission of the family. It is not optional, but fundamental to a family's identity and calling. It is what it does as a community of love in the world.

Finally, the pope uses the "domestic church" imagery to suggest that families must serve the church by being the church.[100] As a "church in miniature," the family evangelizes its members, witnesses to the world, uses its home as a sanctuary (for rituals of prayer and sacramentals), and serves the broader community—for like the church, the family is a servant of humanity.[101] Here again the emphasis is both on the social significance of practices in the home and on the sending forth of the family into the world. The pope's emphasis on the social responsibilities of the family implies that focusing on the family is insufficient. The genius of Catholic teaching on the family is that it refuses to limit families by telling them to just take care of their own.[102]

Transformation of Culture

Although *Ecclesia in America* (*EA*) is not usually considered one of John Paul II's social documents, it addresses social issues comprehensively and best reveals the late pope's integrated understanding of the human person called by faith to love in personal and social relations and to transform culture. Its structure reveals this approach, as the pope begins with encounter with the living Christ. Recalling biblical stories of conversion, he notes that today we find Christ especially in scripture, in liturgy, and in the poor.[103] The conversion about which he speaks is not simply a change in belief. Rather, it is marked by a grace that "enables Christians to work for the transformation of the world, in order to bring about a new civilization."[104] Christians are to strive for constant conversion; it is never finished. One's whole life is to be about living the universal call to holiness in a particular way, a way that includes changing civilization or culture.[105]

Conversion leads, in the pope's schema, to communion with the community of believers who turn to the sacraments for sustenance.[106] Each member of the body of Christ has a particular role to play, but laypeople are especially "called to embody deeply evangelical values such as mercy, forgiveness, honesty, transparency of heart and patience."[107] Families are asked to be domestic churches marked by prayer, sacrifice, and "practical signs of charity," where children might "discover a vocation of service in the community and the church."[108] Throughout the section on communion, the pope returns to the idea of solidarity with the poor as he stresses connections between faith, community, and practice. Significantly, he emphasizes the importance of a faith community through which individuals and families can work together.

When he does deal with solidarity specifically, he turns to the judgment story of Matthew 25 and says, "The awareness of communion with Christ and with our brothers and sisters, for its part the fruit of conversion, leads to the service of our neighbors in all their needs, material and spiritual, since the face of Christ shines forth in every human being."[109] He goes on to speak strongly of the moral vision at the heart of the church's social doctrine, centered on the dignity of persons, which should shape our responses to the many social problems of our day, including foreign debt, government corruption, drugs, the arms race, abortion, euthanasia, the death penalty, marginalization, racism, and immigration. Here, even though the analysis is more similar to traditional Catholic social teaching, the pope never loses sight of his focus on encounter, conversion, communion, and solidarity.

More than other social documents, *EA* appears to approach social ethics more theologically, more personally, and more aware of the need for a culture of charity and justice. Fittingly, the prayer that closes the document is for the families of America: "May they be living witnesses to love, justice, and solidarity; make them schools of respect, forgiveness, and mutual help."[110] Families, while not expected to do everything, have important formative tasks. Their faith, if it is real, ought to lead them to embrace community and solidarity. They may be able to address some of the issues the pope discusses through their votes, but his exhortation indicates that some of their most significant work will be done at home and in community as they teach and witness to the dignity of persons that faith in Christ engenders.

The personalist understanding of solidarity at the core of John Paul II's writing that shapes his approach to work, family, social justice, and culture is also clearly at work in many lay movements active in the church today. The sense that modern society is too big and complex to allow for strong ties, that modern work does not offer satisfaction and connection, that modern churches do not offer strong communities, is widespread. In response, many Christians seek out intentional communities as they look for connections, work, and communities that will help them make sense of their lives. Family-based movements such as CFM, Cursillo, and Marriage Encounter continue, but with diminished numbers, in the United States. However, in most large U.S. cities, one can also point to strong, independent residential or neighborhood communities (usually in poorer sections of town) where people come to experience communion and solidarity more fully. Their work is often a combination of service (hospitality, healing, accompaniment) and political action (protests, advocacy). Though small in number, they offer alternative, personalist ways of living out Catholic social teaching.[111] Faith is linked to social justice, and yet concern for social justice is manifested not only in political initiatives but in daily practices and communal partnerships that build solidarity at the grassroots level.

Conclusion: Families and Social Change

In this chapter I have argued that middle associations such as families play a crucial role in the Catholic tradition on social justice that is often overlooked. In the foundational documents of the Catholic social tradition, in early American appropriations of those teachings, and in the social teachings of John Paul II, there is a prophetic emphasis on what can be done by families in the home, in neighborhoods and workplaces, and in local communities and churches. Social transformation proceeds from below and necessarily involves changes of the heart, ongoing conversion, and countercultural practices that can only begin in the home.

The interpretation of CST outlined in this chapter offers an alternative to the visions of three distinct groups of contemporary CST advocates, as recently delineated by Richard Gaillardetz: neoconservatives, radicals, and liberals.[112] Neoconservatives such as George Weigel, John Neuhaus, and Michael Novak examine the tradition and see approval of free market economics alongside critiques of the culture of death. They are more interested in freeing families from government than getting government to act on their behalf or thinking about how they might contribute to the creation of a more just society. Radicals such as Michael Baxter and David Schindler call for alternative Christian communities of love that oppose capitalist economics and culture. Most numerous and influential are liberals, whom Gaillardetz characterizes as "critical corelational," meaning that they do public theology by engaging in affirmation and critique of aspects of both the tradition and the culture. Gaillardetz favors the latter group for their success in charting a middle course between traditionalist neoconservatives partial to right-wing politics and traditionalist radicals attracted to abandonment of political dialogue.[113]

In my view, however, the major division in social ethics today is not dialogical. The idea of a public square "clothed" in pluralistic discussion where political action can be debated seems to be a given for all but the most radical. The real disconnect is between radicals and neoconservatives who affirm the importance of family and community and more mainstream liberals who do not disagree but talk a great deal more about politics. This divide is reflected in the broader popular dialogue and is much more difficult to bridge. When radicals take seriously "participation in the transformative practices of Christian community," they are still saying something necessary and new.[114] Their valuing of communal and family life is distinct and refreshing, if disconcertingly uncommon.[115]

Even more disconcerting, however, is the reality that none of these groups takes families and middle associations as seriously as CST warrants. Even if most would agree that "the Church, then, should look at social issues through a family perspective because the family is the basic unit of the Church and Society," few include family in their social analysis.[116] Neoconservatives argue for freedom in the private sphere and then seem to leave everyone to fend for themselves. They fail to challenge individuals to heed the call of solidarity beyond the boundaries of family. Liberals work out applications of solidarity in the public realm through analyses of war, economics, and human rights but have little to say about the social ethics of families or communities.[117] Radicals have the most to say about alternative ways of living but frequently leave nuanced analyses behind in order to idealize heroes and saints. What is needed, given the historical and ongoing concern of CST for families and communities, is a social ethics of everyday life with an emphasis on family life, not to replace political analyses, but to work out a crucial missing piece of the Catholic social tradition.

Notes

1. Charles E. Curran, *Catholic Social Teaching, 1891–Present: A Historical, Theological, and Ethical Analysis* (Washington, DC: Georgetown University Press, 2002), 15, 45. Most social ethicists agree. Michael Himes, ed., *Modern Catholic Social Teaching: Commentaries and Interpretations* (Washington, DC: Georgetown University Press, 2005), includes one article on *Familiaris consortio* written by Lisa Sowle Cahill (an encouraging and atypical move), but the index contains few other references to family in other social documents. Coleman, *One Hundred Years of Catholic Social Teaching*, does include a section on family, though

most articles are written by people engaged in pastoral work rather than by theologians. The exception is the article on marriage, again written by Cahill. In her seminal work on the social implications of Catholic theology of the family, *Family: A Christian Social Perspective,* she names compassion as a family value and calls adults to own their political duty to support families in need. Cahill's work focuses more on political reform than the social transformative potential of family life.

2. Thomas Massaro and Thomas Shannon, eds., *American Catholic Social Teaching* (Collegeville, MD: Liturgical Press, 2002), xvi.

3. Clarke E. Cochran and David Carroll Cochran, *Catholics, Politics, and Public Policy: Beyond Left and Right* (Maryknoll, NY: Orbis, 2003), 2. The authors characterize private life as a retreat from public responsibility. Ibid., 21.

4. The distinction between public and private is murky, and while I am employing the terms as they are commonly used, I do not mean to suggest here that family life is wholly private. As I hope to make clear, I am arguing for the social significance of daily practices, thus challenging the idea that "private" life is devoid of "public" or social significance.

5. Marvin L. Krier Mich, *Catholic Social Teaching and Movements* (Mystic, CT: Twenty-third, 2001), 6–10.

6. Ibid., 12.

7. Ibid., 13.

8. Ibid., 14.

9. Ibid., 21.

10. For instance, Curran says pre–Vatican II CST does "not give central importance to the change of heart" and cites as an example *RN,* which only mentions the significance of religion in the last paragraph. Curran, *Catholic Social Teaching,* 46. In his summary of the central themes of *RN,* Mich highlights the economic teachings and refers only briefly to the role of the church in educating citizens. Mich, *Catholic Social Teachings and Movements,* 20–21. He criticizes Leo XIII's arrogant claim that "disorder in society is at root a moral and religious issue" (23–24). Mich judges the concrete proposal of trade-based associations to be unworkable but, more so than others, upholds the insight about the importance of intermediate associations (86). David J. O' Brien and Thomas A. Shannon's summary in *Catholic Social Thought: The Documentary Heritage* (Maryknoll, NY: Orbis, 2003), 12–13, does refer readers to the moral critique of Leo XIII but identifies advocacy of "human rights in the economic order" as his major contribution.

11. Donal Dorr, *Option for the Poor: A Hundred Years of Catholic Social Teaching,* rev. ed. (Maryknoll, NY: Orbis, 1983), 55.

12. Ibid.

13. *Rerum novarum* (1891), no. 5 (hereafter cited as *RN,* followed by number). All citations from papal social documents in this section of the chapter are taken from O'Brien and Shannon, *Catholic Social Thought.*

14. *RN,* nos. 6, 10, and 9.

15. *RN,* nos. 11–12. Many rightly note Leo's mischaracterization of socialism and his blindness to potential goods of socialistic ideas, some of which were adopted by later popes. See Shannon, "Commentary," in O'Brien and Shannon, *Catholic Social Thought,* 135.

16. *RN*, no. 13.

17. *RN*, no. 14.

18. *RN*, no. 19.

19. *RN*, no. 20.

20. Mich, *Catholic Social Teachings and Movements*, 24.

21. Thomas Shannon, "Commentary on *Rerum novarum* (The Condition of Labor)," in *Modern Catholic Social Teaching*, ed. Michael Himes, 128. The most enduring contribution, according to Shannon, was the discussion on the just wage.

22. One might say that Leo XIII wanted social change rather than structural change, because he did not envision a fundamentally equal society, but a society in which the state better protected workers, employers recognized workers' rights, and workers handled their wages wisely.

23. *RN*, no. 23.

24. *RN*, no. 32.

25. *RN*, no. 34.

26. *RN*, nos. 42–43. This claim recalls the guild system recommended by some social movements. It sounds notably unrealistic in today's political climate, although recent discussions of spirituality in the workplace may alter these perceptions. *RN*, no. 45.

27. Leo can justly be criticized for trusting too much in the church's ability to train the faithful in virtue. He does not offer a perfect solution, but his concern with the "private" realm in a document remembered as the founding statement of CST is notable.

28. *Quadragesimo anno* (1931), nos. 83–84 (hereafter cited as *QA*, followed by number).

29. *QA*, no. 88.

30. *QA*, no. 127.

31. O'Brien and Shannon, "Commentary," in *Catholic Social Thought*, 41.

32. Curran, *Catholic Social Teaching*, 10.

33. Mich, *Catholic Social Teachings and Movements*, 65–75.

34. Coleman, *One Hundred Years of Catholic Social Teaching*, 37–38.

35. Christine Firer Hinze, "Commentary on *Quadragesimo anno* (After Forty Years)," in *Modern Catholic Social Teaching*, ed. Michael Himes, 172. Hinze, more than any other moral theologian writing today, appreciates this dimension of CST and works at the intersection of family and social ethics.

36. Second Plenary Council of Baltimore, *Pastoral Letter* (October 21, 1866), no. 27, and Third Plenary Council of Baltimore, *Pastoral Letter* (December 7, 1884), no. 31. All citations of American Catholic social documents are taken from Massaro and Shannon, *American Catholic Social Teaching*.

37. Third Plenary Council, *Pastoral Letter*, nos. 36–45.

38. Second Plenary Council, *Pastoral Letter*, nos. 32–34; Third Plenary Council, *Pastoral Letter*, nos. 60–63.

39. National Catholic War Council, *Program of Social Reconstruction*, February 12, 1919, nos. 24–32.

40. Ibid., no. 40.

41. Bishops' Conference, *Present Crisis*, April 25, 1933, no. 13.

42. Ibid., no. 40.
43. Alfred J. Ede, *The Lay Crusade for a Christian America: A Study of the American Federation of Catholic Societies, 1900–1919* (New York: Garland, 1988), chronicles early Catholic social concerns: intemperance, Sabbath violations, divorce, sex, school reform, and faith renewal.
44. Bishops' Conference, *Present Crisis*, no. 62.
45. National Catholic Welfare Conference, *Statement on the Church and the Social Order*, February 7, 1940, no. 58.
46. Ibid., no. 66.
47. Jeffrey Burns, *American Catholics and the Family Crisis, 1930–1962* (New York: Garland, 1988), 6.
48. Ibid., 17.
49. Ibid., 22.
50. Ibid., 29–32.
51. Ibid., 38–40.
52. Ibid., 68–69.
53. John L. Thomas, *The American Catholic Family* (Englewood Cliffs, NJ: Prentice Hall, 1956), 6.
54. Burns, *American Catholics and the Family Crisis*, 99.
55. Ibid., 128.
56. Ibid., 167.
57. Some dioceses took the U.S. bishops' suggestions further. One example is the "Program for the Christian Family for 1944–45," adopted by the archdiocese of San Francisco that recommended family practices and subjects for discussion each month. Reprinted in Joseph P. Chinnici and Angelyn Dries, ed., *Prayer and Practice in the American Catholic Community* (Maryknoll, NY: Orbis, 2000).
58. Burns, *American Catholics and the Family Crisis*, 170.
59. Ibid., 170–71.
60. Ibid., 173.
61. Ibid., 173–74.
62. Maisie Ward, "Plea for the Family," in *Be Not Solicitous*, ed. Maisie Ward (New York: Sheed & Ward, 1953), 12–13.
63. Burns, *American Catholics and the Family Order*, 188, 187.
64. Ibid., 211.
65. Ed Willock, "Postscript on Poverty and Marriage," in *Be Not Solicitous*, ed. Maisie Ward (New York: Sheed & Ward, 1953), 249–50.
66. Burns, *American Catholics and the Family Crisis*, 279.
67. Ibid., 281.
68. Ibid., 282.
69. Ibid., 293, 294.
70. These included neighborhood actions such as babysitting co-ops, family recreation nights, clothing exchanges, and parish potlucks as well as political actions related to civil rights, labor unions, and urban problems. See Jeffrey M. Burns, *Disturbing the Peace: A History of the Christian Family Movement* (South Bend, IN: University of Notre Dame Press, 1999), 36.
71. See Robert McClory, *Turning Point: The Inside Story of the Papal Birth Control Commission* (New York: Crossroad, 1995).

72. Michael Novak's willingness to read human rights and critique of capitalism out of the tradition is a case in point. See Todd David Whitmore, "John Paul II, Michael Novak, and the Differences between Them," *Annual of the Society of Christian Ethics* 21 (2001): 215–32.

73. David Hollenbach, "Commentary on *Gaudium et spes* (Pastoral Constitution on the Church in the Modern World)," in *Modern Catholic Social Teaching*, ed. Michael Himes, 271–79.

74. Ibid., 279–84. Family and culture are used as examples to illuminate a point about the Second Vatican Council's embrace of legitimate diversity qualified by its transcendent commitment to human dignity but are not treated in their own right. Ibid., 284–87.

75. My colleague, philosophy professor Gregory Beabout, taught me a great deal about *GS* when we taught it together in the fall semesters of 2002 and 2003 at Saint Louis University.

76. M. D. Chenu anticipated much of this analysis in what may be the most important book on work, *The Theology of Work: An Exploration*, trans. Lillian Soiron (Dublin: Gill, 1963).

77. John Paul II, *Laborem exercens* (Washington, DC: United States Catholic Conference, 1981), no. 4.

78. Ibid.

79. Ibid., no. 16.

80. *The Church in the Modern World*, in *Vatican Council II: The Conciliar and Post Conciliar Documents*, rev. ed., ed. Austin Flannery (Northport, NY: Costello, 1988), no. 43.

81. Dorothy Day, *Loaves and Fishes* (Maryknoll, NY: Orbis, 1963), 221.

82. Oscar Romero addresses the reality that many in the world have little choice as to the work they do. Still, he encourages all workers to see their jobs as "priestly work," consecrating it to God. Sermon, November 20, 1977, reprinted in Oscar Romero, *The Violence of Love*, comp. and trans. James R. Brockman (Maryknoll, NY: Orbis, 1988), 10. Those who do have a choice have greater responsibility to respond to social needs.

83. Richard Gaillardetz, "The Ecclesiological Foundations of Modern Catholic Social Teaching," in *Modern Catholic Social Teaching*, ed. Michael Himes, 77.

84. John Paul II, *Sollicitudo rei socialis* (Washington, DC: United States Catholic Conference, 1987), no. 28.

85. Ibid., no. 42.

86. Ibid., no. 41. The pope's insistence that his offering is primarily theological seems designed to return attention to neglected aspects of CST and to check efforts to associate it with specific political programs. It does not deny all interest in political solutions.

87. John Paul II, *Centesimus annus* (Boston: St. Paul Books and Media, 1991), no. 12.

88. Ibid., nos. 35 and 48.

89. See Daniel Finn, "Commentary on *Centesimus annus* (One Hundred Years)," in *Modern Catholic Social Teaching*, ed. Michael Himes, 443.

90. Ibid., 454.

91. Ibid., 455, 457.

92. *Familiaris consortio,* no. 17.
93. Ibid., no. 28.
94. Ibid., no. 37.
95. Ibid., no. 39.
96. Ibid., no. 41.
97. Ibid., no. 42.
98. Ibid., no. 44; and ibid., nos. 44 and 47.
99. Ibid., no. 47.
100. Ibid., no. 21.
101. Ibid., nos. 49–64. Lisa Sowle Cahill also attests to this emphasis in recent Catholic teaching on the family. See Cahill, *Family: A Christian Social Perspective,* 89–91.
102. Cahill claims that "reactions [to *FC*] that minimize the socially radical mission of the Christian family are not numerous and do not seem to have been widely influential." Cahill, "Commentary," in *Modern Catholic Social Teaching,* ed. Michael Himes, 383. However, many theologians downplay the social dimension of *FC*, and few laypeople identify with it. The transformative potential of the document remains unrealized. See, e.g., Janet E. Smith, "The Family: A Communion of Persons," in *A Celebration of the Thought of John Paul II,* ed. Gregory R. Beabout (St. Louis, MO: St. Louis University Press, 1998), 85–104; Donald A. Miller, *Concepts of Family Life in Magisterial Catholic Teaching: From Vatican II through Christifideles laici* (San Francisco: San Francisco Scholars Press, 1996); the influential work of Christopher West (for instance, "A Basic Theology of Marriage," available at www.christopherwest.com); and, as Cahill notes, the new *Catechism of the Catholic Church* (New York: Doubleday, 1995), 446–62.
103. John Paul II, *Ecclesia in America* (Washington, DC: United States Catholic Conference, 1999), no. 10.
104. Ibid., no. 8.
105. Ibid., no. 30.
106. Ibid., no. 35.
107. Ibid., no. 42.
108. Ibid., no. 46.
109. Ibid., no. 52.
110. Ibid., no. 76.
111. John Coleman asserts that lay movements are the new carriers of CST, more important even than encyclicals. See Coleman, "The Future of Catholic Social Teaching," in *Modern Catholic Social Teaching,* ed. Michael Himes, 535–36.
112. Gaillardetz, "Commentary," 79.
113. Ibid., 80.
114. Ibid.
115. An exception is Christopher Wolfe, "Subsidiarity: The 'Other' Ground of Limited Government," in *Catholicism, Liberalism, and Communitarianism: The Catholic Intellectual Tradition and the Moral Foundations of Democracy,* ed. Kenneth Grasso, Gerald V. Bradley, and Robert P. Hunt (Lanham, MD: Rowman & Littlefield, 1995), 81–96. Wolfe notes that limited government allows smaller groups the space to foster virtue but does not comment on the potential of families to contribute to social change.

116. Patricia Voydanoff and Thomas M. Martin suggest ways to close the gap between family and social justice at the pastoral level in *Using a Family Perspective in Catholic Social Justice and Family Ministries* (Lewiston, NY: Edwin Mellen Press, 1994).

117. John A. Coleman recently argued in "Future of Catholic Social Thought," 522–44, that movements and institutions will become increasingly important carriers of the tradition, but his analysis focuses much more on social theory and does not speak to the import of family practices.

CHAPTER THREE

Grace, Sin, and Holy Families

The Limits of a Theology of Ideals

Having established in chapters 1 and 2 that both Catholic sacramental theology and Catholic social teaching point to a need for a social ethic attentive to family concerns, it may seem appropriate to begin analyzing everyday moral issues faced by families, with the hope of sketching what an ideal Christian life might look like. However, before beginning ethical analysis, it is important to address what may be a stumbling block for many readers: an idealized approach to family prevalent in Catholic theology and devotional life. In Catholic liturgy and popular piety, the dominant image of the family is the holy family. This family is most commonly portrayed as abounding in quiet harmony, with each member attentive to the duties of his or her role—Mary, submissive and nurturing; Joseph, quietly protective, a good provider; and Jesus, the holy obedient child.[1] In addition to the holy family, large families who sacrifice financial gain in order to cooperate with God in the creation of new life have been considered ideal. Images of large, pious families gathered at daily Mass or bedtime rosaries, are common in popular Catholic literature, and these families have been frequently invoked as models by the magisterium, theologians, and leaders of lay family movements.[2]

Even today these images often remain with those addressed by Catholic theology and shape responses to everything written about families. John Paul II, for instance, writes, "The family has a mission to guard, reveal, and communicate love, and this is a living reflection of and a real sharing in God's love for humanity and the love of Christ the Lord for the church, his bride," speaking of both an ideal and a reality, a gift and a task.[3] When Catholics read this, images of holy families cannot be far from their minds. The pope asks families to "become what you are" or to live up to the mission that is rightfully yours, to your truest identity.[4] His description of the ideal Christian family has the power to be both inspiring and potentially alienating. Faced with an image that is manifestly different from their own lives, many turn away, assuming that theology about families will elicit feelings of guilt or inferiority. Or, knowing the strengths of their structurally imperfect families, they disregard what seems to be sentimental piety without nuance. In short, images of holy families often stand in the way of right hearing and impair right response.

Any theology of the family needs to address this problem if it is to have any hope of reaching ordinary families. In much of recent Catholic family theology, family difficulties are spoken of as irregularities after the theological vision has been constructed.[5] However, it is not enough to acknowledge the difficulties that broken, flawed, or interfaith families may face in living out an ideal that is constructed without those problems in mind; these problems and imperfections belong to all of us and ought to be reflected in our theological thinking. Literature is a crucial source for correcting this problem, for it "can contribute to our understanding of what it would be like to lead lives of various sorts and thereby help to guide us in constructing our own lives."[6] In this chapter I argue that in order to avoid constructing a potentially alienating, overly idealistic theology of the family, the realities of imperfection, sin, and disunity must be brought to the forefront of theological thinking and writing. In what follows I treat the fiction of Flannery O'Connor as prophetic resource that illuminates the necessity of bringing sin and imperfection to the center of a family ethic situated in the tradition of Catholic systematic theology and social teaching. The concluding section will show that because O'Connor's vision was not only attentive to human finitude but also rooted in solidarity and everyday morality, it provides a good foundation for the kind of family ethics that will occupy the rest of this book.

O'Connor's Gift to Theology

Flannery O'Connor (1925–64), American Catholic writer of two novels and thirty short stories, was criticized in her time for not publishing stories that would inspire a large audience to strive for greater holiness. Her own mother once asked if she thought she was really using the gifts God gave her, writing stories so few people enjoyed.[7] In fact, her stories were notoriously difficult for many people to understand, let alone enjoy. Filled with strange characters seemingly lacking in faith, they are not an obvious choice as a resource for Christian family ethics.

Most who are familiar with O'Connor's letters and essays know that all of her stories concern the inbreaking of grace in the face of darkness and offer the possibility of conversion. However, in O'Connor's stories, only rarely does conversion happen within a family setting. Her stories include no positive portrayals of parents praying with their children, teaching them sound morals, or worshipping in a community of faith. There are no heartwarming homecomings, festive meals, and few significant confrontations. Intact nuclear families are a relatively rare subject in O'Connor's writing. The few that do appear are somewhat less than ideal. Frequently these families' positive view of themselves is revealed to be more distortion than reality. In the well-known story "A Good Man Is Hard to Find," for instance, a family with two parents, two children, and a grandmother set off on vacation in a car trip marked by the grandmother's comments about how few good people are left in the world. O'Connor portrays the grandmother's excessive view of her own goodness by showing her concern with superficial manners that separate "nice people" from everyone else.[8] Only when confronted with a serial murderer named "the Misfit" does the grandmother realize the wrongness of her attempts to classify and separate people.[9] Traditional families may first appear in O'Connor's stories in picturesque settings, but it is their imperfection rather than their ideal status that is significant. In a tradition dominated by holy families, these stories can provide balance. O'Connor's potential contribution to Christian family ethics lies in her portraits of nonideal families who reveal the importance and difficulty of faith and the frailty of human beings. Her work should push us to bring forward a theological vision of marriage and family that is attentive to both grace and finitude.

Seeing: Acknowledging the Importance and Difficulty of Faith

O'Connor's stories bring readers back to the most crucial issue in the lives of religious persons. Behind traditional practices and ethical demands central to most theology on the family lies the question of faith. O'Connor thought of herself as a moralist because her stories concerned the presence of evil. However, the crucial moral issue for her was seeing rightly—that is, through the eyes of faith. She sought to enable her audience to see evil where they might otherwise miss it and to encourage in them the sorts of small steps toward better faith her unlikely heroes take. In the terms of moral theology, fundamental option is primary for O'Connor.[10] "What, ultimately, is one's life about?" she forces her readers to ask.

One might argue that O'Connor would have been more effective as a moralist concerned with right seeing if she wrote stories about good rather than evil. However, she was convinced that stories involving the pious practice of good people would not reveal faith for her secular or lightly Christian audience. Thus she exaggerated to show how people run from faith or only just glimpse it. "When you can assume that your audience holds the same beliefs you do," she famously said, "you can relax a little and use more normal means of talking to it; when you have to assume it does not, then you have to make your vision apparent by shock—to the hard of hearing you shout, and for the almost-blind you draw large and startling figures."[11] Using this method, she sought to reveal not "what we ought to be but . . . what we are at a given time and under given circumstances."[12] Her work depicts reality—most people struggle with faith, and many more affirm it but do not get very far in living it.

Her characters, then, are not heroes or saints. By "focusing on characters who, far from representing the faith, are set apart by it," O'Connor restores an understanding of the difficulties that human beings can have living without God, whether they are nominally Christian or not.[13] She gives readers characters claimed by faith against their will or despite their attempts to run, so the need for faith and the poverty of existence without it come through.[14]

This approach differs from most Catholic theology on the family, in which faith is assumed. Most theologians exhort Christian families to live more actively Christian lives, while mourning the waywardness of the world and its encroachment on "the family."[15] However, given the reality of mixed marriages (40% and growing) and varying degrees of commitment among people of faith, O'Connor's realism is a good corrective.[16] Plurality, doubt, and lives unmarked by faith exist not only "out there" in the world but also "in here"—in the church and in Christian families.[17] Acknowledging this is the precondition for authentic grappling with moral dilemmas central to family ethics.

Concern that such an approach will leave out the majority of less than perfect believers would be unwarranted, for O'Connor does not simply speak in black-and-white terms of accepting or rejecting faith. Rather, she writes about the struggle of keeping faith and taking it seriously. This nuanced understanding of faith, though sometimes hard to discern in the midst of casts of grotesque characters, is central. As she put it,

> I don't think you should write something as long as a novel around anything that is not of the gravest concern to you and everybody else, and for me this is always the conflict between an attraction for the Holy and disbelief in it that we breathe with the air of our times. It's hard to believe always but more so in the world we live in now. There are some of us who have to pay for our faith every step of the way and who have to work out dramatically what it would be like without it and if being without it would be ultimately possible or not.[18]

In families, the difficulty of belief and life without faith are perhaps even harder to see than in individuals because families are likelier to engage in traditional faith practices. Yet, even for them, larger questions of what faith really means and how it shapes life from the center out—or does not—remain unasked and unanswered. O'Connor's narratives beg readers to ask those questions.

Hazel Motes, hero of the novel *Wise Blood* struggles with faith.[19] Tempted by atheism, he tries to run from the faith of his ancestors. He mocks his grandfather's life as a preacher by going from town to town, standing on top of his big car and preaching the church without Christ. Many of O'Connor's intellectual readers believe Hazel to be a hero because he rejects and mocks the simplistic faith of southern fundamentalism. However, O'Connor writes that in Hazel's character, there are "a number of conflicting wills in one person."[20] His struggle is difficult, because as much as he wants to, he simply cannot leave faith alone. This, O'Connor reveals in the second edition of the novel, is why she admires him.[21]

In fact, many of her characters are baptized members of a church who nonetheless find it hard to live up to the ethical implications of their faith. In "The Displaced Person," Mrs. McKinley, a landowner, tries to be a good Christian woman by inviting the displaced Guizac family to work on her property and by trying to treat all of her workers as well as she can, but she is blind to the real moral evil around her.[22] She cannot see that her black workers deserve more than her tolerance of their supposed moral weakness and lax work ethic or that her view of her own largess depends on a false picture of her independence. She, like the rest of her household, does not want to recognize Mr. Guizac's goodness, and in the end she and the others watch as he is plowed under by a tractor.[23] Yet these people are not so evil that they can be dismissed. Readers sympathize with characters who, so like themselves, stand by in the face of moral atrocity because they fail to see it for what it is.[24]

Despite O'Connor's pessimism about human nature, she offers hope in her portrayals of people who are not perfect but searching. Though they might go through most of their daily lives unperturbed by questions of faith, in the end, most of the characters reveal themselves to be spiritually hungry.[25] Ordinary people, O'Connor maintains, want to see.

And there is much to see when one's eyes are opened. The contrast between Mrs. McKinley and the priest in "The Displaced Person" makes this clear. The priest alone notices and appreciates the beauty of Mrs. McKinley's peacock, though others think him an idiot for making a fuss over the animal.[26] Mrs. McKinley thinks that "the DP" (as Mr. Guizac is called in the story) is her salvation because he works hard, but the DP, like all the others who cultivate her land, is not real to her.[27] Instead of seeing them as persons like herself, she insists that they are all "the same" or "extra."[28] The priest, however, sees the DP as the Christlike person he is, but he also sees the humanity of the white and black people who work the farm, and of Mrs. McKinley herself.[29] His vision is a source of hope that grace can break in even in a place where such inhumanity has occurred.

O'Connor's stories recognize that the first moral question is one of vision or faith. Though it is no doubt easier to assume that one's audience shares one's own convictions, it is more honest to acknowledge the struggles many people have just in trying to believe. A compelling vision of Christian ethics must speak to people at a variety of stages of faith and unfaith because all of these people are inside the church today.

Sin and Finitude

O'Connor's understanding of the difficulty of faith for modern persons is accompanied by a pessimism about human nature that could be seen as a diminishment of gains the church has made since Vatican II. In particular, the church's growing optimism about human persons and its move away from a focus on sinfulness that previously dominated Catholic theology would seem to differ from O'Connor's emphasis on human finitude. Catholic theology on marriage in particular has benefited from more attention to the spiritual significance of loving relationships.[30] While few would want to return to pre–Vatican II theology, overly idealized ways of talking about families can be almost as harmful as overly dark descriptions, alienating people because of their distance from reality. Yet traditional discussions of original sin are difficult for contemporary Christians to hear, because they seem at odds with modern ideas about the goodness and perfectibility of human beings.

O'Connor's stories paint portraits of evil that assume sound Christian teaching about the dual nature of human persons marked by grace and sin. Of the novelist, she writes, "His concern with poverty is with a poverty fundamental to man. I believe that the basic experience of everyone is the experience of human limitation."[31] Her characters are stark symbols of limitation rather than realistic depictions. Characters that remind readers of their limits were important to O'Connor, for she believed it is because "we are afflicted with the doctrine of the perfectibility of human nature by its own efforts that the vision of the freak in fiction is so disturbing. The freak in modern fiction keeps us from forgetting that we share in his state."[32]

Contemporary theology centering on family can often fall into the language of perfectibility. In John Paul II's discussion of the family as domestic church, for instance, he writes that "the Christian family has a special vocation to witness to the paschal covenant of Christ by constantly radiating the joy of love and the certainty of the hope for which it must give account."[33] The language of calling, vocation, and mission animates ethical writings about families and seems to ask of them unanimity, certainty, and constancy that are often in short supply in the real world.

O'Connor's fiction does not deny the high vocation of families, but it recalls another piece of Christian understanding of human beings—their failures in joy, hope, and love, their experience of being insufficient in themselves. In "The Displaced Person," Mrs. McKinley labors under the illusion that everyone is dependent on her and misunderstands herself as financially rather than spiritually poor, failing to recognize her true needs.[34] In contrast, the priest and the DP are both humble and content to do what they can in imperfect situations. Reading O'Connor's stories schools readers in recognizing human limitation.

Often characters in O'Connor's stories know they need faith but are told by others that they do not, further revealing how human beings struggle to accept their finitude. In "The Lame Shall Enter First," Rufus, foster child of Sheppard, "will not accept explanations of his behavior that omit forgiveness or the need for it."[35] Though Sheppard wants to deny or explain away Rufus's bad behavior, Rufus will not be comforted by cheap grace. He, like many of O'Connor's characters who look evil on the surface, is not willing to change, but at least he knows who he is. What is more, he insists on his need for redemption, even in the face of Sheppard's attempts to convince him that Christianity is standing in the way of his growth. At the end of the story, Sheppard's attempts to reach Rufus are all rejected because they deny Rufus's desire to acknowledge his own finitude.[36] Similarly, in "A Good Man Is Hard to Find," the Misfit, who murders the grandmother, knows that Jesus has "thrown everything off balance" even if he is afraid to truly live with the implications of that claim, and the grandmother realizes obliquely by the end that these things are more important than the manners she has been prattling on about.[37] O'Connor corrected readers who saw the grandmother as an unrepentant witch, noting that those in the South know many old ladies like her.[38] Though deeply flawed, in contrast to those around them, the grandmother and the Misfit both perceive their neediness, and O'Connor held out hope that both would come around in the end.[39]

O'Connor used the grotesque to illuminate human imperfection. She explained that she was "not simply showing us what we are, but what we have been and what we could become."[40] The power of O'Connor's stories is in their ability to portray evil that is so extreme and yet convince readers that they are not so very different from these characters. The Misfit is not just a crazy murderer but also someone who knows that if Christ died for us, "it's nothing for you to do but throw away everything and follow Him," yet chooses to keep doing what he likes.[41] It is a rare reader who cannot see herself in this honest, if brutal, man. Similarly, when Hazel Motes of *Wise Blood* blinds himself trying to live without Christ, the ordinary struggles of ordinary people who harm themselves attempting to prove their self-sufficiency are illuminated.[42] Better than sweeping attempts to describe imperfection, the use of the grotesque helps readers see what is wrong with their lives and opens them to the possibility of grace.[43] Seeing these enlarged characters lends urgency to moral deliberation. If these characters need Christ, do we? If they have said no, what would it mean to say yes?

The recognition of finitude, so evident in O'Connor's fiction, should affect the way Christians think about families. O'Connor offers a reminder of how hard it is for human beings to see their own weakness. If our theology sounds more appropriate for people whose faith is always secure, whose understanding and embrace of the cross is beyond reproach, then something is off balance. Talking about the crosses people must bear is not enough. Ordinary people need to be able to visualize what the cross might mean in an ordinary life and think about how they fit into a theological vision from where they are right now.[44]

Grace, Sin, and Finitude in Christian Marriage

Much of contemporary Catholic theology on marriage suffers from a failure to take the reality of human imperfection as seriously as O'Connor did. Its optimistic portrayal of married life seems alien to the reality of most. This optimism stems from good intentions. Contrary to earlier theologies of marriage, contemporary theology confidently attests that the married state of life is an excellent way to live out a Christian vocation. Language of marriage as an inferior way has all but disappeared from the tradition. Even John Paul II, who maintains the traditional view of celibacy as the higher path, calls it so because the celibate gives up the love and grace of marriage—one of the highest goods human life has to offer.[45] Lay theologians are largely silent on the distinction between the two paths of Christians, preferring to focus on the joys and struggles of the path chosen by most. Contemporary theology is free to move beyond earlier suspicions that sexual passion and family care would be distractions from the spiritual life. Its aim has been to explore the spiritual and moral meaning of sacramental marriage, to describe how grace is present not only in the juridical bond of marriage but in the lives of married people and their children. However, though recognition of the grace present in Christian marriage is important, overly idealistic visions of spousal love can inadvertently obscure the reality of human finitude and, importantly for my purposes, the social import of Christian marriage. The best of contemporary theology holds grace and sin together in the context of an outward-turning marriage. It underlines the grace present in loving relationships, calls couples to solidarity, and recognizes the depths of human sinfulness. It is this theology that can speak with authenticity to the church broadly conceived.

One of Pope John Paul II's most significant contributions to Catholic theology is his elevation of married life. For him, the sacrament of marriage is "the specific source and original means of sanctification for Christian married couples and families." It "is in itself a liturgical action, glorifying God." It gives couples "the grace and obligation of transforming their whole lives into a 'spiritual sacrifice.'"[46] Self-giving love is for the pope the point of human existence and the heart of marriage. He believes that in drawing close to one another and giving more of themselves, wife and husband become better human beings and better Christians. Though few people recognize the language of growing in holiness, most of those who believe know that they experience God's love in their most intimate relationships. They can see that over time they get better at sacrificing their own wants for those who are close to them. Their marriages are sacramental, not just because they are faithful, fruitful, and lifelong, but because they are loving relationships through which God can be deeply known.

John Paul II carries the tradition further not only by seeing sacramental grace in marriage itself but by extending sacrament to include family. His decision to speak of family as a communion is profound, for it captures sacramental presence using a word that evokes eucharistic presence and community or even communing. The bodily presence of family life is raised up. The pope implies a similarity between the intimate encounter of Eucharist and the intermingling of lives that occurs in a family. Family values of acceptance, encounter, dialogue, availability, and sacrifice are implicitly affirmed. The pope puts forth the idea that because the dignity of each person is recognized in a profound way in the family, it is "the most effective means for humanizing and personalizing society" by "making possible a life that is human."[47] We come to understand the value of persons here and bring this understanding forward into society. As well, those outside a family are brought to a deeper understanding of human dignity when they see and experience the love that holds a family together. It is a love that proclaims, "This is what God is like; God loves us like this." This understanding of sacrament pertains not simply to juridical bonds or marriage liturgies but also to human relationships.

Even though the language of sacramental grace is most prominent in the pope's theological treatment of marriage, the cross is never far from his thoughts. The pope claims that a lifelong marriage covenant is the necessary context for the internal and external goods of familial communion to flourish. He writes that married couples "are a permanent reminder to the church of what happened on the cross; they are for one another and their children witnesses to the salvation in which the sacrament makes them sharers."[48] The comparison of married love to the love expressed on the cross is crucial. Loving one's spouse is sometimes analogous to the sacrifice of Christ, who would not stop loving no matter what it cost him. It is a rare family that does not experience some of the cross in their marriage, and yet, the pope claims, they are called to fidelity, for their "deeply personal unity . . . demands indissolubility and faithfulness in definitive mutual giving."[49] The strength of John Paul II's theology is that it offers recognition of both loving communion and suffering in Christian marriage.

Still, the total self-giving the pope advocates can be criticized as overly ideal. Is it really possible for ordinary human beings to be completely selfless? Lay theologians writing on marriage offer a corrective by bringing their own experiences as married people into dialogue with Catholic theology. Their writings bring marital theology down to earth with a greater recognition of human finitude.

Bernard Cooke's well-known understanding of marriage as a sacrament of friendship is a prime example. Cooke worries that the older sacramental theology led Catholics to think that when people get married they are able to make special withdrawals from the bank of grace.[50] This notion is not very convincing, as most know of Christian marriages that seem lacking in grace, and many have the experience of trying to make a withdrawal but coming up short. Instead, Cooke claims, married couples should understand that they are grace to each other, to their children, to everyone around them.[51] This sounds radical, but it really is not. Love is the most profound human experience. We experience love in friendship, and marriage is the ultimate friendship, wherein God communicates to us through the love of others. This is the sacrament, the grace of God's love poured out on us through those who love us. Though Cooke is not significantly less idealistic than the pope, by naming marriage as friendship he allows people to connect with the concept of sacramentality that many still link to a bond or ceremony rather than to the relationships that are most central to their lives. If total self-giving seems unattainable, friendship—even lifelong, deep friendship—remains a widely shared experience.[52]

A theology that locates sacramental grace in the self-giving of the spouses can also be justly criticized for overlooking how sexism can distort marital love. Even today, many women are too willing to sacrifice, while men can be simultaneously unaware of and attached to male privilege.[53] Lay theologians attempt to make the language of sacrament more conscious of sexism so that it points toward true mutuality. In a recent essay, Herbert Anderson argues that if marriage is to image God's love, it must mirror God's justice as well. Just love, he claims, requires "a willingness of all persons in a family to regard each other as persons of worth, renew relations when they are broken, and restore [any] imbalance of power."[54] Just love includes sacrifice for the larger good of the marriage, gratitude for sacrifices made, and continuing attention to fairness in the distribution of sacrifices and to the claiming of specific roles and virtues. Reliance on socially determined parts should ultimately give way to true openness to the gifts and desires of each person. The commitment of the couple should be to the growth of each individually and to the good of the family as a whole. This is the same love and sacrifice that John Paul II writes about, tempered by the insistence that marriage must be just as well as intimate.[55]

A theology of marriage that truly reckons with human finitude will require serious recognition of how sexism distorts efforts at communion, as well as how difficult intimate marital union is to attain in the first place. Deepening communion is hard work and, in the rush of contemporary family life, easy to avoid. Many couples today, even those who rarely travel or work late, know that sometimes in the rush of jobs, activities, meals, and housework, in the dance of dividing and conquering, they can fall into bed exhausted from their efforts without having had a meaningful conversation, let alone having spent the day together. There is so much to occupy a family's days, and intimacy is often not sought out or protected. It is far easier to walk through the early years of married life filled with young children, homemaking, and career building and fail to connect with a spouse. It may be harder still when growing children seek independence or aging parents require care. However, as Florence Bourg writes, a vision of marriage as a sacramental covenant can help married couples see each other in a new light, not apart from, but in the midst of, the chaos of modern family life. According to Bourg, "A family where Christian sacramental vision is operative may experience the same 'falling short of ideals' as any other family. But they dare to believe, if nothing else, that God remains with them."[56] This vision of marriage recognizes the grace found in a loving, mutual union of imperfect human beings who often fall short of the total self-giving toward which they aim.

If all families are limited in their potential to achieve total self-giving, some families are especially challenged. Catholic theology gives little attention to families dealing with problems of divorce, poverty, racism, abuse, or addiction. In *Familiaris consortio*, John Paul II briefly treats those families who cannot meet the ideal of a healthy, two-parent family in a section called "Pastoral Care of the Family in Difficult Cases," which tries to deal firmly but compassionately with mixed marriages, cohabitation, separation, divorce, remarriage, and so forth.[57] Though the pope says too little about the potential for these families to experience grace in the midst of imperfection, he does name many people who find themselves in circumstances that make family life exceptionally hard: migrant workers, those in the armed forces, refugees, homeless persons, single-parent families, those suffering from addiction, those experiencing discrimination, the elderly, and those isolated from religious communities. While he offers strategies for how churches should try to help these families, he also says something interesting about the advantages these otherwise disadvantaged families have: "These are circumstances in which . . . it is easier to help people understand and live the lofty aspects of the spirituality of marriage and the family, aspects which take their inspiration from the value of Christ's cross and resurrection, the source of sanctification and profound happiness in daily life, in the light of the great eschatological realities of eternal life."[58]

There may be more openness to experiencing grace in families in which scarcity or loss make faith and interdependence more obviously necessary.[59] Even, and perhaps especially, in the depths of human weakness and in the face of imperfect attempts to love, God remains present and active.[60] Key strains of the contemporary Catholic tradition affirm that this is true not just for families that are structurally broken or facing serious problems but also for those that are broken in more ordinary ways, that is, for all families. Often it is in a family's imperfection that grace is revealed. In their brokenness, their need for God and each other is made clear.

For instance, Joanne Heaney Hunter writes that families are called to become Christ for one another. Like Eucharist, she says, they are blessed and broken. She emphasizes the dying and rising that takes places at so many stages of marriage: when young adults enter marriage and must give up some of their freedom, when parents suffer as children continually seek independence and experience the pain of growing up, when parents welcome back children who have made serious mistakes, when spouses care for their own frail, elderly parents.[61] Families become known to each other in the breaking of bread over a lifetime. As they are broken through suffering, they open themselves to greater familial communion. Thus, "God builds on the imperfection present in every family life, and makes it holy."[62]

Theologians in the post–Vatican II generation tend to be even more conscious of the difficulties of achieving perfect union.[63] Richard Gaillardetz's consciousness of human finitude pushes him to put less emphasis on the actions of married men and women and more emphasis on God's abiding presence. He reminds Christian spouses that "their communion with each other is, at the same time, communion with God . . . the ground and source of our existence who sustains us and abides in us."[64] Gaillardetz does not revert to an earlier view of marriage that fails to recognize the value of and need for the work of love, but he does recognize that husbands and wives do not make grace present on their own, and he knows that God is present not only when they love each other well. Rather, "God is [also] found in the 'between' of the relationship of husband and wife," in the solitude and pain, in the waiting through the wintry seasons of a marriage, in the "sense of absence, longing, and the embrace of the limits of the relationship."[65] Christians who have passed through these seasons can know that God is present, even when they fail to live up to the potential of their marriage vows.

The key point here is not that the efforts of human beings make grace present but that in their "faithful endurance . . . they will discover their marriage as grace."[66] This is hard to recognize because modern-day Catholics may be more likely to think they have to do everything on their own, but in the best of contemporary Catholic theology, there is an insistence that despite our flawed efforts God remains steadfast, pouring out love. As David McCarthy puts it, "If marriage in the church is a grace, then marriage and family life will be sustained despite our ambiguous choices and our lack of interpersonal expertise."[67] Especially during the down times of marriage, spouses may make a conscious choice to rely on the covenant they have made. Even if they know they will not leave their spouse, working on their problems is not always possible. So they keep going, trusting that the marriage will pull them through, and very often it does.[68] According to McCarthy, marriage is "structured to accommodate dysfunction."[69] It allows for grace and redemption despite sin and suffering.

The best of Catholic sacramental theology of marriage does not assume perfect love. Rather, this theology sees God working in and through limited human efforts. Although the contemporary Catholic tradition can be justly criticized for minimizing the roles of sin and finitude, most lay theologians do give some attention to the reality of married life that includes light and darkness, steadfast love and failure to love. Far less attention is given to the 40 percent of couples with mixed-faith marriages or to the many more who struggle with faith or its expression. A family ethic that hopes to speak to a broad audience will have to reckon more closely with the witness of Flannery O'Connor, who took the messy reality of grace and sin, faith, and unbelief as her starting point and still managed to find grace and point the way—however bleakly—toward a life of discipleship. This does not mean going back to the days when marriage was viewed as the second best vocation, but it does mean viewing this life in all its complexity in order to avoid alienating, overly idealistic visions that do not speak to ordinary families.

Sin, Grace, and Solidarity

A family ethic that begins with finitude and sin is likely to be faulted for being too focused on private failings and individual salvation. After all, most Christians are already conscious of sins of failure in relationships or personal integrity, more so than social sins such as paying unjust wages or damaging the environment. Those writers who mourn the presence of sin in the family are more likely to be talking about sexual sins or divorce, not racism or social injustice. Flannery O'Connor herself seems an unlikely source for the sort of socially conscious family ethic argued for in this book.

However, I want to contend that O'Connor does provide a good model for family ethics, both because of her portrayal of solidarity and because of her concern with local or personal efforts at eradicating social sin.

Flannery O'Connor is commonly viewed by those who understand her theological perspective as a writer concerned with sin and grace in general, not with specific moral issues. Much of her writing centers on highly unusual situations rather than on ordinary ethical dilemmas. In her essays and letters, she insisted that she had no interest in politics or social issues.[70] Yet a close reading of her stories reveals that for most of her characters evil is associated with pride and exclusion, while grace is linked to humility and reaching out beyond one's social class or race. With her stories, O'Connor gives flesh to the often amorphous moral value of solidarity, embodying a distinctly Christian sensibility about the responsibility to extend compassion beyond the boundaries of family. Though O'Connor is not commonly viewed as a social moralist, in fact, her moral vision of imperfection is directly linked to key themes of Catholic social ethics that are central to the theological vision at the heart of this book: solidarity and the significance of the moral life of families.

A Christian family ethic is inherently social. As I argued in chapters 1 and 2, scripture, liturgy, sacramental theology, and Catholic social teaching all point toward a Christian family ethic that involves dual callings to serve one's own as well as the broader communities in and outside the home. In particular, there is a mandate in Catholic family theology to embrace those who are poor and defenseless. Yet, in a society in which "family first" seems a necessary message to counter dominant trends encouraging focus on career and the self, it is often difficult to take seriously as a moral failing the neglect or mistreatment of needy persons in our own midst.

O'Connor offers specific, penetrating illustrations of pride that impedes connection with others, as well as genuine—if partial and flawed—attempts to seek connection, and overwhelming visions of the good that center on inclusive community. Much more effective than general exhortations to solidarity, her stories invite readers to reach beyond themselves and extend their understanding of family.

Many of O'Connor's stories center on a character who is blissfully ignorant of his or her own self- or family-centeredness. Mrs. McKinley, in "The Displaced Person," speaks frequently and disparagingly of the poor white and black workers on her farm. Though she takes in the DP, she is unnerved by his work ethic and worries that he will outgrow his position. When distressed by the DP's attempts to bring his cousin over from a Polish work camp by marrying the young woman off to a black man on the farm, Mrs. McKinley declares, "I am not responsible for the world's misery."[71] Refusing to acknowledge her common bond with the people who work her land, she maintains an illusory independence until the end of the story, when all have left her and she is alone with worsening health and eyesight, with little hope of ever seeing rightly.[72]

Similarly, Ruby Turpin, in the story "Revelation," thinks little of the blacks and poor whites she meets in the doctor's office.[73] O'Connor tells how Mrs. Turpin sorted the people around her into classes. She puts colored people, white trash, homeowners, home-and-land owners like herself, and rich people in their appropriate places. Once she imagines that Jesus says, "All right, you can be white-trash or a nigger or ugly," giving herself a perfectly unsolvable dilemma.[74] In the climactic scene, a college girl in the doctor's waiting room who has heard enough of Mrs. Turpin's nonsense throws a book at her and says, "Go back to hell where you came from, you old wart hog." Mrs. Turpin is stunned because she, "a respectable, hard-working, church-going woman . . . had been singled out for the message, though there was trash in the room to whom it might justly have been applied."[75] O'Connor portrays pride without shame as primary sin.

Conversion, fittingly, is often represented by a more inclusive or expansive attitude to those normally thought of as outside one's family and class. Near the end of "The Displaced Person," Mrs. McKinley does not change her views completely, but when her physical suffering makes it impossible to maintain belief in her own independence, she does begin to perceive that she is not so unlike the other displaced persons around her.[76] In "A Good Man Is Hard to Find," the grandmother reaches out for the Misfit, calling him her own son, right before he shoots her.[77] Her ability to see connections between people has greatly improved. In "Revelation," Mrs. Turpin comes slowly to see herself clearly as the wart hog she is, and this opens her to receiving a revelation of the last judgment, in which the last (blacks and poor whites) had become the first, and the first (those "accountable as they had always been for good order and common sense and respectable behavior") had become the last.[78] The beginning of her conversion is marked by a vision of humanity at odds with her previous racism and classism. The accusations in stories like "Revelation" beg readers to ask, "How am I an old wart hog, and who knows it better than I do?" More forceful than exhortations to solidarity, O'Connor's stories cry out for the reader's critical self-reflection.

However, O'Connor does not simply leave readers wallowing in guilt. In her own way, she offers a vision of what could be, and usually it concerns solidarity. Ruby Turpin's revelation of all the "classes" of people walking together to heaven is a dream of unity O'Connor's readers could hardly imagine.[79] Solidarity is a crucial part of the mystery O'Connor's best characters come to see—the central ethical ideal she believes is mocked by the way most people live. It is a great deal more than inclusivity or a vague feeling for others. At its core, O'Connor's writing concerns "the isolated individual striving toward or resolutely avoiding, true communion with others."[80] Her stories provide glimpses of grace to encourage the striving for it, and grace, in almost every case, involves unity among people for whom it does not come easily.

The journey toward communion is a crucial part of a Christian theology of the family. In *Familiaris consortio* John Paul II speaks about family as communion and conveys the bodily and spiritual coming together of persons with each other in the presence of God.[81] He writes that "the fostering of authentic and mature communion between persons within the family is the first and irreplaceable school of social life, an example and stimulus for the broader community of relationships marked by respect, justice, dialogue, and love."[82] He rightly points to how the experience of family communion schools family members in solidarity and calls families to social responsibility. However, we have to know what lack of communion or solidarity really looks like to understand why it is such a tragedy and to desire its opposite. In her stories O'Connor gives us a vision of uncommunion within and outside families. Without communion, human beings look ugly. O'Connor holds up a mirror and forces readers to confront their own failings, with the hope that they will be moved to keep striving, not just for personal salvation, but for increasing solidarity beyond the boundaries of family.

Flannery O'Connor's stories concern communion and solidarity, but they are not "social issues" stories. The solidarity envisioned is distinctively local, and thus it is particularly relevant for Catholic family ethics. While racism and classism were inevitably crucial components of fiction set in the South of the 1950s and 1960s, the central moral issues of O'Connor's work are far less grandiose: humility and the right treatment of those to whom one is closely connected. Some criticize O'Connor's insistence on being apolitical, but her commitment to writing about life in small communities is in some sense quintessentially Catholic. For as Andrew Greeley claims, "Catholic social theory . . . has espoused decentralization . . . in focusing on the local community, indeed on the family itself, as the essential nucleus of a healthy society."[83] This local focus can be seen in stories revealing "the communal action of grace" that are so common among Catholic writers like O'Connor.[84]

A local focus in Catholic literature does not imply that global or national issues lack importance. Rather, it is an assertion that local issues are also significant, that ethical conflicts experienced in families and small communities are meaningful and deserving of attention as well. In Catholic social ethics, advocating decentralization means favoring local control wherever possible and supporting a rich local culture of associations. For a Catholic theology of marriage, it should mean paying attention to morally significant ordinary happenings in family and community life.

This is precisely what does not happen enough in most theology on marriage. In traditional theological discussions of the husband and wife who image Christ and the church, there is affirmation of the spiritual importance of the marriage bond, of fidelity, and even of the sacrifice a life of fidelity requires.[85] In the more recent theology of John Paul II, there is more attention to the sacramental quality of the self-giving relationship between husband and wife and some in-depth, thick description of how this plays out in the sexual realm.[86] Still, the language is very general and can seem disconnected from ordinary married life. Although the identification of the social mission of the family is prophetic and strong, there is still a tendency to focus attention on the two spouses and on their sexual relationship in particular. This focus in official Catholic teaching is limiting because marriages are situated in families and communities, and sexual love, while important, is but a small part of the lives of married couples. Moreover, as I pointed out in chapter 1, the newest theology of marriage from lay theologians is just beginning to attend to the ordinary. There remains a great need to engage in moral discussion of other dimensions of family life.

Fittingly, the key moments in O'Connor's stories are located in the local moral realm between political ethics and sexual ethics. Ruby Turpin, in "Revelation," learns that she needs to replace the "spiritual vanity" that keeps her up at night sorting classes with a dose of humility.[87] At the end of the story, readers are left with the hope that her grandiose vision of a march to heaven led by the least will lead her not to join in political protest but to stop thinking of the poor whites and blacks around her as lesser beings and start treating them with respect. Sheppard of "The Lame Shall Enter First" seems truly moved by Rufus's rejection of him.[88] Although he will not be able to make up for his neglect of his own son, perhaps he will take the words of the boys he works with more seriously and be open to the idea that he too stands in need of something beyond himself. The grandmother in "A Good Man Is Hard to Find" does not survive her attacker, but if she had, she most likely would not have become an advocate for criminals' rights, but she may have tried to pass on to her grandchildren a sense of their connection to all people rather than encouraging them to set themselves apart by their good manners.[89] The small dilemmas at the core of O'Connor's work are not lacking in significance.

Moreover, although O'Connor is viewed more as an observer of communities than of families, in fact most of her stories concern how family members treat one another. Mrs. Turpin, in "Revelation," fails to appreciate her daughter; Sheppard ignores his own son's grief over the loss of his mother; and the parents in "A Good Man Is Hard to Find" seem blissfully unconnected to their children (which is why the grandmother is left to instruct them in manners and morals). Often O'Connor's stories give us parents shocked into recognition of their misunderstanding and neglect through the intervention of a stranger. Sometimes there are heartbreaking moments of self-knowledge that lead to change. Sally Fitzgerald once noted that O'Connor was concerned with original sin, and "if she stuck with family relationships and situations as a ground, it was because she wrote of obscure, 'unimportant,' people, and some kind of family community is where most of us live, and where even our cosmic dramas are enacted and our souls won or lost."[90] Families, Fitzgerald suggests, are the loci of most people's significant moral struggles, and thus they are a crucial part of the local ethics to which O'Connor rightly directs our attention.

O'Connor was convinced that social change begins from below. On the civil rights issue of her time, she controversially insisted that laws forcing integration were unhelpful. She supported civil rights for blacks but was convinced that real change would come gradually through the transformation of culture. "The South has to evolve a way of life in which the two races can live together with mutual forbearance. You don't form a committee to do this or pass a resolution; both races have to work it out the hard way."[91] Her stories, which often involve people trying "to work it out"—sometimes well and sometimes badly—point those who seek social change back to the local realm of family and community.

O'Connor drew much of her philosophy from Jacques Maritain, who wrote of the habit of art as a virtue that perfects the subject.[92] Sally Fitzgerald proposes that, while O'Connor clearly acquired the habit of art, she also strove for the habit of being, "an excellence not only of action but of interior disposition and activity that increasingly reflected the object, the being, which specified it, and was itself reflected in what she did and said."[93] This habit is clearly reflected in her letters, which reveal her very deliberate way of living. Her stories also concern the habit of being or how people go about their everyday lives with or without reference to faith.

O'Connor paid attention to the everyday because she believed in "the essential mystery of a 'here and now,' no matter how superficially devoid of meaning, in which displaced individuals exercise a profound moral freedom."[94] All of her stories raise the question, "What are you going to do with your freedom?" The situations that bring about change are often extraordinary, but the changes themselves are small and familial or local, though no less significant. O'Connor explained that her work concerned mystery and manners: "The mystery . . . is the mystery of our position on earth, and the manners are those conventions which, in the hands of the artist, reveal that central mystery."[95] That mystery, she knew, is right in front of us: in neighborhoods, communities, and families.

Conclusion: Beginning with Imperfection, Moving toward Solidarity

What ought Christians to take from O'Connor? One of O'Connor's last and best stories provides a helpful compass. In "Parker's Back," an interracial married couple remain faithful to each other but share little warmth or understanding. Parker is distinguished mainly by the tattoos that cover most of his body, except for his back. His wife is notable for her violently strong faith, which Parker does not share. A near-fatal tractor accident shakes Parker up and sends him back to a tattoo artist to ask for a large portrait of Christ on his back. When he arrives home, he expects his wife to understand the change that has come over him, but she does not recognize the face on his back. "Don't you know who it is?" he cries. "It ain't anybody I know," she says.[96] And failing to recognize the image of Christ in her husband, she beats him, leaving red welts on his back, hardening her heart as he cries.[97] Grace goes unrecognized in her partner, and the unity that marriage is supposed to embody is destroyed in their estrangement. Violence flows directly out of misperception, revealing distance between husband and wife, black and white, faith and practice. In stories such as this, readers can see that the characters need God most desperately. Their turning away from God is almost always manifest in their turning away from each other, while turning toward God is signaled by right treatment of loved ones and strangers and by greater humility that enables people to see themselves and others clearly. As we think about sacramental marriage and ponder how two human beings could possibly image God's love, it is good to spend time in O'Connor's world to see grace both in the ordinary and in heartbreaking human frailty.

The fiction of Flannery O'Connor offers much wisdom for a Catholic theology of the family. By portraying human sinfulness in all its intensity, O'Connor reminds us of the human need for God, the depth of human finitude, the fundamentally important struggle for solidarity, and the moral significance of everyday life in family and community where habits of being are cultivated over time. Moral theology often offers an ideal vision of how things ought to be and speaks with compassion about exceptions to the rules. O'Connor pushes us to go further. Her stories draw us to sin and call out, as Parker does, "Look at it! Don't just say that! *Look* at it!" Instead of responding, as Parker's wife, "I done looked," we are called to spend time with imperfection in human relationships, pondering how seeing grace even here can expand our understanding of family and aid our journey toward greater faith, humility, and solidarity.[98]

A Catholic family ethic informed by O'Connor's fiction has much to offer a world in which people respond to fragmentation by seeking a soul mate to complete them, saving them from the messiness of the world. As I pointed out in chapter 2, the romantic story told so often in our culture is terribly limited. There is some truth in it—most spouses do find peace resting in each other's embrace. But it is also in their ordinary daily lives, their brokenness, and their efforts to reach beyond themselves that they witness to the human quest to love God and to God's willingness to love us. Our brokenness is an indication of our need for God and others. The best of the

Catholic tradition wisely calls us to see and embrace this reality of marriage, to reach out to God, to each other, and to others in need, finding an answer to fragmentation (both personal and social), not in a solitary, perfect union of two, but in a lifelong belonging that is loving, broken, and open to others, in marriage made for all who Flannery O'Connor so rightly called "rough beasts slouching toward Bethlehem."[99] It is from this vantage point that I offer the analyses of everyday practices that will occupy the remainder of the book.

Notes

Portions of this chapter appeared originally in Julie Hanlon Rubio, "Flannery O'Connor and a Catholic Theology of the Family," in *God's Grandeur: The Arts and Imagination in Theology*, ed. David Robinson, *College Theology Society Annual* 52 (2006): 110–27.

1. See, e.g., *Familiaris consortio*, no. 86. These themes are more fully developed in John Paul II, *Redemptoris custos* (On the Person and Mission of St. Joseph in the Life of Christ and of the Church, 1989), www.vatican.va/holy_father/john _paul_ii/apost_exhortations/documents/hf_jp-ii_exh_15081989_redemtoris-custos_en.html (accessed November 15, 2008).
2. See Bernard Haring, *Marriage in the Modern World* (Westminster, MD: Newman Press, 1965). While admitting the legitimacy of limiting and spacing births by natural means, Haring holds up the sacrifice of families with more than the standard two offspring in a world hostile to children. Ibid., 314–23. He cites the *Code familial de l'Union de Malines*, no. 57, which reads, "Properly understood, the law of community demands of every family community the greatest number of children which—all things considered—the couple can not only fittingly have but educate in a fitting manner," and an address of Pius XII to the larger families of Italy. Ibid., 315, 321. See also Willock, "Postscript on Poverty and Marriage," 250. Willock likens families in the lay Marycrest community to saints who take vows of poverty, saying, "Most families I know who are trying to practice holy poverty have to a great degree solved the problem of luxuries. They haven't any. This happy state is usually achieved by accepting the beggars that God sends whether by way of the door or by way of the womb."
3. *Familiaris consortio*, no. 17.
4. Ibid.
5. Ibid., nos. 77–86. See also McCarthy, *Sex and Love in the Home*, who addresses irregularities in a chapter added to the second edition. My own *Christian Theology of Marriage and Family* is similarly flawed, addressing broken families in only one chapter.
6. Philip L. Quinn, "Tragic Dilemmas, Suffering Love, and Christian Life," *Journal of Religious Ethics* 17 (Spring 1989): 152.

7. Flannery O'Connor, "To Cecil Dawkins," in *The Habit of Being: Letters of Flannery O'Connor*, ed. Sally Fitzgerald (New York: Noonday Press, 1979), 326.

8. Flannery O'Connor, "A Good Man Is Hard to Find," in Flannery O'Connor: *The Complete Stories* (New York: Noonday Press, 1971), 119.

9. Ibid., 132.

10. Josef Fuchs describes the fundamental choice this way: "Grace, therefore, calls, and is accepted or refused in the center of the person. . . . [G]race makes its way from the centre of a man and his basic freedom into all areas of life, into the many acts of free choice and beyond those into the formation of the world." Fuchs, "Basic Freedom and Morality," in *Introduction to Christian Ethics: A Reader*, ed. Ronald P. Hamel and Kenneth R. Himes (New York: Paulist, 1989), 197. Richard A. McCormick, drawing on the major moral theologians of his day, agrees that faith transforms the person at the level of worldview, motivation, and style of life. McCormick, "Does Faith Add to Ethical Perception?" in *Readings in Moral Theology No. 2: The Distinctiveness of Christian Ethics*, ed. Charles E. Curran and Richard A. McCormick (New York: Paulist, 1980), 170. In noting the agreement of most Christian ethicists with the claim that faith is the fundamental moral issue, I am not ignoring the reality of differing views as to how much faith influences ethics but rather emphasizing the relatively uncontroversial nature of the claim to faith's fundamental status, a reality that is starkly portrayed in O'Connor's stories.

11. Flannery O'Connor, "The Fiction Writer and His Country," in *Mystery and Manners: Occasional Prose*, ed. Sally Fitzgerald and Robert Fitzgerald (New York: Noonday Press, 1969), 34.

12. Ibid.

13. Paul Elie, *The Life You Save May Be Your Own: An American Pilgrimage* (New York: Farrar, Straus and Giroux, 2003), 153.

14. Ibid. Not all people feel adrift without faith. O'Connor spoke and speaks primarily to those who already share or come to share her faith and her sense of its significance. Yet the fullness of life may still be lacking for those who cannot bring themselves to believe.

15. Recall John Paul II's plea, "Family, become what you are." *Familiaris consortio*, no. 17, and his discussion of the situation of the world today, which includes much more darkness than light (no. 6). Even the most recent theology on the family rarely addresses unbelief. See my *Christian Theology of the Family*; McCarthy, *Sex and Love in the Home*; and Bourg, *Where Two or Three Are Gathered*.

16. Lee M. Williams and Michael G. Lawler, "Religious Heterogamy and Religiosity: A Comparison of Interchurch and Same-Church Individuals," *Journal for the Scientific Study of Religion* 40 (2001): 465–78. The Pew Research Center's Forum on Religion and Public Life reported in February 2009 that while 85 percent of women and 79 percent of men are affiliated with a religion, only 63 percent of women and 49 percent of men say that religion is very important in their lives, only 66 percent of women and 49 percent of men pray daily, and only 44 percent of women and 34 percent of men attend a worship service weekly. The data are drawn for the U.S. Religious Landscape Survey, completed by Pew in 2007. See http://pewforum.org/docs/?DocID=403 (accessed February 15, 2009).

17. In a recent article, Paul Elie argues for a shift in how we read O'Connor. Whereas she pitted the church against the world, we must see the blurring of the two, acknowledge doubt among Christians, and understand her stories as addressed not only to "them" but to us. See Paul Elie, "What Flannery Knew: Catholic Writing for a Critical Age," *Commonweal*, November 21, 2008, 12–17.
18. Flannery O'Connor, "To John Hawkes," in *The Habit of Being: Letters of Flannery O'Connor*, ed. Sally Fitzgerald (New York: Noonday Press, 1979), 349–50.
19. Flannery O'Connor, *Wise Blood*, in *3 by Flannery O'Connor* (New York: Signet, 1983).
20. Ross Labrie, *The Catholic Imagination in American Literature* (Columbia: University of Missouri Press, 1997), 220–21, describes O'Connor's conception of free will as it applies to Hazel, who struggles to reconcile divine will with his will and the wills of others.
21. O'Connor, *Wise Blood*, 2.
22. Flannery O'Connor, "The Displaced Person," in *Flannery O'Connor: The Complete Stories* (New York: Noonday Press, 1971), 194–235.
23. Ibid., 234.
24. Labrie, *Catholic Imagination*, 16.
25. O'Connor, "Displaced Person," 231.
26. Ibid., 198, 200. O'Connor, famous for her collection of peacocks and other exotic birds, often uses birds as symbols of Christ.
27. Ibid., 203.
28. Ibid., 224, 225.
29. Ibid., 235.
30. Michael Lawler describes these changes in *Marriage and Sacrament: A Theology of Christian Marriage* (Collegeville, MN: Liturgical Press, 1993), 65–71.
31. Flannery O'Connor, "The Teaching of Literature," in *Mystery and Manners: Occasional Prose*, ed. Sally Fitzgerald and Robert Fitzgerald (New York: Noonday Press, 1969), 131.
32. Ibid., 133.
33. *Familiaris consortio*, no. 2.
34. O'Connor, "Displaced Person," 217, 221.
35. Labrie, *Catholic Imagination*, 219. See O'Connor, "The Lame Shall Enter First," in *Flannery O'Connor: The Complete Stories* (New York: Noonday Press, 1971), 445–82.
36. Even more tragically, Sheppard's neglect of his own son leads Rufus to suicide and Sheppard to despair. O'Connor, "Lame Shall Enter First," 82.
37. O'Connor, "A Good Man Is Hard to Find," 132.
38. O'Connor, "On Her Own Work," in *Mystery and Manners: Occasional Prose*, ed. Sally Fitzgerald and Robert Fitzgerald (New York: Noonday Press, 1969), 110.
39. Ibid., 112–13.
40. O'Connor, "On Her Own Work," 118.
41. O'Connor, "A Good Man Is Hard to Find," 132.
42. O'Connor, *Wise Blood*, 108.
43. Granville Hicks wrote that O'Connor used extreme characters to portray reality: "In these times the most reliable path to reality, to the kind of reality that seems to her important, is by way of the grotesque." Quoted in Rosemary M.

Magee, *Conversations with Flannery O'Connor* (Jackson: University Press of Mississippi, 1987), 84.

44. Florence Caffrey Bourg does an excellent job of talking about the need for attention to growth in moral perfection in *Where Two or Three Are Gathered*, 66–68.

45. John Paul II, *Familiaris consortio*, no. 16,

46. Ibid., no. 56.

47. Ibid., no. 43.

48. Ibid., no. 13.

49. Ibid.

50. Bernard Cooke, "Christian Marriage: Basic Sacrament," in *Perspectives on Marriage: A Reader*, 2nd ed., ed. Kieran Scott and Michael Warren (New York: Oxford University Press, 2001), 48.

51. Ibid., 58.

52. Michael Lawler's theology of marriage has a similar focus on relationship. See his *Marriage and Sacrament*. See also William P. Roberts, *Marriage: It's a God Thing* (Cincinnati, OH: St. Anthony Messenger Press, 2007).

53. Lisa Sowle Cahill justly criticizes Michael Lawler and others for uncritically accepting the language of mutual self-giving without referring to the sexist potential of the concept. Because men and women are conditioned differently, they hear this language in distinct ways. See Cahill, "Equality in Marriage: The Biblical Challenge," in *Marriage in the Catholic Tradition: Scripture, Tradition, and Experience,* ed. Todd A. Salzman, Thomas M. Kelly, and John J. O'Keefe (New York: Crossroad, 2004), 71–73.

54. Herbert Anderson, "Between Rhetoric and Reality: Women and Men as Equal Partners," in *Mutuality Matters: Family, Faith, and Love,* ed. Herbert Anderson et al. (Lanham, MD: Sheed & Ward, 2004), 78.

55. Including justice as a fundamental component of sacramental marriage need not undercut love. As philosopher Pauline Kleingold points out, "If both spouses care about achieving a just marriage, claims of justice can even be welcomed ('I'm glad you mentioned it.') instead of having to be interpreted as the opening of hostilities and the end of affection." See "Just Love? Marriage and the Question of Justice," in *Mutuality Matters: Family, Faith, and Love,* ed. Herbert Anderson et al. (Lanham, MD: Sheed & Ward, 2004), 34.

56. Bourg, *Where Two or Three Are Gathered*, 118.

57. *Familiaris consortio*, nos. 77–85.

58. Ibid., no. 77.

59. The U.S. bishops make a similar point about families that have experienced divorce. They call all families holy, for "wherever a family exists and love still moves through its members, grace is present. Nothing—not even divorce or death—can place limits upon God's gracious love." It is possible that divorce provides additional opportunities to become open to the loving compassion of others. See United States Conference of Catholic Bishops, *Follow the Way of Love* (Washington, DC: United States Catholic Conference, 1994), 11.

60. Florence Caffrey Bourg points out that in contemporary Catholic theology this traditional concept might be more precisely expressed as "God works in us with us," leaving room for human agency, however imperfect. See *God Working in Us*

without Us? A Fresh Look at Formation of Virtue (New Orleans, LA: Yamauchi Lecture Series, 2004), 12.

61. Joanne Heaney Hunter, "Toward a Eucharistic Spirituality of Family: Lives Blessed, Broken, and Shared," in *Marriage in the Catholic Tradition: Scripture, Tradition, and Experience,* ed. Todd A. Salzman, Thomas M. Kelly, and John J. O'Keefe (New York: Crossroad, 2004), 128–30.

62. Ibid., 132. On this theme, see also Bourg, *Where Two or Three Are Gathered*, 133.

63. In his recent survey of contemporary Catholic theology on marriage, Charles E. Curran notes that post–Vatican II moral theology was rooted in the theological contributions of the council (the importance of conscience and an optimism about the goodness of life in the modern world and marriage in particular), while the newest theology draws more from the experience of married life, which is more mixed. See Curran, *Catholic Moral Theology in the United States: A History* (Washington, DC: Georgetown University Press, 2008), 214–16.

64. Gaillardetz, *Daring Promise,* 43.

65. Ibid., 44, 69.

66. McCarthy, *Sex and Love in the Home,* 204.

67. Ibid., 206.

68. Linda Waite's research shows that even couples that are most dissatisfied with their marriages tend to get through difficult times and emerge satisfied if they are willing to maintain their commitments. See Linda J. Waite and Maggie Gallagher, *The Case for Marriage* (New York: Broadway Books, 2000), 148–49.

69. McCarthy, *Sex and Love in the Home,* 274.

70. In one interview, she stated, "The writer has no responsibility for topical subjects" and should focus instead on the "human condition which he may approach indirectly through individuals, be they black or white." See *Conversations with Flannery O'Connor,* ed. Magee, 80, 81. In other interviews, she admitted concern about racial problems but insisted that more could be achieved by changing manners than laws. Ibid., 109.

71. O'Connor, "Displaced Person," 223.

72. Ibid., 235.

73. Flannery O'Connor, "Revelation," in *Flannery O'Connor: The Complete Stories* (New York: Noonday Press, 1971), 490.

74. Ibid., 491–92.

75. Ibid., 502.

76. O'Connor, "Displaced Person," 235.

77. O'Connor, "A Good Man Is Hard to Find," 132.

78. O'Connor, "Revelation," 508.

79. Ibid., 508–9.

80. Farrell O'Gorman, *Peculiar Crossroads: Flannery O'Connor, Walker Percy, and Catholic Vision in Postwar Southern Fiction* (Baton Rouge: Louisiana State University Press, 2004), 12.

81. *Familiaris consortio,* no. 43.

82. Ibid.

83. Andrew Greeley, *The Catholic Myth: The Behavior and Beliefs of American Catholics* (New York: Scribner, 1990), 258–59.
84. Labrie, *Catholic Imagination*, 10.
85. Thomas Aquinas, *Summa Theologica* III, supp. Q. 42.
86. *Familiaris consortio*, nos. 13, 32.
87. O'Connor, "Revelation," 219.
88. O'Connor, "Lame Shall Enter First," 481–82.
89. O'Connor, in "A Good Man Is Hard to Find," depicts the grandmother reaching out to the Misfit in recognition of their shared humanity, 132.
90. Sally Fitzgerald, introduction to *3 by Flannery O'Connor* (New York: Signet, 1983), xxiii.
91. C. Ross Mullins Jr., "Flannery O'Connor: An Interview," in *Conversations with Flannery O'Connor*, ed. Magee, 104. O'Connor may be justly criticized for not seeing the importance of civil rights laws and even for not appreciating the evil of race relations in the South, as Elie points out in *Life You Save*, 327–28. Still, the focus on change from below portrayed in her stories is not thereby discredited.
92. Sally Fitzgerald, introduction to *Habits of Being*, by Flannery O'Connor, ed. Sally Fitzgerald (New York: Farrar, Straus and Giroux, 1979), xvii.
93. Ibid.
94. O'Gorman, *Peculiar Crossroads*, 12.
95. O'Connor, "Teaching of Literature," 124.
96. Flannery O'Connor, "Parker's Back," in *Flannery O'Connor: The Complete Stories* (New York: Noonday Press, 1971), 529.
97. O'Gorman notes that the woman "cannot see the presence of God in the flesh of her own husband." O'Gorman, *Peculiar Crossroads*, 104. He claims that Catholic writers such as O'Connor share "a common emphasis on the concrete and a faith that the immediate world itself holds a mystery and a meaning that does not have to be imposed by the artist but is already present, if only recognized." Ibid., 108. O'Connor shifts attention to the mystery of the ordinary.
98. O'Connor, "Parker's Back," 529.
99. O'Connor adapted the phrase from W. B. Yeats's poem "The Second Coming," which can be found in W. B. Yeats, *Selected Poems and Two Plays of William Butler Yeats*, ed. M. L. Rosenthal (New York: Collier Books, 1968), 91.

Part II / Practices

CHAPTER FOUR

Practicing Sexual Fidelity

Why Practices?

The first three chapters of this book argue for attention to ordinary life (especially the lives of families), emphasize the union of the personal and the social in Christian theology of marriage and Catholic social teaching, and point to the grace found in human finitude rather than perfection. Having laid the groundwork, in this chapter I turn to analyzing the ordinary through a set of five practices. I could proceed otherwise, through case studies or personal narratives, for instance; however, I have chosen the concept of practice to orient this ethic of ordinary life. Why? My assumption is that intentional practices are necessary if believers are to live out their faith in a culture wedded to other truths. If ordinary middle-class life is marred by a fundamental disengagement from what ought to matter for Christians, living distinctly is not something that can be left to saints and martyrs.

The language of practice is associated with the work of philosopher Alisdaire MacIntyre, who upholds the importance of actions that shape human persons in the context of their traditions.[1] Stanley Hauerwas builds on MacIntyre's work and gives his ideas Christian context with a focus on character and discipleship. For Hauerwas, being a disciple of Christ means engaging in specific practices with a Christian community devoted to a particular way of life. The church, Hauerwas claims, must "be a people of virtue—not simply any virtue, but the virtues necessary for remembering and retelling the story of a crucified savior."[2] If we want to be Christian, we must live deliberately out of step with the mainstream by adopting distinctive patterns of life or practices.

While marriage is certainly not always a countercultural space, a marriage centered on alternative practices can be, according to Kieran Scott, "a protest against a meaningless, self-centered, commodity-driven life."[3] Building on John F. Kavanaugh's classic analysis of consumerism in *Following Christ in a Consumer Society*, Scott outlines five cultural deficiencies and offers five practices of resistance.[4] First, to combat a loss of interiority or self-knowledge, he suggests solitude and centering prayer. Second, to counter the loss of solidarity, he commends "wasting time" on the covenantal relationships, giving those we love the gifts of presence and attention. Third, to combat pervasive injustice, he advises increasing our commitment to justice, beginning in the home. Fourth, to counter the craving for consumption, he recommends throwing off cumber and embracing simplicity. And fifth, to prevent a flight from vulnerability that prevents us from fully giving ourselves to both family and those on the margins, he counsels compassion. In all five areas, the intent is to choose practices that will enable Christians to live what Kavanaugh calls the personal form—"a mode of perceiving and valuing men and women as irreplaceable persons whose fundamental identities are fulfilled in covenantal relationship."[5] In the context of this book I consider sex as fundamental to the practices of relationship and compassion, eating as a dimension of practicing relationship and justice, tithing in relation to the practice of simplicity, serving as a way of practicing compassion, and praying as a form centering. All five can be seen as practices of resistance embedded in ordinary life marked by Christian commitments to God and neighbor.

Sex may seem a particularly odd choice with which to begin. After all, what does sex have to do with resistance? Can sex be understood as a practice like prayer, fasting, or simplicity? Or, as one of my students asked, "With sex, isn't it just yes or no?" Though it may seem odd to think about sex in marriage as a fundamental practice of resistance, there are good reasons for doing so. I understand practice, with Craig Dykstra and Dorothy Bass, as an intentional, shared action, situated in the context of a tradition, ordinary in outward appearances but transcendent in its association with fundamental human goods.[6] This understanding of practice allows for a different way of thinking about sex that will allow us to imagine what sort of sex life married couples could have and ponder what goods they ought to seek. Fidelity to a practice of sex in marriage that is oriented to relationship and compassion could be a powerful response to the loss of solidarity and flight from vulnerability, key markers of the consumer society.

In my consideration of sex as a practice, I outline debates that have obscured the importance of the practice of sex, describe the current situation using recent social science literature, and identify goods toward which good sexual practice ought to aim. I argue that faithful sexual practice in marriage requires an ongoing, regular commitment to pursue the goods of vulnerability, self-sacrifice, self-love, and bodily belonging with one's spouse. Sexual practice devoted to these goods has an essential place within a Christian family ethic oriented to a life full of communion and solidarity. It is an appropriate yet ordinary place to begin to consider how Christian families can resist harmful aspects of the culture by practicing their faith.

Sexual Ethics: Moving beyond Controversy

Much of the discussion of sex in Christian ethics is devoted to arguments about controversial issues. Underlying these debates are disagreements about what sex is for. Before moving forward to discuss the practice of sex in contemporary Christian marriage, it is necessary to understand the issues that still consume much of sexual ethics, even while noting emerging progress toward a better conversation.

Modern debates have their origin in the deficiencies of pre–Vatican II sexual ethics. For example, *Modern Youth and Chastity*—a theologically significant work written by moral theologian Gerald Kelly—was an influential part of the pre–Vatican II popular communication of traditional Catholic sexual morality.[7] It is well remembered by most Catholics who came of age before the council. The document makes a strong case against premarital sex (and other premarital acts that may bring a person to the near occasion of sin) and is, in the main, representative of the pre–Vatican II approach to sexual ethics: natural law dominated, negative in tone, and focused on rules.[8] It gives little attention to what constitutes good sex in marriage. Chastity is promoted as a virtue, and sex is judged to be good within its proper confines, but these are minor concerns in a work devoted to limiting unchaste sexual acts.[9]

A negative, acts-centered approach to sex pervaded pre–Vatican II official Catholic teaching on marriage. In his 1931 encyclical *Casti connubii*, Pius XI describes how "man and wife help each other day by day in forming and perfecting themselves in the interior life," affirming the centrality of the relationship between the spouses.[10] However, his discussion of sex is limited to the marital rights that men and women acquire by contract and the procreative potential of sexual acts.[11] Earlier documents were even more wedded to portraying procreation as the primary end of sex, so much so that the idea of sex as something worthy of the attention of married couples seeking intimacy in their relationship is never considered.[12]

The 1968 encyclical *Humanae vitae* attempted to remedy the deficiencies of pre–Vatican II sexual theology. The document is praised by theologians of many different perspectives for bringing positive, personalist language into official Catholic theology on marriage.[13] Marriage is described as a "reciprocal personal gift of self" involving a quest for "mutual personal perfection," as well as collaboration with God "in the generation and education of new lives."[14] Spousal love is said to be as marked by four characteristics. It is, first, fully human in that "husband and wife become one only heart and one only soul"; second, total, "a very special form of personal friendship"; third, faithful, requiring a fidelity that, though difficult, is "a source of profound and lasting happiness"; and fourth, fecund, spilling over into new life.[15] The sexual acts of married couples are for "expressing and consolidating their union" as well as collaborating in the generation of new life.[16] This increased recognition of the unitive meaning of sex in marriage was long overdue, but it was overshadowed by the controversy the encyclical provoked over contraception.[17]

During his long papacy, Pope John Paul II expanded the positive conversation begun by *Humanae vitae* while defending traditional norms. With his theology of the body, he offered a language for talking about the meaning of sexual gestures that elevated the unitive aspect of sexual acts.[18] The pope's strong affirmation of sexual love and his method of "reading" loving actions opened up a new way of understanding how sex brings husbands and wives closer together. His views have greatly contributed to the richness of post–Vatican II theological writing on sexuality. However, not all agree with the specific ways in which Pope John Paul II reads the body and evaluates sexual actions.[19]

In the last forty years, there has been a watershed in Catholic sexual ethics as laypeople have brought their experience to the table and engaged in vigorous debate. Some conservative theologians have found in John Paul II's writing a theology that fully explains and justifies *Humanae vitae.*[20] They have tended to emphasize the fecund nature of sexual love. The key claim is that full self-donation includes fertility because fertility is a dimension of the self. In addition, they emphasize the importance of self-mastery in a sexual love that aims to be fully human.[21] The richness of this theology has filtered back into the sexual experience of couples who practice natural family planning (NFP), as they speak of the connection between loving union and openness to life.[22] Liberal theologians often object to John Paul II's highly spiritualized language, his deep concern about desire, his focus on the self-control necessary for chastity, and his highly gendered understanding of what goes on in the sexual lives of married couples.[23] De-emphasizing fertility, they aim to describe a sexual love between spouses that is total in its personal and spiritual dimensions. They see sex as an essential part of the daily growth in mutual love between husbands and wives.[24] The experience of sexual pleasure is, they assert, crucial to the unitive meaning of sex.[25] Liberals value procreation but prioritize other aspects of sexual love, namely vulnerability and intimacy. The experience of sex in marriage aided by contraception clearly informs their understanding of sex as relational communion.[26]

While these divisions run deep, overlap between the two groups is also discernible. In contrast to theologians of earlier generations who wanted to either criticize or defend magisterial teaching, theologians today want to speak of growth in sexual virtue and describe the personal and spiritual meanings of sexuality.[27] Fundamentally new questions are being asked: What makes sexual love fully human? What does it mean to give one's whole self to one's spouse? What is true fidelity? What constitutes fruitfulness? As unprecedented numbers of laypeople have come to study theology, a rich body of attempts to answer these questions has developed.[28]

Today, both liberals and conservatives value self-giving, intimacy, mutuality, sexual pleasure, and the connection between sex and the transcendent.[29] Moreover, "there is a freshness in this conversation that allows for further growth in sexual ethics and practice, because instead of trying to prove each other's positions illegitimate, this new generation is simply attempting to situate their sexual practice in the context of Christian living."[30] In this particular cultural moment, focusing on the potential contributions of both groups to a conversation about sexual practice is paramount. It is time to give attention to sexual lives of married couples, because there is much more to say than yes or no.

Sex, Fidelity, and Infidelity: The Situation

In order to think about what good Christian sexual practice ought to be, we need to understand the current situation. If theologians are to write with authenticity about good sex in marriage, in addition to mining the resources of scripture and tradition, they must know something of what married couples actually experience. Much of pre–*Humanae vitae* sexual ethics can be justly criticized for leaving out experiential knowledge of this kind. The result was discourse on sexuality that few Catholics could relate to their own sexual practice. Since 1968, the experience of sex in marriage has figured prominently in the theological writings. However, most theologians rely on their own personal experience only.[31] More comprehensive knowledge of sexual experience will allow for the development of better theology and ethics with more potential to speak to Christian married couples.[32] Moreover, an exploration of the situation in sexual ethics is no different from similar explorations that are common in social or medical ethics. Knowledge of the situation, with its blessings and problems, is crucial to any argument for an ethical practice.

Social scientific knowledge of sex between married people is not as comprehensive as it could or should be. Many of those who analyze the results of sex surveys note the paucity of good studies.[33] Sex outside of marriage is much more frequently examined. Moreover, much of the information gathered on sex in marriage is limited to the relatively objective categories of frequency and satisfaction. As stated by the authors of a decade review of studies of sex in marriage, "Unfortunately, if scholars were to use the corpus of empirical-based knowledge about marital sexuality to paint a picture of marital sexuality for the public, it would not be a very detailed or richly colored picture."[34] Still, although the available information is imperfect, it is certainly worth examining.

What constitutes a "sex life" for most married couples? The duration of an average sexual encounter is relatively short, "only 15 to 60 minutes for most couples."[35] On average, married couples have sex 6.5 times per month, or one to two times per week.[36] Studies have consistently shown that sexual frequency in marriage declines over time.[37] Married couples have sex an average of 12 times a month in their early twenties, but that figure falls to 8.5 times in their early thirties, 6.5 in their early forties, 5.5 in their early fifties, 2.5 in their early sixties, and less than one for those 75 and older.[38] Other than age, factors significantly associated with a decline in sexual frequency include marital duration, pregnancy, and the presence of young children in the household.[39] Many studies, though not all, find a connection between commitment to work, school, and parenting and lower levels of sexual frequency.[40] Factors such as higher levels of education, the presence of older children in the home, and marital satisfaction are associated with higher levels of sexual frequency.[41]

What exactly most couples do when they have sex, the quality of their sexual encounters, their feelings about their experiences, and the frequency and quality of sexual interactions other than intercourse have not received serious attention, so knowledge of sex in marriage is limited.[42] Nonetheless, theologians would do well to keep this snapshot picture in mind. Though it may only account for an hour or two of a couple's week and can be expected to decline in frequency over time, most couples find the practice important and pleasurable enough to continue throughout their marriage.

Moreover, married couples are generally satisfied with their sex lives, more so than those in dating or cohabiting relationships.[43] Some researchers posit that marital commitment allows for deeper satisfaction, because spouses have the time and energy to devote to each other and enough practice to know how to make each other happy.[44] Others link sexual satisfaction to the quality of sexual interaction, equity between partners, and the degree of self-disclosure present in the sexual relationship, all qualities that are more likely to be present in marriage.[45] Sexual satisfaction is positively associated with sexual frequency, even though frequency declines at a faster rate than satisfaction over time.[46] According to social scientists, relatively infrequent reports of sexual disinterest or dysfunction are both cause for worry and an indication that couples expect sex to be regular and pleasurable and miss sex because it serves an important function in their marriage.[47]

Marital satisfaction and sexual satisfaction are interrelated, though it is difficult to discern exactly how. Marital satisfaction is negatively correlated with infidelity, and sexual infrequency is associated with higher levels of infidelity.[48] Generally speaking, low frequency levels do lead some spouses to seek satisfaction elsewhere, while more sexually satisfied partners are less likely to stray. Although different couples will find satisfaction at different frequency levels, the regular presence of sex is generally helpful, and its decline is harmful to marital satisfaction, at least until the later stages of life.

Although this sketch of sex in marriage is suggestive, given the lack of substantive qualitative research in this area, it also helpful to examine studies of infidelity. In fact, infidelity has been the subject of a great deal of research.[49] Notably, in the United States, despite strong disapproval of extramarital sex (EMS; 80 percent say EMS is always wrong), 25 percent of married men and 15 percent of married women admit to at least one act of infidelity.[50] Though nearly all married persons expect marital fidelity of themselves and their partners, fidelity is a promise that a substantial number are unable to keep.[51]

Why do so many spouses break their vows? Those with strongly negative views of infidelity are more likely to be faithful, while those with higher education, higher income, and liberal attitudes toward sex and infidelity are more likely to be unfaithful.[52] In addition, most research shows that those who hold religious beliefs and, more important, attend religious services are more faithful in marriage, because "this exposure seems to help people to adhere to the norms of [their] community," while detachment from a local faith community is a predictor of infidelity.[53] Still, while beliefs about commitment and participation in a faith community translate into fidelity in many cases, opportunity is also a strong predictor of infidelity.[54] Even those with strong beliefs are vulnerable to infidelity if they work longer hours, work in intense situations with members of the opposite sex, and/or travel for their jobs.[55] Moreover, while most studies find an association between marital dissatisfaction and infidelity, some do not. It is disturbing that "many people who engage in extramarital intercourse are quite satisfied with their marriages."[56]

Studies of infidelity help fill out our understanding of the experience of sex in marriage. Clearly, sexual fidelity is not easy. Knowing the lure of opportunity even for people who hold traditional views on marriage and are satisfied with their marriages, those who seek to prevent adultery may draw attention to certain risk factors and counsel married couples to avoid certain kinds of temptation.[57] However, for my purposes, the more important task is drawing upon what we know about sex as it is currently experienced in order to encourage sexual practice that fits within the Christian life of discipleship. If Christianity can say little more about sex than sex is good, as long as it is between people who respect and value one another in some way, something is wrong. We now have a plethora of sexual guides written by Catholics and Protestants that promote sex using familiar language of romance and pleasure.[58] Surely Christians ought to have something distinctive to say about what sex means when two people who are married engage in it and about why they ought to engage in the practice of sex at all.

What does sex have to do with a life of discipleship? In what sense can it constitute resistance? If discipleship involves resistance to mainstream culture, and if sex in our culture is often marred by depersonalization, sex in Christian marriage should aim toward deeper intimacy rather than objectification or even mere satisfaction. A good sexual practice would aim to bind couples in the married love that John Paul II appropriately calls "communion."[59] Such a practice would constitute a way of resisting the depersonalization and lack of intimacy that permeate our culture, even in marriage. It would provide a strong base for a familial life centered in personal relationships and commitment to the common good.

Sex as Practice: Seeking the Good

Contemporary Christians may be able to say, "Sex is good," but we are far from knowing what we mean. While we have left *Modern Youth and Chastity* behind, we are not yet ready to discard post–Vatican II discussions linking sexual pleasure to the holy. Yet we also stand in need of an alternative to the purely romantic or hedonistic approaches to sex prevalent in popular culture. In this chapter I attempt to follow the lead of John Paul II by locating the goodness of sex in authentic self-giving. Truly human sex, the pope states, "by means of which man and woman give themselves to one another . . . is by no means something purely biological, but concerns the innermost being of the human person as such."[60] The pope indicates a deep respect for the depth of married sex, though he does not tell us exactly what it means to give our "innermost being" to another. I suggest that pleasure is central to the giving of one's self and to sex's deeper meaning.

Pleasure and self-gift are not really two separate dimensions of sex at all. Rather, it is in and through the giving and receiving of sexual pleasure that self-gift occurs. Luke Timothy Johnson has written, "Amid all the talk of self-donation and mutuality, we should also remember, 'plus, it feels good.'"[61] However, pleasure is not simply another aspect of sexual experience. We need to think about how pleasure can be a means of intimacy and unity, about what it is about engaging in this intensely pleasureful act that brings two people closer together. I argue that having good sex requires attending to the goods of vulnerability, sacrifice, self-love, and bodily belonging through mutual sexual pleasure. This is the central paradox of sex: In seeking pleasure we find generosity, intimacy, even communion. As Christina Traina says, sex seems designed so that "we get more than we ask for."[62]

Vulnerability

Good sex involves the vulnerability of self-exposure that is symbolized but not fully encompassed in nakedness. There is a certain risk not only in baring oneself before another but also in seeking or longing for another person. Edna McDonagh speaks movingly of the vulnerability in married sexual friendship within which spouses "reveal and cherish more of each other's distinctiveness, strangeness and otherness. All of this is heightened by their sexual otherness, the desire it kindles and the fear it may provoke in its very strangeness."[63] Vulnerability means acknowledging that one's own needs cannot be met by oneself alone and must be met through entering more deeply into relationship. At times, physical and emotional desires for sexual connection can be overpowering. Admitting this and then allowing another person to be the one who tries to meet those desires is risky, because the desires of different persons are distinctive and finding a satisfying practice for two different people is not always easy. Perhaps the desired spouse will not be equally desirous. Perhaps one spouse will be uneasy with the other's sexual longing or with the ways in which that spouse wants to find sexual pleasure. Perhaps one will grow frustrated with the process before the other does. Speaking desire aloud is risky, even with a beloved spouse who is always "other," even when deeply loved and deeply known.

While some measure of self-control is necessary if one is to take one's partner's needs seriously, having sex also requires a certain measure of abandon. Protestant theologian Mary Pellauer writes frankly of the vulnerability that giving into that abandon brings: "The middle is often confusing. I often do not know exactly what I want or need at this time. This stage does not supply me or my partner with clear guidance about how to satisfy these deep undercurrents. Sometimes I flail around. But in the farther reaches of this phase, I would do anything to make this last forever."[64] Pellauer describes the longing, the frustration, and the imperfection of ordinary sex in marriage. She locates the risk of sex both in expressing desire and in accepting pleasure. "That my pleasure was important to him, this was hard to accept, to let in. That he would refuse his own release till I had mine, that he was willing to persist in trying to bring my release/ecstasy, that he reveled in it: This shook me very deeply. . . . I experience it as grace, an instance of his vulnerability-to-me reaching out to meet my vulnerability to him."[65] The grace of which Pellauer speaks comes because one spouse is willing to be vulnerable in expressing desire and because the other is willing to answer that call.

It is the vulnerability of sex that causes most contemporary theologians to argue that sex belongs in committed relationships, usually marriage. Karen Lebacqz's short essay "Appropriate Vulnerability" argues that there is too much risk in sex with those who are not mutually committed: "Sexuality has to do with vulnerability. Eros, the desire for another, the passion that accompanies the wish for sexual expression, makes one vulnerable. It creates possibilities for greater joy but also for greater suffering. To desire another, to feel passion, is to be vulnerable, capable of being wounded."[66]

Lebacqz finds appropriate vulnerability in the lack of shame Adam and Eve feel despite their nakedness and advises that it can most often be found in marriage because of the safety commitment brings.[67] Her claims resonate because many know the sting of inappropriate vulnerability and the security and satisfaction of committed sex.

If sex outside marriage may be make one too vulnerable, it follows that sex within marriage can be appropriately risky. Of marriage, Lebacqz says that partners are able to risk exposure and failure "in a mutually vulnerable and mutually committed relationship."[68] Couples who consistently work to open themselves to each other, to reveal more and more of their desires and their love, are training themselves in intimacy. A sexual relationship like this "becomes a school for love. It teaches us that we bare our full selves, not only our bodies but our feelings, desires, fears, and commitments and offer ourselves to the loved spouse who loves us, that we are rewarded not only by physical pleasure but with intimacy that offers us closeness, communion, stimulation, and companionship."[69] While self-exposure within marriage is far less risky than casual sex, if taken seriously it can be far more demanding.

Good sex requires a commitment to deepening vulnerability, or to increasing sexual and emotional openness between two people.[70] Spouses can work toward more intimacy and self-disclosure not only through conversation but through the "holy play" of sex.[71] Deepening intimacy requires a commitment to a process that can last a lifetime. Because human beings are always becoming and growing, relational commitments can never be static. Spouses have to be faithful within the growing, evolving relationship to which they are committed. If "the whole of life is potentiality, [then] . . . we have to accept responsibility . . . for the deeply personal process of continued actualization of our potential."[72] A lifelong commitment enables growth and actualization of our potential over time. "Fidelity as process then is submission to this ongoing conversion of heart which is necessary to be true to one's initial commitment in faith and love."[73] Just as becoming oneself is an ongoing task, so is becoming married, and it requires a commitment to ongoing growth in vulnerability.[74]

Conversely, deciding not to risk vulnerability is not virtuous. As Christine Gudorf writes, "Going through the motions of sex, without having first gone through the struggle to understand, disclose, and compromise around differences is sex without symbolic meaning."[75] It is sex without vulnerability. If sex outside of marriage is a lie because it does not express the joining that bodies speak, sex without vulnerability is not fully truthful either. The tradition has often spoken of desire as if it were given; the only ethical challenge was controlling it. Contemporary writers speak from experience of desire as risk, as struggle, as ethical demand. The vulnerability of desire is more of a good to be sought than an appetite to be controlled. It is the path to true intimacy in marriage.

Sacrifice

Though the understanding of sex as self-gift is widespread in contemporary theology, the Christian tradition has not always associated sex with giving or sacrifice. Historically, marital sex has been associated with lust and pleasure, justified first only by procreation, later because it kept spouses from seeking sexual pleasure elsewhere, and later still because it promoted the union of the spouses. If sacrifice was involved, it was the sacrifice of the wife who was encouraged to acknowledge the "marital right" of her husband to sex even if she was not interested.[76] Because sex involves pleasure, engaging in it was viewed as duty or self-indulgence rather than self-sacrifice or gift.

However, contemporary theologians tend to agree that a good sexual relationship both requires sacrifice of the spouses and develops their capacity to sacrifice. The language of self-gift suggests that sex is more than the individual pursuit of pleasure.[77] Rather, when two people are really making love, they are also freeing themselves of self-centeredness in order to enter more fully into the life of their spouse. Sidney Callahan notes that this is sometimes difficult, for "just as the mind flees God, the nonintegrated self evades full sexual focus on another by relapsing into rational thought, irrelevancies, or drifting into self-absorption," yet it is worth disciplining oneself, for "a collected, integrated self cannot only give more but can give more easily."[78] Giving oneself to one's spouse requires suspending self-absorption and is fundamental to good sexual practice, even if every sexual act will not reach the heights of intentional, pure, and total self-giving.[79]

Imperfect human beings will no doubt struggle to maintain this level of sacrifice. Yaweh's covenant with Israel can be seen as a model for marriage. The Israelites continually stray, hardening their hearts, and keeping their covenant only superficially. They need to be in deeper relationship with God. Eventually God calls them back, "ask[ing] for a radical transformation of their entire way of life."[80] He tells them that fidelity must no longer be living by the law in a habitual, routine, external manner only. It must spring from their deepest selves, as an unreserved surrender. "Fidelity means intimacy with God."[81] Christians seeking wisdom for relationships can take from sacred history the truth that fidelity means intimacy, which begins with a recognition of superficiality and limits of self-sufficiency, and continues as a process of progressive self-surrender. Knowing that self-giving begins with self-knowledge, spouses can work on knowing and being faithful to their true selves.[82] Comfortable with who they are and in touch with their interiority, they can risk intimacy and fidelity. Spouses may sometimes struggle to be fully present to each other, but through the sacrificial work of being present they have the potential to find greater intimacy and fulfillment.

Because intimate sex involves two people with different sex drives, sexual histories, sexual preferences, and personalities, finding a practice that works for both of them will require sacrifice on the part of both. There will be sacrifice when one chooses to be open to sex or to forgo sex in response to the needs of the other. As studies show that sexual frequency declines over time but that high frequency is associated with sexual and marital satisfaction, the need for negotiation and sensitivity to changing needs and desires will continue.[83] Few theologians today would welcome a return to the language of marital rights, but many acknowledge that sex that is truly giving requires self-sacrifice so that each can adequately recognize the needs of the other.[84] There is no one standard of frequency; couples need to find a balance that is right for them. However, the prevalence of sexual and marital dissatisfaction suggests that many look elsewhere for physical and emotional attention when they could turn to their spouses. If the covenant of marriage is to be experienced and deepened, couples have to find a regular sexual practice that is agreeable to both. The sacrifice this entails should be shared rather than avoided.

Sacrifice may also be experienced in times of intentional fasting from sex. Couples who practice NFP experience sacrifice in times of planned abstinence. They find peace in doing what they believe God asks of them and take joy in nurturing neglected aspects of their relationship (both spiritual and emotional) when sex is not an option.[85] Still, most acknowledge the discipline involved in orienting their sex lives around the women's natural cycle rather than their own individual desires. They are being schooled in sacrifice. Chastity, some have argued, prepares couples for the sacrifices they must make for others both inside and outside the family.[86]

Sacrifice is also involved in the self-control couples need to be good sexual partners. NFP advocates note that times of abstinence involve a measure of self-mastery that is necessary for good sex. Sex when called for is then fully human because not driven by blind instinct.[87] This insight can be affirmed as long as legitimate desire is not at issue. However, self-control is also necessary to honor one's partner's need for pleasure. Gudorf calls men in particular to greater self-control and persistence in helping their wives achieve orgasm.[88] John Paul II goes even further in advocating mutual, simultaneous orgasm, which involves a great deal of self-control.[89] In all of these cases, faithful sexual practice both involves sacrifice and increases the capacity for it.

Some theologians have been critical of the emphasis of traditional Catholic theology on sacrifice in sexual relationships. Mitch Finley, for instance, believes that a lingering sense that couples can have too much self-indulgent sex lies behind advocacy of NFP. Instead, he argues that because sex is so personal and spiritual, couples should no more seek to avoid sex than avoid Mass.[90] On the one hand, his caution seems correct: sex is not some dark pleasure that one is better off without. It is, rather, a sometimes easy and sometimes difficult practice to which spouses are called to be faithful. On the other hand, good sexual practice might involve sacrifice because couples sometimes need something other than sex. If a full spiritual life involves regular Sunday Mass, it might also call for meditation, a retreat, or a nightly examination of conscience, depending on individual needs. Even if Mass has privileged status, all are paths to intimacy with God. Similarly, whether because couples are respecting the natural rhythms of a woman's cycle or abstaining from sex because of a need to walk, talk, or sleep instead, they ought to sacrifice when necessary in order to be faithful to each other in their sexual practice.

Sacrifice is also involved in the commitment to continue having sex over time, even when sex becomes routine. This insight is perhaps not well-recognized in the tradition, because sex is perceived as something couples always desire. However, during many periods in a couple's marriage, there are challenges to keeping up a regular sex life: pregnancy, illness, travel, children and parents requiring physical care, demanding jobs, personal difficulties, and so on. Couples who nonetheless refuse to let their sexual practice die are seeking the sacred in the ordinary and affirming it, even when it might be easier not to. Though this is not the sort of sexual sacrifice traditionally upheld, in this situation as in many others, both having sex when one would rather not and not having sex when one would favor it can be forms of sacrifice necessary for good practice. A sexual ethic for marriage demands sacrifice in putting one's own needs aside for the other, developing self-control, submitting to times of sexual fasting, and working on a sexual relationship over time, even when such work may be painful and demanding.[91]

Self-Love

A good sexual practice would be unbalanced if it emphasized self-sacrifice at the expense of the good of the self. To seek one's own pleasure in sex one must consider oneself worthy of receiving pleasure. One must be able to recognize and pursue one's owns desires. This dimension of sexual love is sometimes underemphasized in contemporary conservative thought, just as self-sacrifice can sometimes be overlooked in liberal thought. However, when rightly understood as intimately related to the traditional good of union, self-love can be recognized as an essential dimension of good sexual practice. In the work of John Milhaven, for instance, the pure enjoyment of sex is celebrated. He reports that his friend Fergie describes his experience of falling asleep next to his wife in terms that sound almost hedonistic: "As I slope down with Julie to sleep, thoughts float off. I don't think. I enjoy. I enjoy myself. . . . It's hard to describe since it lasts only seconds and I scarcely notice it happening. The bliss is not just in the losing of tension, concerns, thoughts, etc. Voluptuous fullness takes over me. I am filled by the pleasure of swelling desire and the pleasure of desire collapsing into sweet satisfaction. Gluttonous, needy, triumphant desire of the enveloping darkness."[92]

Fergie's concern is with his own pleasure, but the context for his pursuit of joy is clearly a marriage in which both he and Julie are deeply known and loved. He writes, "I don't think of Julie as I go off to sleep. She's not in my mind. But she's in my legs, torso, and arms. Not in my head. Without thinking of it, I know her there going to sleep like me. I know her knowing me the same way. This must be why that trust rises swiftly and fills us."[93] His pleasure is anything but solitary and cannot be fairly described as self-centered because he finds his center by uniting his body and soul with his wife's. Gudorf goes so far as to place mutual sexual pleasure at the center of sex. Claiming the tradition has stressed self-sacrifice too much, she insists that "love of neighbor must begin with love of self."[94] Pleasure alone seems insufficient to ground a Christian sexual ethic, but the insight that seeking sexual pleasure is a legitimate form of self-love is important, as long as its connection to union is recognized. Nurturing the thirst for pleasure is crucial because it pulls spouses toward embrace.

Of course, most theologians now affirm the good of sexual pleasure for men and women in marriage, but they "generally presume it to be . . . automatic."[95] However, Patricia Beattie Jung makes a strong case that cultural norms make it more difficult for women to experience pleasure.[96] She notes that 26 percent of women regularly do not experience climax, 32 percent report a lack of interest in sex, and 23 percent say sex is not pleasurable for them.[97] Certainly, more women today expect to experience sexual pleasure, but some continue to be frustrated or are content to let it go. Grabowski argues that even though the tradition has not paid a great deal of attention to this problem, "a case can be made that psychologically and theologically this sexual release within the context of bodily union is not unrelated to the gift of self that intercourse signifies."[98] In other words, if, on the one hand, women pursue their own sexual pleasure (a practical expression of their self-love) and their husbands commit to helping them achieve it, their sexual practice will be more pleasureful and giving for both. If, on the other hand, women and men focus solely on male pleasure, men will sacrifice less or give less of themselves, and women will participate less fully in sex and give less of themselves. Sex that is not grounded in self-love is not likely to be fully giving or fully unifying, while sex that begins in self-love is likely to be better on both counts.

In fact, in sexual relationships, self-love, self-gift, and union are intimately connected. Allowing oneself to experience pleasure is a way of loving oneself and a way of giving oneself to one's partner. Gudorf rightly notes the intertwining of self-love and other-love, showing that sex involves not a contest of wills or drives but a dance in which seeking pleasure for oneself gives pleasure to one's partner and experiencing the pleasure of one's partner is a source of one's own pleasure.[99] The good of self and neighbor are so intertwined as to be inseparable. As Jung puts it, "Our sexuality draws us into one another's arms—and consequently into an awareness of and concern about the needs of that other."[100] Putting self-love in a central place in sexual practice can help Christian couples achieve a fuller sexual life together that is both more pleasureful and more unitive.

Moreover, self-love legitimately pursued for the sake of greater goods—in this case, marital union—usually results in greater capacity to give. As Bonnie Miller-McLemore points out, caring for oneself allows one to be a better giver for "a mother cannot genuinely recognize the needs of the other unless her own subjectivity is recognized."[101] Feminist theologians have shown that women often struggle with self-love, preferring to put the needs and desires of others before their own.[102] The tradition is better at insisting on the sin of self-indulgence than the sin of failing in self-love, and women are particularly adept at taking this message to heart. Yet those who do not love themselves are often less able to achieve mutually loving relationships. An inability to love oneself is ultimately a block to intimacy. Good sexual practice must include both seeking pleasure and receiving it, along with attending to one's partner's needs to do the same.

Couples who give themselves permission to seek and experience pleasure will strengthen their marriage and find that they have greater energy for working for the good of others beyond their children, according to some theologians.[103] Paradoxically, a sexual practice that seeks self-love can result in greater unity between spouses and a stronger capacity to work together for others. In marriages where spouses care enough about themselves to make mutual sexual pleasure a priority, the love and warmth they generate can then be shared with their children and with others to whom they are committed. Nurturing their communion through self-love and self-sacrifice paradoxically enables their greater love for others. This is what Kieran Scott is getting at when he links failures in self-knowledge, solidarity, and vulnerability, and counsels centering, spending time in relationship, and extending compassion.[104] Knowing and valuing ourselves and loving and being loved by the person to whom we are most deeply committed are good practices—celebrations of human dignity and intimacy. They provide a rich foundation from which love can be extended to others, even the most vulnerable. Loving ourselves, knowing we are loved and practiced in loving another, we are free to love even more.

Bodily Belonging

Adultery strikes most people as fundamentally wrong because it constitutes a blow to what we assume to be true: Marriage means pledging your body and soul to another. Admittedly, there is some discussion at the margins of Christian theology about the possibility of moral sexual relationships outside of marriage, if it contributes to the growth and fulfillment of both spouses.[105] However, the vast majority of Christian theologians—whether liberal, conservative, or moderate—assume that infidelity is wrong. Exploring why adultery is seen as such a strong violation of marriage may help us to build a positive vision of bodily belonging toward which sexual practice ought to aim.

Traditionally, infidelity has been viewed as a violation of the marriage covenant. Adultery is clearly forbidden in the Hebrew Bible (Exod. 20:14; Deut. 22:22) and condemned by Jesus (Mark 10:19), despite his forgiving response to the women caught in adultery (John 8:1–11). Though women's status as men's property no doubt was the primary reason that the writers of the Hebrew Bible treated adultery as objectionable, the idea of the marriage covenant becomes more central to their understanding of the ethical demands of marriage over time.[106] Paul specifies the body rights that come with covenant marriage when he tells husbands and wives that they can expect both sex and fidelity in marriage (1 Cor. 7:2–5). The exclusivity of the Christian marriage covenant built on scriptural foundations requires sexual fidelity.

Although scriptural language for marriage is covenantal, the language the tradition has used to condemn adultery has often been more contractual. Augustine calls sexual fidelity one of the three goods of marriage, saying, "Married people owe each other not only the fidelity of sexual intercourse for the purpose of procreating children—this is the first association of the human race in this mortal life—but also the mutual service, in a certain measure, of sustaining each other's weakness, for the avoidance of illicit intercourse."[107] This rather thin notion of fidelity as committing to sexual exclusivity in order to avoid greater evil is carried forward in pre–*Humanae vitae* church documents. *Casti connubii*, for instance, cites Augustine when claiming that "what belongs to one of the parties by reason of this contract sanctioned by divine law, may not be denied to him or permitted to any third person."[108] Pope Pius XI rejects the criticism that laws against adultery are born of a "rigid attitude. . . a narrowing of mind and heart, something obsolete, or an abject form of jealousy," and claims that both natural instinct and scripture point to the immorality of third-party sexual relations.[109]

In the more recent tradition, contractual arguments have given way to personalist claims. Most prominent in the Catholic tradition are explanations of how the one-flesh union of the couple would be contradicted by adultery. John Paul II does not explicitly address adultery in *Familiaris consortio*, but the language of total self-gift that lies at the center of his description of marriage makes such an act unthinkable. How could spouses who "'are no longer two but one flesh' and . . . called to grow continually in their communion through day-to-day fidelity to their marriage promise of total mutual self-giving" possibly give their bodies to anyone else?[110] Moreover, strong claims about the need to give one's whole self to one's spouse so that sex does not become a lie seem to rule out self-giving to multiple partners.[111] One cannot simultaneously divide oneself between two persons and give oneself fully. In earlier writings, John Paul II makes a more explicitly personalist argument against adultery, noting that while it is not incorrect to say that marital sex is the right of the spouses or to say that adultery is a violation of this right, sex in marriage is more importantly "the regular sign of the communion of the two people," and adultery is not simply a breach of that contract but "a falsification of that sign."[112]

The communion of husbands and wives that is violated by infidelity is not only symbolized but deepened by sexual practice within marriage. There is a deep connection between body and spirit. In and through a good practice of sex, spouses seek ever greater intimacy and union. With good sex, they aim to belong more and more to each other. How does this happen?

Each sexual act is seen by some theologians as a bodily reenactment of a couple's marital vows. Drawing on John Paul II's theology of the body and canon law regarding the necessity of sex to seal the covenant promises of sacramental marriage, John Grabowski holds that sex is "an activity that seals the covenant relationship between man and woman in marriage. As such, sex has an anamnetic quality in that it is a recollection and enactment of what the couple promise in their vows to one another."[113] Grabowski invests sex with spiritual and relational significance that it has historically lacked by connecting the practice of sex to liturgy and highlighting its role in solidifying spousal bonds. Sexual union is not just bodily significant—it is spiritually significant precisely in its bodiliness. Through the body, the sexual and the spiritual are linked together. Our sex drive, according to William May, is "integrally personal" if ordered by chastity.[114] May posits that marriage is a "communion in being" and that sex "is intended to foster this communion in being." Sex is how husbands and wives communicate their communion.[115] With their bodies they speak their desire to live for each other.

The procreative potential of sex deepens its capacity to link a couple bodily as well as spiritually. Paul Ramsey speaks of the implications of the traditional teaching that unitive and procreative meanings are inscribed in the very nature of sex.[116] Ramsey holds that sex "is quite definitely a matter of our*selves,* of our souls *de profundis* . . . the I-saying subject desires in all its desiring, and what is desired is not a *what* . . . but a *who,* another I-saying one who is a presence in his or her body and therefore accessible for creaturely life-in-community."[117] Sex that involves our very selves also tends toward procreation.[118] For Ramsey, this means that sexual acts not involving the self or not within the context of a marriage open to children are lacking something fundamental. He writes that even assuming perfect contraception, "God joined sexual love and procreation together in our beings" so that, "when a man engages in sexual intercourse with a woman with whom he would not will to have a child . . . or when he begets a child with a woman to whom he does not want to give himself in love or in relation to whom he does not want the sex act to have fruition in strengthening the bond of love between them," it is to "put asunder what God has joined together."[119] Conversely, to have sex in the context of loving marriage is to give oneself to another with the expectation of lifelong love and, in most cases, shared nurturing of children.

The traditional marriage formula, "With my body, I thee wed," is more intelligible in contemporary theology because we have largely put behind us dualist thinking and suspicion of desire in order to embrace bodily belonging. Adrian Thatcher points out that Christians have turned to Trinitarian imagery to understand human beings as fundamentally relational and desire as the good impulse that draws us together. Desire is not a state of imperfection to be overcome; it is "what brings us out of ourselves, rescue[s] us from private selfhood, drive[s] us to seek the arms of our beloved, to reach out from ourselves, to learn to love."[120] Physical desire, then, is a reminder of human neediness and interconnection, and sexual union is an expression of both, which makes it an apt practice for marriage.

Yet contemporary theologians also warn that we must be careful not to overstate the significance of any one sexual act. David McCarthy rightly criticizes the common claim that "sexual desire moves us toward a complete unity of selves."[121] He suggests that every sexual act cannot be an act of total self-gift, even in marriage. "Not in an instant, but over time, we come to belong. . . . [W]hat we do today gains its meaning in relation to yesterday and what we will do tomorrow. For sex to have depth, it needs extended bodily communion over time."[122] Sex is ordinary—part of a bodily life lived in common in the context of the household. Yet, like all good practices, it also points toward the transcendent, precisely because the bodies of husbands and wives come together so many times during their common life.

In any sexual encounter, husbands and wives may recall moments of their sexual life together: their wedding night and honeymoon; those nights when they wanted to conceive a child; times when they came together after a long absence, a difficult pregnancy, or a period of estrangement; times when they sought comfort because of the illness or death of a family member or personal failure; the celebratory sex of anniversaries and good news. Their many sexual encounters fade into each other, yet as bodies change, children are born and grow, and commitments shift, still there is this practice, this ritual they enact again and again, uniting their bodies and commingling their lives.

Faithfully enacting the ritual over time will mean accepting change. Young newlyweds with perfectly lean bodies and untiring enthusiasm for sex differ from new parents who are exhausted by the physical demands of child care, from middle-aged parents mature in body and busy with many commitments, from retirees with aging bodies alone in the house with time to spare, from couples in the last stages of life whose bodies are beginning to fail them. The fidelity of marriage must be a "mobile fidelity [to] persons . . . that are growing and changing."[123] To continue in fidelity to a good practice throughout a marriage is to continue to risk and grow in a belonging that seeks one-flesh union.

Conclusion: From Intimacy to Community

In this attempt to construct a sexual practice for Christian spouses, I have tried to move beyond old impasses that led to a focus on sexual sin rather than sexual practice, and to be responsive to social science data on the experience of sex inside and outside of marriage. I have attempted to build on contemporary theological writing in order to describe sex as practice oriented to specific goods. I have suggested that maintaining a sexual practice oriented to vulnerability, self-sacrifice, self-love, and bodily belonging is essential to Christian marriage. Sex is a practice through which spouses grow in the bodily and personal intimacy necessary for true communion.

A positive Christian sexual ethic assumes the potential of sex to speak the commitment of marriage vows, not in explicit promises or earth-shattering experiences, but in the very ordinary repetition over time of a bodily act that says, "I still want to be with you. I will always want to be with you." Such a practice ought to be attentive to four goods basic to sex. Vulnerability requires a disciplining of desires to a relationship, a reasonable limitation to free one's attention for one particular other. We say, in effect, "I'm not going to any place or to anyone else. I'll pour my relational energy into you." Thus committed, spouses are free to be increasingly vulnerable to one another over time.

Good sexual practice will involve self-sacrifice and self-love. True self-giving love can only come about through self-love that inspires a desire to be vulnerable. On the one hand, if both spouses do not desire pleasure for themselves, they are not fully loving themselves or connecting with their spouse. On the other hand, spouses who do not seek the pleasure of their partner fail to embrace a necessary measure of sacrifice that love requires. Both self-giving and self-seeking involve the kind of risk that engenders deep relationship.

Finally, bodily belonging is perhaps the most significant good sought in married sex. Though couples share many bodily experiences, sex is unique to marital friendship and plays a key role in the development of one-flesh unity. If couples are faithfully committed to remaining connected, not just emotionally but physically, they will seek to maintain the sexual side of their life together. Honoring and nurturing sexual desire will bring them together bodily, emotionally, and spiritually. It will continue to open each spouse to the other, and that opening will not only nourish the communion of their married life together but will prepare them to open themselves to others. Thus sex is a foundational practice for family ethics, the first practice of resistance to which married couples committed to love and solidarity ought to be faithful.

Notes

Portions of this chapter appeared originally in Julie Hanlon Rubio, "Practicing Sexual Fidelity," *Josephinum* 14, no. 2 (2007): 269–91.

1. Alisdaire MacIntyre, *After Virtue,* 2nd ed. (Notre Dame, IN: University of Notre Dame Press, 1984). Practices are defined and linked to virtue in chap. 14.
2. Stanley Hauerwas, *The Peaceable Kingdom: A Primer in Christian Ethics* (Notre Dame, IN: University of Notre Dame Press, 1983), 103.
3. Kieran Scott, "A Spirituality of Resistance for Marriage," in *Perspectives on Marriage: A Reader,* ed. Kieran Scott and Michael Warren (New York: Oxford University Press, 2001), 403, 404.
4. John F. Kavanaugh, *Following Christ in a Consumer Society: The Spirituality of Cultural Resistance,* 25th anniversary ed. (Maryknoll, NY: Orbis, 2006).
5. Scott, "Spirituality of Resistance," 403.
6. I am drawing on the rich discussion of practice in Craig Dykstra and Dorothy C. Bass, "A Theological Understanding of Christian Practices," in *Practicing Theology: Beliefs and Practices in Christian Life,* ed. Miroslav Volf and Dorothy C. Bass (Grand Rapids, MI: Eerdmans, 2002), 13–32. See also Dorothy C. Bass, ed., *Practicing Our Faith* (San Francisco: Jossey-Bass, 1997).
7. Gerald Kelly, *Modern Youth and Chastity* (St. Louis, MO: Queen's Work, 1943), 3. This book is described in the introduction as an attempt "to give to young men and women of approximately college age a clear, adequate presentation of the Catholic moral teaching on chastity."

8. Ibid. The core of the text is chapters 10 and 11, which describe in great detail the practical moral principles toward which the whole text leads.

9. There are three chapters on chastity near the end of the book. Chastity is defined as "the habit of regulating the use of the generative faculty according to the principles of reason and of faith." Ibid., 52. The focus is on developing the virtue in order to control the sexual appetite and avoid mortal sin. Only in the last of these chapters is an attempt made to speak of chastity as "the most practical expression of sincere love for Christ." Ibid., 97.

10. *Casti connubii* (1931), in Gerald C. Treacy, ed., *Five Great Encyclicals* (New York: Paulist, 1939), no. 23.

11. Ibid., nos. 6, 9, and 12, and nos. 11–15, respectively.

12. See Leo XIII, *Arcanum*, in Claudia Carlen, ed., *The Papal Encyclicals, 1878–1963* (Raleigh, NC: McGrath, 1981).

13. Paul VI, *Humanae vitae* (Washington, DC: United States Catholic Conference, 1968).

14. Ibid., no. 8.

15. Ibid., no. 9.

16. Ibid., no. 11.

17. A selection of significant works include Janet Smith, *Why Humanae Vitae Was Right: A Reader* (San Francisco: Ignatius Press, 1993); Ronald Lawler, Joseph Boyle, and William E. May, *Catholic Sexual Ethics: A Summary, Explanation, and Defense* (Huntington, IN: Our Sunday Visitor, 1985); Charles Curran and Richard A. McCormick, eds., *Dialogue about Catholic Sexual Teaching* (New York: Paulist, 1993); and William Shannon, ed., *The Lively Debate: Responses to Humanae Vitae* (New York: Sheed & Ward, 1970).

18. See John Paul II, *Reflections on Humanae Vitae: Conjugal Morality and Spirituality* (Boston: St. Paul Books and Media, 1984), 29–40.

19. For instance, Charles E. Curran, *The Moral Theology of John Paul II* (Washington, DC: Georgetown University Press, 2005), 160–201; and Margaret Farley, *Just Love: A Framework for Christian Sexual Ethics* (New York: Continuum, 2006), 309, both raise critical points and find little of significance. David Cloutier, "Composing Love Songs for the Kingdom of God? Creation and Eschatology in Catholic Sexual Ethics," *Journal of the Society of Christian Ethics* 24, no. 2 (2004): 71–88; and McCarthy, *Sex and Love in the Home*, 42–49, see more to praise in the pope's work, though they worry that it overidealizes sex and marriage.

20. See, e.g., John Grabowski, *Sex and Virtue: An Introduction to Sexual Ethics* (Washington, DC: Catholic University Press of America Press, 2003); and Mary Shivanadan, *Crossing the Threshold of Love: A New Vision of Marriage* (Washington, DC: Catholic University of America Press, 1999).

21. See Mary Shivanadan, "Natural Family Planning and the Theology of the Body," *National Catholic Bioethics Quarterly* 3, no. 1 (2003): 25.

22. For an analysis of the wealth of experiential reflection on NFP, see my "Beyond the Liberal/Conservative Divide on Contraception: Wisdom from Practitioners of Natural Family Planning and Artificial Birth Control," *Horizons* 32, no. 2 (2005): 270–94.

23. See, e.g., Luke Timothy Johnson, "A Disembodied 'Theology of the Body': John Paul II on Love, Sex, and Pleasure," *Commonweal*, January 26, 2001, 11–17; and

Cristina Traina, "Papal Ideals, Marital Realities: One View from the Ground," in *Sexual Diversity and Catholicism*, ed. Patricia Beattie Jung, with Joseph Andrew Coray, 269–88.

24. See Jack Dominian, "Sex within Marriage," in *Sexuality and the Sacred: Sources for Theological Renewal*, ed. James B. Nelson and Sandra P. Longfellow (Louisville, KY: Westminster John Knox Press, 1994), 264–76.

25. See Christine E. Gudorf, *Body, Sex, and Pleasure: Reconstructing Christian Sexual Ethics* (Cleveland, OH: Pilgrim Press, 1994), 81–138.

26. Rubio, "Beyond the Liberal/Conservative Divide on Contraception."

27. Among the most significant works are Grabowski, *Sex and Virtue*; Shivanadan, *Crossing the Threshold of Love*; Joseph A. Selling, *Embracing Sexuality: Authority and Experience in the Catholic Church* (Burlington, VT: Ashgate Press, 2001); Jack Dominian, *Let's Make Love: The Meaning of Sexual Intercourse* (London: Darton, Longman, and Todd, 2001); Evelyn and James Whitehead, *Marrying Well: Possibilities in Christian Marriage Today* (Garden City, NY: Doubleday and Company, 1981); Gudorf, *Body, Sex, and Pleasure*; Patricia Beattie Jung, with Joseph Andrew Coray, ed., *Sexual Diversity and Catholicism*; McCarthy, *Sex and Love in the Home*; Lisa Sowle Cahill, *Sex, Gender, and Christian Ethics* (Cambridge: Cambridge University Press, 1996); Farley, *Just Love*; Kieran Scott and Harold Daly Horell, eds., *Human Sexuality in the Catholic Tradition* (Lanham, MD: Rowman & Littlefield, 2007); Gareth Moore, *The Body in Context: Sex and Catholicism* (New York: Continuum, 2001); David Cloutier, *Love, Reason, and God's Story: An Introduction to Catholic Sexual Ethics* (Winona, MN: St. Mary's Press, 2008); Todd A. Salzman and Michael G. Lawler, *The Sexual Person: Toward a Renewed Catholic Anthropology* (Washington, DC: Georgetown University Press, 2008).

28. On changes in the field of theology, see Florence Caffrey Bourg, "The Dual Vocation of Parenthood and Professional Theology," *Horizons* 32, no. 1 (2005): 26–52; and Sandra Yocum Mize, *Joining the Revolution in Theology: The College Theology Society, 1954–2004* (Lanham, MD: Rowman & Littlefield, 2007).

29. Rubio, "Beyond the Liberal/Conservative Divide on Contraception."

30. Ibid., 291.

31. See, for instance, Traina, "Papal Ideals, Marital Realities"; or Rosemary Radford Ruether, "Birth Control and the Ideals of Marital Sexuality," in *Moral Theology No. 8: Dialogue about Catholic Sexual Teaching*, ed. Charles E. Curran and Richard A. McCormick (New York: Paulist, 1993). Exceptions would be Grabowski, *Sex and Virtue*, and Shivanadan, *Crossing the Threshold of Love*, both of whom cite studies of NFP users with small sample sizes; Christine Gudorf, *Body, Sex, and Pleasure*, and Patricia Beattie Jung, "Sanctifying Women's Pleasure," in *Good Sex: Feminist Perspectives from the World's Religions*, ed. Patricia Beattie Jung, Mary E. Hunt, and Radhika Balakrishnan (New Brunswick, NJ: Rutgers University Press, 2001), 77–95, include social scientific analysis in their work.

32. William Mattison argues that the theology of the body is overly romantic and insufficiently attentive to the realities of human sinfulness. His claim that married people seem less interested in the theology of the body is also significant. See "'When they rise from the dead, they neither marry nor are given to

marriage': Marriage and Sexuality, Eschatology, and the Nuptial Meaning of the Body in Pope John Paul II's Theology of the Body," in *Sexuality and the U.S. Catholic Church: Crisis and Renewal,* ed. Lisa Sowle Cahill (New York: Herder & Herder, 2006), 32–51.

33. Vaughn Call, Susan Sprecher, and Pepper Schwartz, "The Incidence and Frequency of Marital Sex in a National Sample," *Journal of Marriage and Family* 57 (August 1995): 639, found 1 article on marital sexuality out of 533 articles on human sexuality between 1987 and 1992. The authors utilize data from the large National Survey of Families and Households in their study.

34. F. Scott Christopher and Tiffani S. Kisler, "Exploring Marital Sexuality: Peeking inside the Bedroom and Discovering What We Don't Know—But Should!" in *The Handbook of Sexuality in Close Relationships,* ed. John H. Harvey, Amy Wenzel, and Susan Sprecher (Mahwah, NJ: Lawrence Erlbaum Associates, 2004), 371–72.

35. Call, Sprecher, and Schwartz, "Incidence and Frequency of Marital Sex," 641.

36. Waite and Gallagher, *Case for Marriage,* 82. See also F. Scott Christopher and Susan Sprecher, "Sexuality in Marriage, Dating, and Other Relationships: A Decade Review," *Journal of Marriage and Family* 62 (November 2000): 1001–3.

37. Call, Sprecher, and Schwartz, "Incidence and Frequency of Marital Sex," 640. This study found that decline is mostly steady, but there is a significant drop-off after the first year. See also Christopher and Kisler, "Exploring Marital Sexuality," 372.

38. Call, Sprecher, and Schwartz, "Incidence and Frequency of Marital Sex," 646. The large drop-off after age sixty is mostly due to an increase in couples who stop having sex altogether.

39. Ibid., 647–48.

40. Ibid., 650. Authors posit that despite time pressure, those who want to make time for sex do.

41. Ibid., 650.

42. Christopher and Kisler call for social science to investigate "how marital sexuality is woven into the normal fabric of marital and family life," in "Exploring Marital Sexuality," 382.

43. Christopher and Sprecher, "Sexuality in Marriage," 1003; Waite and Gallagher, *Case for Marriage,* 82–83.

44. Waite and Gallagher, *Case for Marriage,* 88–89.

45. Christopher and Sprecher, "Sexuality in Marriage," 1004. Social and demographic factors are not associated with satisfaction.

46. Ibid. See also Christopher and Kisler, "Exploring Marital Sexuality," 373, who report a slightly weaker association.

47. Christopher and Kisler, "Exploring Marital Sexuality," 375.

48. Adrian J. Blow and Kelley Hartnett, "Infidelity in Committed Relationships II: A Substantive Review," *Journal of Marriage and Family Therapy* 31, no. 2 (2005): 222.

49. Adrian J. Blow and Kelley Hartnett provide a comprehensive review of recent studies and analyze their limits in "Infidelity in Committed Relationships I: A Methodological Review," *Journal of Marital and Family Therapy* 31, no. 2 (2005): 183–96. Infidelity is most often defined as extramarital intercourse

(EMS), but there is some movement toward defining it as any sexual or emotional act outside the primary relationship. Ibid., 186, 191–92. In addition, as Christopher and Kisler point out, there is increasing concern about the rise of internet infidelity via pornography websites or chat rooms. "Exploring Marital Sexuality," 376. Given the difficulties of ascertaining when friendships become instances of infidelity, for the purposes of this chapter, I will define infidelity as EMS.

50. Blow and Hartnett, "Infidelity in Committed Relationships II," 221. This widely accepted, longitudinal study show levels that are disturbing, but not as high as the 50 percent to 75 percent figures sometimes seen in the popular press. There is less infidelity in marriage than in dating or cohabitation.

51. The United States is unusually intolerant of infidelity in principle. Ninety-nine percent of married individuals expect fidelity of their spouses and say that their spouse expects the same of them, and 80 percent say EMS is always wrong. However, in other countries, the percentage of those disapproving of adultery is far lower (67 percent in Britain and Italy, 36 percent in Russia, 58 percent in Japan). Men's affairs are also viewed as more acceptable in some African, Latin American, and Asian countries. See Judith Treas, "Infidelity," in *International Encyclopedia of Marriage and Family Relationships*, vol. 4, 2nd ed., ed. James J. Ponzetti (New York: Macmillan Reference USA, 2000), 299–308.

52. Blow and Hartnett, "Infidelity in Committed Relationships II," 224–25.

53. Ibid., 223. See also Judith Treas and Deirdre Giesen, "Sexual Infidelity among Married and Cohabiting Americans," *Journal of Marriage and the Family* 62 (February 2000): 59.

54. Blow and Hartnett, "Infidelity in Committed Relationships II," 226.

55. Ibid., 227. See also Treas and Giesen, "Sexual Infidelity," 59.

56. Treas, "Infidelity," 899. See also Blow and Hartnett, "Infidelity in Committed Relationships II," 222, who note that women are more likely to engage in emotional affairs when they are dissatisfied with their marriages and that all those who engaged in infidelity with coworkers were more satisfied with their marriages than others who cheated on their spouses. This suggests that dissatisfaction does predict for significant affairs, but satisfaction may not protect in situations with significant opportunities for EMS.

57. Christians ought not respond to this data by avoiding male-female friendships. The Christian tradition affirms the value of these relationships in community. Rodney Clapp argues that fearing male-female friendships "reinforces the impoverished, overly narrow idea that a member of the opposite sex can be only a love object or a casual acquaintance." Clapp, *Families at the Crossroads: Beyond Traditional and Modern Options* (Downers Grove, IL: Intervarsity Press, 1993), 110.

58. See, for instance, Gregory K. Popcak, *Holy Sex: A Catholic Guide to Toe-Curling, Mind-Blowing, Infallible Loving* (New York: Crossroad, 2008). In a recent article, David Van Biema, "And God Said, 'Just Do It,'" *Time*, June 26, 2008, notes the increase of seminars in Christian churches on good sex.

59. *Familiaris consortio*, nos. 18–20.

60. *Familiaris consortio*, no. 11.

61. Johnson, "Disembodied 'Theology of the Body,'" 15.

62. Traina, "Papal Ideals," 280. Traina writes, "Greater sexual desire for my husband yields, paradoxically, greater generosity toward him: fuller self-gift. From my point of view this manifests God's brilliance."

63. Edna McDonagh, *Vulnerable to the Holy in Faith, Morality, and Art* (Dublin: Columba Press, 2004), 91.

64. Mary Pellauer, "The Moral Significance of Female Orgasm," in *Sexuality and the Sacred: Sources for Theological Reflection,* ed. James B. Nelson and Sandra P. Longfellow (Louisville, KY: Westminster John Knox Press, 1994), 157.

65. Ibid., 157.

66. Karen Lebacqz, "Appropriate Vulnerability," in *Sexuality and the Sacred: Sources for Theological Reflection,* ed. James B. Nelson and Sandra P. Longfellow (Louisville, KY: Westminster John Knox Press, 1994), 258. Donna Frietas's book, *Sex and the Soul: Juggling Sexuality, Spirituality, Romance, and Religion on America's College Campuses* (New York: Oxford University Press, 2008), vividly showcases the lack of vulnerability in the sex lives of most college students who substitute pleasure for intimacy.

67. Lebacqz, "Appropriate Vulnerability," 259–60. Lebacqz does not rule out the possibility of appropriate vulnerability in other kinds of committed relationships.

68. Ibid., 260.

69. Christine Gudorf, "Why Sex Is Good for Your Marriage," reprinted in *Human Sexuality in the Catholic Tradition,* ed. Kieran Scott and Harold Daly Horell (Lanham, MD: Rowman & Littlefield, 2007), 129. McDonagh goes further, claiming that vulnerability in marital friendship prepares us for vulnerability to the holy. McDonagh, *Vulnerable to the Holy,* 92.

70. Richard J. Foster, *The Challenge of the Disciplined Life: Christian Reflections on Money, Sex, and Power* (San Francisco: HarperCollins, 1985), 164.

71. Ibid., 163–64. The connection between play and self-disclosure is not fully explored here or, for that matter, in many theological works.

72. Rita Zeis, "Fidelity as Process: Being and Becoming," in *Fidelity: Issues of Emotional Living in an Age of Stress for Clergy and Religious,* ed. John Hart (Whitinsville, MA: Affirmation Books, 1980), 55.

73. Ibid., 65.

74. Bernard J. Bush, "I Do for Life," in *Fidelity: Issues of Emotional Living in an Age of Stress for Clergy and Religious,* ed. John Hart (Whitinsville, MA: Affirmation Books, 1980), 76. This sense of journey is helpful and perhaps underdeveloped in some John Paul II's writings on marriage.

75. Gudorf, "Why Sex Is Good for Your Marriage," 129.

76. In the classic textbook used in Catholic seminaries until Vatican II, *Moral Theology* (Westminster, MD: Newman Bookshop, 1945), 557, Fr. Heribert Jone writes, "Rendering the marriage debt is a grave obligation, especially when the petitioner is in danger of continence or would have to make a great sacrifice to overcome temptation." A good overview of development in the tradition is Joseph A. Selling, "The Meanings of Human Sexuality," *Louvain Studies* 23 (1998): 22–37.

77. Note, e.g., embrace of the concept by Grabowski, who argues that all human beings "are created for love" and "fulfilled in the self-donation of love" (*Sex*

and Virtue, 125), and by Gudorf, who sees in orgasm a surrender of self-control, "a little death, a losing of oneself," that can potentially open people up to become more self-giving in all areas of their lives (*Body, Sex, and Pleasure,* 108–9).

78. Sidney Callahan, *Beyond Birth Control: The Christian Experience of Sex* (New York: Sheed & Ward, 1968), 140.

79. Married theologians tend to be realistic about what self-gift entails in any one sexual act. For example, Grabowski writes, "Spouses give themselves to each other as they are (joyful, anxious, tired, energetic, preoccupied, attentive, etc.)." Grabowski, *Sex and Virtue,* 69.

80. Vincent M. Bilotta III, "Lived Fidelity to the Sacred: Responding to my Hunger for Depth," in *Fidelity: Issues of Emotional Living in an Age of Stress for Clergy and Religious,* ed. John Hart (Whitinsville, MA: Affirmation Books, 1980), 99.

81. Ibid.

82. Ibid., 109.

83. Call, Sprecher, and Schwartz, "The Incidence and Frequency of Marital Sex," 650.

84. See, for instance, Grabowski, *Sex and Virtue,* 125; and Gudorf, *Body, Sex, and Pleasure,* 119.

85. The positive literature on NFP is vast. See especially Paul *Murray,* "The Power of *Humanae Vitae:* Take Another Look," *Commonweal,* July 15, 1994, 14–18.

86. Gregory R. Beabout and Randall Colton, "If You Want Justice, Work for Chastity," unpublished paper, 2003; and David Matzko McCarthy, "Sexual Utterances and the Common Life," *Modern Theology* 16.4 (2000): 443–59.

87. Shivanadan, "Natural Family Planning," 25.

88. Gudorf, *Body, Sex, and Pleasure,* 85. Gudorf carefully distinguishes between control and repression.

89. Karol Wojtyla, *Love and Responsibility,* trans. H. T. Willetts (San Francisco: Ignatius Press, 1993), 272–73.

90. Mitch Finley, "The Dark Side of Natural Family Planning," *America,* February 23, 1991, 207.

91. This is particularly difficult in situations when one partner has experienced sexual abuse. Clearly, the victim of abuse should expect care and understanding from her or his spouse throughout the healing process. Only later would mutuality in sacrifice be appropriate, and even then, deference to the survivor's needs would be necessary.

92. John Giles Milhaven, "Sleeping Like Spoons," in *Sexuality and the Sacred: Sources for Theological Reflection,* ed. James B. Nelson and Sandra P. Longfellow (Louisville, KY: Westminster John Knox Press, 1994), 88.

93. Ibid., 89.

94. Gudorf, *Body, Sex, and Pleasure,* 115.

95. Jung, "Sanctifying Women's Pleasure," 81.

96. Ibid., 84–89.

97. Ibid., 82. All figures are from the 1992 National Health and Social Life Survey.

98. Grabowski, *Sex and Virtue,* 141, allows that this ideal may not always be realized.

99. Gudorf, *Body, Sex, and Pleasure,* 115–16.

100. Jung, "Case for Sexual Fidelity," 94.

101. Bonnie Miller-McLemore, *Also a Mother: Work and Motherhood as Theological Dilemma* (Nashville, TN: Abingdon, 1994), 103.

102. Valerie Saiving, "The Human Situation: A Feminine View," in *Womanspirit Rising: A Feminist Reader in Religion,* ed. Carol P. Christ and Judith Plaskow (San Francisco: HarperCollins, 1979), 25–42. See also Mary Stewart VanLeeuven, "The Christian Mind and the Challenge of Gender Relations," in *Sexuality and the Sacred: Sources for Theological Reflection,* ed. James B. Nelson and Sandra P. Longfellow (Louisville, KY: Westminster John Knox Press, 1994), 120–30.

103. Gudorf, *Body, Sex, and Pleasure,* 138.

104. Scott, "Spirituality of Resistance," 404–9.

105. James Nelson, "Varied Meanings of Marriage and Fidelity," in *Perspectives on Marriage,* ed. Kieran Scott and Michael Warren (New York: Oxford University Press, 1993), 103, defines fidelity as "a commitment of emotional and physical intimacy with the partner; it means caring for the growth and fulfillment of each as a person[;] . . . it involves willingness to explore ways of opening the self to the partner at the deepest possible level, risking the pains that may come; it includes openness to secondary relationships of emotional intimacy and potential genital expression, but with the commitment to the primacy of the marriage."

106. John J. Collins, "Marriage in the Old Testament," in *Marriage in the Catholic Tradition: Scripture, Tradition, and Experience,* ed. Todd A. Salzman, Thomas M. Kelly, and John J. O'Keefe (New York: Crossroad, 2004), 12–20. Prophetic critiques of divorce and adultery come in later prophetic books such as Malachi and Hosea.

107. Augustine, "The Good of Marriage," excerpted in *The Book of Marriage: The Wisest Answers to the Toughest Questions,* ed. Dana Mack and David Blankenhorn (Grand Rapids, MI: Eerdmans,2001), 77.

108. Pius XI, *Casti connubii,* no. 19.

109. Ibid., no. 73.

110. *Familiaris consortio,* no. 19. The pope does note that their "communion is radically contradicted by polygamy."

111. Ibid., no. 32.

112. John Paul II, *Blessed Are the Pure of Heart: Catechesis on the Sermon on the Mount and Writings of St. Paul* (Boston, MA: St. Paul Editions, 1983), 108, from a sermon, "Adultery: A Breakdown of the Personal Covenant," preached on August 27, 1980.

113. Grabowski, *Sex and Virtue,* 47–48.

114. May, "Sexuality, Fidelity, and Marriage," 282–83.

115. Ibid., 286.

116. Aquinas also understands adultery as an offense against procreation and chastity, though he defines adultery as a species of lust and is more concerned with chastity, *Summa Theologica* II-II, Q. 145, art. 8.

117. Paul Ramsey, "A Christian Approach to the Question of Sexual Relations Outside of Marriage," *Journal of Religion* 45, no. 2 (1965), 102.

118. Ibid.,105.

119. Ibid., 109.
120. Adrian Thatcher, "Intimate Relationships and the Christian Way," *Modern Believing* 44, no. 1 (2003): 6.
121. McCarthy, *Sex and Love in the Home*, 43.
122. Ibid, 45–46.
123. Whitehead and Whitehead, *Marrying Well*, 390.

CHAPTER FIVE

The Practice of Eating

Love, Justice, and Mercy

In this chapter I continue to consider specific practices that mark family life and ask how families might shape those practices in accord with the theological framework outlined in the first three chapters of this book. The first choice of a practice was somewhat easy, for sex is probably the practice that most distinguishes Christian marriage, even if it is rarely examined and virtually never advocated as a crucial part of the Christian moral life for married persons. Choosing additional family practices was difficult, as there are so many possibilities. However, because I contend that the ordinary daily life deserves more attention, I leave aside issues that traditionally occupy theologians concerned with family. As I argue that in the Christian tradition families are called to be socially concerned, I consider only practices with potential to serve the good of families themselves and the good of others. In order to avoid constructing an overly ideal ethic as the best of Catholic theology and literature counsel, I strive to acknowledge human imperfection and focus on small efforts toward solidarity.

Eating, the focus of this chapter, is perhaps the most common and necessary family practice. While individuals in families can and do eat in a variety of ways, when families gather over meals, those meals are formative. In coming together to eat, a family recognizes bonds they share, shapes its members' characters, and sends them forth to be certain kinds of people. This is true whether families intend it or not. Around a table, a family becomes more of who it is—faithful or jaded, contentious or loving, open or closed, or something in between.

I argue that a good eating practice can both contribute to the growth of family members as a Christian community and function as a way for them to live out their commitment to the common good. On my way to discussing good eating, I analyze current eating practices of American families and turn to the Christian tradition for wisdom about eating, focusing on Jesus's meals in the gospels and the liturgical practice of Eucharist. Reading the tradition on food yields two seemingly competing values: Christian identity and inclusivity or compassion. For Christians, a good eating practice must balance these two values. It must be marked by mercy, even as it is oriented to love and justice.

Family Meals in the Twenty-first Century

In *Sharing Food: Christian Practices for Enjoyment*, Christian ethicist L. Shannon Jung urges readers to work toward "a deeply satisfying way to eat" centered on shared meals.[1] In the last two decades most adults have been made aware of the importance of family meals for the good of their families. In doctors' offices, television commercials, and school-sponsored mailings, they have been warned of the dire consequences of not sitting down to dinner with their children and encouraged to take advantage of the benefits of doing so. A recent *Time* magazine cover story brings together a plethora of studies showing that the more often a family eats together, the less likely children are to drink, smoke, take drugs, be overweight, have eating disorders, get depressed, or consider suicide, and the more likely they are to do well in school, delay sex, avoid drugs, eat healthy food, have a good vocabulary, and use good manners.[2] Many parents have heard the message. According to a 2005 longitudinal study by the Center on Addiction and Substance Abuse at Columbia University, the percentage of adolescents eating with families increased 23 percent between 1998 and 2005.[3] This improvement is laudable.

Still, only about 55 percent of twelve-year-olds and 26 percent of seventeen-year-olds report that they regularly eat meals with their families.[4] Because more women are in the workforce, professionals are more likely to work late, working-class adults hold service jobs that require more evening hours than the factory jobs their parents may have held, children and teens engage in more extracurricular activities, and few families have an adult at home who is free to make a meal each day, sitting down to a home-cooked meal has become much more difficult. Thus even many of those who know the benefits of family meals find themselves unable to make them a priority on a regular basis.

Eating meals together is associated not only with strong families but with strong communities. Robert Putnam's well-known book *Bowling Alone* chronicles the remarkable decline in family meals through the 1990s. Putnam notes that, from the 1970s until the 1990s, the percentage of married Americans who agreed that their whole family usually eats dinner together declined by one-third, from 50 percent to 34 percent.[5] These data actually understate the scope of change in American habits because they only deal with married couples, while the proportion of adults living alone doubled during the same period.[6] Clearly, a majority of Americans do not regularly eat the evening meal with significant others. The gravity of this change can be overstated, as there are plenty of other ways for families to connect. However, Putnam's research shows that "virtually all forms of family togetherness became less common over the last quarter of the twentieth century."[7] He worries about "loosening family bonds."[8] Although meals are not everything, "since the evening meal has been a communal experience in virtually all societies for a very long time, the fact that it has visibly diminished in the course of a single generation in our country is remarkable evidence of how rapidly our social connectedness has been changing."[9] A fundamental way in which the sociality of human beings has been expressed is in serious decline.

Moreover, the decline in family gatherings is not an isolated example of declining sociality. Putnam's data show that the decline in family meals has been accompanied by a decline in other social gatherings. For instance, there has been a decrease in social visiting. Whereas the average family entertained friends at home fourteen to fifteen times per year in the late 1970s, by the late 1990s they did so only eight times—a decline of 45 percent in two decades.[10] Dinner parties have not given way to meeting at restaurants, as both going out to see friends and having friends over declined from the 1970s to the 1990s.[11] Contrary to popular wisdom, dining out (alone or with others) has increased very little over the last several decades.[12] Moreover, people patronize bars, nightclubs, and taverns 40 to 50 percent less often than they did twenty years ago. So "the practice of entertaining friends has not simply moved outside the home, but seems to be vanishing entirely."[13]

Although a causal relationship is impossible to prove, the parallel decline in family practices and community practices is suggestive. In a busy world, people have less time to be in relationship with family, friends, and neighbors. Social connections are in decline in many arenas. It may be that when families fail to gather themselves in their homes their own members are less likely to become the kind of people who join in community with others.

When a majority of families, and many more single people, do not sit down together for an evening meal, it is not surprising that other communal bonds suffer. Eating is a seemingly ordinary family practice that profoundly affects the social order. Yet the Christian tradition rarely gives attention to eating as an ethical practice. Even in Catholic teaching on the family, nowhere are family meals called a requirement for virtuous living. No instructions are given for eating meals in a particularly "Christian" way. Yet there is in the tradition great wisdom about eating that may inform this attempt to construct a practice of resistance to individualistic cultural trends.

Eucharist: Communion and Calling

The meals remembered and celebrated by the Christian community can illuminate the meaning of ordinary meals of believers. Patrick McCormick writes that when Christians eat consciously they can reflect on many familiar stories from their tradition that center on eating: the Last Supper, the miracle of the loaves and fishes, God's provision of food for the Hebrew people wandering in the desert, Jesus's promise of a heavenly banquet, and God's creation of the Earth that provides sustenance.[14] These stories form a narrative through which Christians may understand their own eating practice.

Fundamental to this narrative is the interplay between human neediness and divine giving. To be human is to be in need—of food, drink, rest, justice, meaning, and so on—and the Christian story tells of God's desire to fulfill those needs. McCormick claims that hunger itself is powerful if pondered, for "the hungry know they need God, and their hunger has made a space in them to celebrate God's bounty."[15] The Christian story that tells of human need and divine blessing calls out for gratitude. Recognizing God's blessing does not at first seem novel, but it is difficult to keep in mind in a culture where focus on achievement, busyness, and agency encourage forgetfulness of human dependence on God. Thus thinking about eating through the lens of Christian tradition involves the difficult work of letting go of this cultural paradigm and embracing a sense of need and gratitude. Eucharist means to give thanks.[16]

Eucharist fulfills the fundamental human need for communion with God and others. The gathering of a community around a table can be experienced as communion, for, as one theologian notes, "every time we eat with others, we commune with them."[17] The ancient practice of joining Eucharist and eating a meal is a reminder that all food is sacred. Through this joining, personal experience of the real presence of God in the eucharistic bread becomes shared communion. We are fed not only by the food of God's presence but by the experience of receiving God with others. Eucharist aims for this sort of communion, even if Eucharist as experienced is limited by an imperfect grasping of human neediness, an imperfect understanding of the significance of Christ's real presence in the transformed bread and wine, and an imperfect realization of Christian community in a given parish.[18]

Eucharist is not only about gratitude and communion; it is about being sent forth. It is a way to celebrate the unity of the church in itself and invite members to make the church present in the world. David Hollenbach claims that sacramental celebrations provide important insights into the church's social role.[19] Hollenbach sees in the communion meal a moral imperative. Because Eucharist is the sacrament that symbolizes the unity of all persons in Christ, and because this unity is symbolized by the sharing of food, it makes sense to think of both gathering as a community and feeding the hungry as central to Christian life. In the sharing of food with each other and those in need, Christians celebrate who they are. The command to do justice is deeply embedded in the most central celebration of Christian identity and community.

The connection between Eucharist and social justice is also implied in our participation in a ritual given by Jesus to his disciples so that they would remember him. As Monika Hellwig claims, when we eat at God's table, we are obligated to take up the cause of Jesus; we cannot separate the message from the messenger.[20] To eat his body is to assent to his mission to bring good news to the lowly. This calling to continue Jesus's work is not individual but communal, for just as the Last Supper solidified the bonds of the community gathered around Jesus, so too the Eucharist is meant to be a transformative moment for a Christian community. As Ela puts it, "The Eucharist is real only in the transformation of a divided people into the oneness of Christ."[21] Hellwig goes so far as to say that transubstantiation can be understood in part as the transformation of the community.[22]

To be transformed by Eucharist, a Christian community is to model its life after the life of Jesus, knowing that his ministry was healing, welcoming, and preaching to people who were marginalized in his own society. The Jesus who preached that the last would be first, told the story of Lazarus and the rich man, and announced that those who fed the hungry and clothed the naked would be on the right side on Judgment Day also identified himself with the bread sent from heaven.[23] Thus when Jesus finally gathers the disciples for the Last Supper the night before he dies and, as John has it, washes their feet, he is telling them once again who he is and who they must be—and he tells them with a meal, a meal that becomes the model for the church's Eucharist.[24]

Because Jesus was universal and nondiscriminatory in his love, his followers are called to a lifestyle that includes "the serious practice of universal (non-exclusive) charity that is the exercise of the creative love of God."[25] However, this is not to say that only charitableness is required of Christians. When believers recall and celebrate Christ's death and resurrection in the Eucharist, they remember Jesus's radical challenge to the world and prepare themselves to take up that challenge. David Powers calls attention to the eschatological dimensions of this memorial, claiming that it "places communities and human enterprises under judgment, or alerts them to what is now commonly called the apocalyptic sting of the gospel proclamation, the submission of all human reality in its corporate and historical totality to a judgment that puts it face to face with Christ."[26] Powers suggests that celebrating the Eucharist points toward future perfection, places the world under judgment, and calls all who participate to follow Jesus in engaging the powers that hold the world back from being what it ought to be, knowing the cost of such engagement. Commitment to both nondiscriminatory love and structural change are implied by remembrance of Jesus in the Eucharist. Relationship with God, participation in community, and the call to do justice in the world are all bound up together in this simple practice.

Eucharist as celebrated this way can serve as a model for family meals. Church communities can exclude or alienate. They often fall short of great liturgy and great homilies. Yet communal celebration of Eucharist still calls forth gratitude, aims at communion, and sends members forth to do justice. The important thing is that the practice of Eucharist continues and the Christians who participate in it strive to become people of love and justice. Similarly, in spite of real imperfections, continuing the practice of family meals is key. As with Eucharist, if the family meal is neglected, family members' sense of themselves as community will suffer, and so will their understanding of what they are about.

Eating with/as Sinners: Practicing Mercy at the Table

Viewing Christian meals through the lens of the Eucharist yields a more substantive understanding of what Christian families ought to be about when they gather to eat. They are not simply focusing on their emotional bonds in order to ensure personal success and family closeness. Rather, they are binding themselves to one another in a community oriented to Christ and to living out Christ's mission. Their unity, shared identity, and commitment to social justice are crucial to their gathering and this implies the need for a distinctive eating practice.

However, the reality of family life makes this sort of gathering seem impossible. Families are diverse—in faith traditions, in faith commitments, and in ideas about what it means to live out Christ's mission. Families are flawed—not conscious enough of their own neediness, less than fully grateful for their privileges, too fractured to achieve communion, and not interested enough in social justice. How, then, can a theology of Eucharist serve ordinary families? Who could possibly measure up to this standard? I argue that the witness of Jesus provides a radical lens through which to view the eucharistic model because he did not avoid questions of sin, difference, or worthiness. Holding Jesus's eating practice in tension with the ideals of eucharistic theology offers possibilities for constructing a viable Christian practice of eating today.

Over the past thirty-five years, a great many scripture scholars have affirmed that Jesus enjoyed many meals with outcasts and sinners.[27] The relative silence of critics and the number and prestige of advocates of this thesis combine to make a solid case that Jesus ate with people who were considered by most in his time to be sinners.[28] All three of the synoptic gospels record the charge that Jesus ate with tax collectors and sinners (Matt. 11:19; Mark 2:15; Luke 7:34, 15:12, 19:7). There is no record of Jesus's excluding anyone from his table because of sin or scandal. The early Christian community struggled with this issue, but Jesus, apparently, did not.

Jesus's inclusive meals disturbed many of his contemporaries. Recent scholarship has emphasized that meals were central teaching moments for Jesus, intimately related to his mission and message, and possibly among the causes of his death.[29] Clearly inclusivity was disturbing to many. As New Testament scholar Marcus Borg points out, in the ancient Near Eastern world sitting down to a meal with another person was a sign of approval, and refusing to do so was a mark of disrespect.[30] Within Judaism, and more particularly within the Pharisaic sect, who are most often cast as critics of Jesus's eating practices, table fellowship assumed an even greater importance, as it was linked to personal holiness.[31] Thus Jesus's practice was disturbing because he challenged predominant ideas about the links between meals, holiness, and the identity of the Jewish people before God.

Despite near consensus by scholars on the historicity of inclusive meals and the scandal those meals engendered, there is considerable disagreement about the meaning of the term "sinner" and thus about with what sort of sinner Jesus shared meals.[32] According to Borg, while Jesus does not appear to have eaten with Gentiles, he did break with many in his tradition by taking meals with Jews who engaged in work that was considered unclean and at least potentially immoral, Jews marginalized because they did not uphold the Jewish law as strictly as the Pharisees believed they ought, and Jews who were engaged in the deliberate breaking of the Jewish law.[33] Joachim Jeremias characterizes those in the fourth and last category as persons who "notoriously failed to observe the commandments of God," while New Testament scholar E. P. Sanders simply says they were "the wicked . . . who sinned willfully and heinously and who did not repent."[34] For my purposes, this fourth category is most important, though it is clear that people in all categories would have been considered sinners in Jesus's day. Barbara Taylor writes that if Jesus's meals were held today, they might include "an abortion doctor, a child molester, an arms dealer, a garbage collector, a young man with AIDS, a Laotian chicken plucker, a teenage crack addict, and an unmarried woman on welfare with five children by three different fathers."[35] It is highly probable that Jesus ate with the sort of people that some contemporary Christians see as sinners.

Still, even if most believe that inclusive meals with sinners did occur, the significance of the meals is considerably less clear. Was Jesus inviting sinners to his table with the hope that conversion would follow? Was he deliberately eating with anyone in order to show his disdain for social distinctions? Was he questioning the focus of his contemporaries on purity? Each of these theories will be explored in the following paragraphs, and I argue that each is a partial explanation of Jesus's practice. Taken together, they offer a plausible understanding of what meals with sinners meant in the context of Jesus's time and provide a model for Christian families trying to discern the ethical dimensions of their meals today.

In many of the situations in which Jesus is accused of eating with sinners, he responds by explaining that he is trying to save them. In one case (Mark 2:15–17), he compares himself to a doctor who comes to heal the sick. In another case, he implicitly links his practice to the saving action at the center of three parables: the lost sheep, the lost coin, and the lost son (Luke 15:1–32). In each case, characters standing for God (the shepherd, the woman, and the father) rejoice when they find what was lost, without troubling themselves about how their contact with the found objects will affect them. Many scripture scholars claim that Jesus's meals are symbols of his concern for finding those who needed him, or his offers of salvation to the lost.[36] For these authors, the meals with sinners are easily comprehended once situated in the context of Jesus's mission to call people to repentance and new life. Just as pastors today travel among the lost in order to spark conversions, Jesus wanted to bring new life to sinners in his society. Contemporary believers with similar concerns, it might be argued, could justifiably eat with sinners.

However, Sanders convincingly argues that Jesus's meals were particularly offensive because he ate with people while they were still sinners and in doing so offered them forgiveness before they had repented and reformed.[37] For instance, Jesus eats with Levi and his tax collector friends (Luke 5:29–32), he eats with Pharisees (Luke 7:36), and he allows a sinning woman to approach the table in order to wash his feet (Luke 7:37–50). Sanders's analysis brings to light the more radical nature of Jesus's eating praxis. It is undeniable that Jesus went among the lost in order to offer salvation, but he ate with sinners before any discussion about salvation had taken place, before any new promises had been made. Jesus's choice of eating companions must mean something more.

Recent New Testament scholarship indicates that Jesus's meals with sinners were radical because of the way they challenged the social hierarchies of his day. In first-century Palestine, meals were symbols of the way society was structured. An invitation to a meal was an extension of social acceptance. A host expected that he would be invited to his guests' homes in return. The honor/shame code of the society was reinforced when those who would bring a host honor were included and when those who would not bring honor were excluded.[38] In this context, eating with sinners or social outcasts made no sense. Inclusive meals were a threat to the order of the society in which Jesus lived. Instead of respecting the social norms of his culture, Jesus seems to have offered what Jerome Neyrey calls "new maps of persons," by "eating across the board."[39] John Dominic Crossan, who celebrates Jesus's "random and open commensality," goes even further and argues that Jesus ate with anyone, "negating the very social function of the table."[40] In the simple action of eating, the social order was broken open.

Acknowledging this aspect of the meals with sinners is important to understanding the social significance of Jesus's practice. Clearly, Jesus undermined his own status as a religious leader in his society when he chose to eat with people who were considered beneath him. He did not claim the honor that could have been his by virtue of his purity. Rather than spend most of his time among friends and supporters, he sought out those who did not understand or approve of his ways. His meals with sinners are not only occasions in which Jesus extends forgiveness to those who want to change but also instances in which he brings into question his society's ways of distinguishing the honorable from the disreputable, the worthy from the unworthy.

The practice of eating with sinners represented a break with purity codes that were central to some forms of Judaism in Jesus's time. Theologian John Elliott is especially clear on this point. For him, the meals represent a new food code within a new religious system in which mercy is more important than purity in one's relationship with God. Elliott argues that unlike the Pharisees who advocated a reform program in which households would conform to temple purity codes, Jesus suggested with his practice that the ethos of the household—which prized mercy and hospitality over purity concerns—should remain intact and become a model for the temple.[41] It was not necessary to keep oneself pure by avoiding unclean foods or people; imitating the mercy and compassion of God was more important. Borg is even more emphatic in his claim that Jesus's table fellowship was "a critique of holiness as the dominant paradigm of the people of God."[42] Like the Good Samaritan who practices love by helping a stranger (and risking impurity, unlike the rabbi who refused to stop), Jesus eats with the impure, implicitly criticizing the way in which, for some, the quest for holiness could obstruct the exercise of compassion. Jesus would not allow such a quest to interfere with ministry. While he shared with the Pharisees a desire to reform Judaism by calling Jews to a higher standard, his program was different because he redefined holiness as mercy rather than separation.[43]

Thus the meals with sinners that were significant symbols of Jesus's expansive forgiveness and lack of respect for social ordering were also and, perhaps most important, indications of what was central to his moral vision. In practicing inclusion, Jesus reveals his faith in a compassionate God who would not leave anyone out of the celestial banquet. As Elisabeth Schüssler Fiorenza claims, "The power of God's *basileia* is realized in Jesus's table community with the poor, the sinners, the tax collectors, and prostitutes—with all those who 'do not belong' to the 'holy people,' who are somehow deficient in the eyes of the righteous. . . . Jesus's *praxis* and *vision* of the *basileia* is the mediation of God's future into the structures and experiences of his own time and people."[44] In eating with sinners and outcasts, Jesus was revealing human compassion and modeling divine mercy.

However, while the prominence of the meal tradition in the gospels indicates that the early church identified with Jesus's inclusive practice and felt challenged "to take on itself the same scandal Jesus took on himself," there is little evidence of early Christian meals with the sort of people contemporary Christians saw as sinners and little record of Christian reflection on Jesus's practice.[45] Still, even though Jesus's example is not specifically invoked, the debate between Peter and Paul over eating with Gentiles can be seen as an argument about how best to honor the gospel value of open commensality.[46] In Galatians 2:14, Paul accuses Peter of not honoring the truth of the gospel because of his refusal to eat with Gentiles.[47] In the book of Acts, Peter's conversion on the issue of inclusive table fellowship is described in detail. In the beginning of Acts 10, Peter is hesitant to eat with Gentiles, and his concern over a meal becomes a symbol of a crisis about who the Christian community is and what it is about. In the dramatic conclusion of the story, Peter hears the voice of God telling him to eat with Cornelius, a Gentile. He relents, claiming that God has told him that there are no unclean foods or unclean persons (Acts 10:28). According to Elliott, in this pivotal case, purity codes relating to food and company have been rescinded by God, who has told Peter that no person is unclean.[48] Peter eats with Cornelius, who is praised for his prayer and almsgiving. "The implication," says Elliott, "is that Cornelius' prayers and alms in his home are equivalent to or a replacement of the 'clean' sacrifices at the Temple. . . . Deeds of mercy (alms) and prayer now take the place of Temple sacrifice as the sign of union with God."[49]

The story of Peter shows that among the early Christians, eating with Gentiles had become a mark of the Christian movement. Note, too, though purity is the main focus of this story, social hierarchies are also overturned when Peter eats with a class of people who were considered beneath him. Moreover, though Peter does not offer forgiveness to Cornelius, his implicit acceptance of Cornelius is an analogous act, for he eats with Cornelius before receiving any confirmation of his faith. Thus all three meanings of Jesus's meals with sinners are reflected in this one early Christian conversion to open commensality.[50] In this practice, the early church seems to be implicitly honoring the example of Jesus.

However, Paul specifically advocates exclusion from ritual meals within the Christian community. Paul tells his fellow Christians not to worry about eating with immoral people as long as they are non-Christians, but he also warns them "not to associate with any one who bears the name of brother if he is guilty of immorality or greed, or is an idolater, reviler, drunkard, or robber—*not even to eat with such a one*" (1 Cor. 5:11–13, emphasis mine).[51]

What can explain this seeming contradiction? Most commentators note the change in context. Paul (and eventually Peter) ate with Gentiles in the context of a mission of conversion. They de-emphasized ritual purity but still sought moral purity within the church. With their leadership, the Jesus movement became a community of disciples that Paul compares to the body of Christ. In this body, purity was again important. It was crucial to establish Christian identity in opposition to the world.[52] Paul seemed to think that exclusion was necessary to preserve the identity, purity, and unity of the church. Being a Christian was supposed to mean taking on a new identity and acting in new ways. If some in the Corinthian community asserted their freedom to do whatever they wanted to while claiming to be Christian, Paul argued that they were wrong.[53] Paul advocated excluding sinners of certain kinds from meals of the Christian community so that the church would remain united in faithfulness to Christ.

This exclusion continued as the church developed, primarily out of concern for unity. Canons from early church councils show that Christians who were guilty of willful murder, involuntary homicide, divination, and other scandalous behavior were excommunicated for years at a time in order to preserve church unity.[54] Only later were some repenting sinners reinstated as full members of the community. Although councils seemed more concerned with eucharistic meals than ordinary meals, believers are also warned not to communicate or pray with excommunicated persons or heretics. Most patristic commentators explain that the purity of the church demands avoiding sinning brothers.[55] Clement of Alexandria's comments are typical: "Neither in discourse or food are we to join, looking with suspicion on the pollution thence proceeding, as on the tables of the demons."[56] General advice to keep away from false teachers, heretics, and any persons who were excommunicated from the Christian community was common, for "the taint of sins can be communicated as if contagious, wherever a man mixes himself with sinners."[57]

A second important reason for exclusion was concern for the soul of the sinner, who needed the opportunity to repent of his sins and right his relationship with God.[58] Cyprian writes that it would be more sinful to ignore the sin, for "how can the medicine of permissiveness profit anyone? What if a physician hides the wound and does not allow the necessary remedy of time to close the scar? To not require repentance makes the way easy for new dangers. To do that is not *curing* someone. If we are honest, it is slaying him."[59] Clearly, the early Christians believed that exclusion from table fellowship was for the benefit of the sinner as well as the community.

However, concerns about identity and unity were far more pervasive. Andrew McGowan, whose *Ascetic Eucharist* shows the diversity of eucharistic practice among early Christian communities, claims that "Christian uses of food could express self-definition and separation of the group from the wider society."[60] The eating practices of different Christian communities distinguished Christians from pagans, rich Christians from poor Christians, ascetics from those who loved luxury, the pure from the impure.[61] Many early Christian texts go beyond Paul to include warnings about the dangers of eating with unbelievers.[62] Food and guest lists are used to mark early Christian identity by excluding both rival Christian groups and those of other faiths.[63] The witness of the early church includes many more references to exclusion than inclusion.

The abundance of material on the subject suggests some diversity in practice, but the patristic writings seem to imply that those whose practice was lax were in the minority. Attempts to solve the problem of laxity included requirements that someone entering a new community must carry a letter certifying his eligibility for communion, and appeals to recognize the authority of the bishop over excommunication—the only way to guarantee consistency in practice.[64] The push of the early patristic writers was overwhelming for unity in exclusion for the sake of the sinner and the church.

Despite the hopeful signs in Acts, early Christian meals seem to have departed from the practice of Jesus. Jesus's inclusive table fellowship represented an offer of forgiveness, a challenge to social hierarchy, an embrace of mercy, and a rejection of the idea that eating with people who sinned made one impure. Jesus honored the dignity of people in his community who were considered ritually and morally unclean, and he called his followers to do likewise.[65] Though he preached an uncompromising message of conversion, when at table he often asked for conversion from those who would never have considered themselves sinners while embracing those he was expected to ignore. With his actions, his parables, and his meals, he invited his followers to replace concerns about moral purity with concerns about mercy, justice, and compassion. It seems difficult to justify not recognizing such a significant practice.

However, the context of Jesus's ministry is distinct from that of the early church. While Jesus's meals were inclusive, signifying fellowship in the present and acceptance at a future messianic banquet, as early churches shaped their eucharistic practice, there was a perceived need to define the community by stressing the worthiness of participants.[66] The Old Testament concept of purity returned as a means of unifying the church, and thus Origen speaks of how serious sin excludes one from the church by diminishing his sanctity, and Cyprian justifies exclusion because sin makes impossible the sacramental sign unity that the Eucharist is supposed to embody.[67] Only sin "serious enough to cast doubt upon the sincerity of their baptismal metanoia" would qualify, but there is little doubt among patristic sources that such sin existed and had to be rooted out.[68]

The inclusive meals of Jesus and the boundary-breaking meals with Gentiles contrast with the consistent theme of the early fathers that the community must not be polluted with sin. If the very existence of the meals with sinners stories indicates early Christian identification with the Jesus who invited outcasts to his table, concern with the fragile unity of the new church is also evident right from the beginning. Many contemporary authors who explore the eating stories in early Christianity place much more emphasis on the memory of Jesus's radical example than on the later concern with purity. Yet even they acknowledge that there was a constant tension between hierarchy and equality implicit in the banquet tradition of the ancient Mediterranean world, and the early Christians inherited this tension without resolving it.[69] In essence, Christian meals, like all good banquets, were supposed to celebrate and extend friendship or, in Paul's theological system, build up community. In the judgment of many Christian leaders, the good of the community sometimes justified exclusion, at least temporarily. Without such boundaries, the church could not be the church. For the early Christians, being church required some exclusion, even as it also required praying for, seeking out, and welcoming back repentant sinners.

Eating, an ordinary practice of the household, is a key vehicle for the central message of Jesus's mission. Forgiveness, solidarity, and mercy are all embedded in a practice central to ordinary daily life. What goes on in the home becomes a model for society. The social import of family life is made clear, as Jesus's meals suggest a close connection between practice, faith, and social concern. At the same time, because the meals are only rarely gatherings of committed disciples alone, the gospels do not promote an elite model of Christian community. The struggles of the early church around Eucharist reveal the difficulty of remaining faithful to this witness. The *basileia* evoked by Jesus's meals suggests there is room at the table for everyone—strong believers and wary skeptics, wise elders and those whose faith is still young, saints and sinners, those who are found and those who are still lost, those who belong and those who are just passing through. The limited use of exclusion by the early church inspired by true compassion and a desire for unity should give us pause, but for contemporary Christians, Jesus's radical and merciful eating practice is the more important witness.

Love and Justice at the Table: Practices within the Practice

Christian families can construct an eating practice that is loving and just as well as merciful by drawing on wisdom from the Eucharist and Jesus's meals with sinners. Like Eucharist, family meals are formative of family bonds and family mission in the world. Just in gathering, families make concrete their commitment to be together and orient themselves to a larger good. Moreover, meals are not simply preparation for something beyond the family. Families can practice social justice by preparing meals for others and advocating on behalf of the hungry, but family meals themselves can also be occasions for doing the work of justice in the home.[70] Through adopting just eating practices, families can contribute to social change, taking up the challenge given to them by Catholic social teaching.

Choosing to eat intentionally is a practice with formative power. Families make a countercultural choice by prioritizing evening meals, thinking about where the food they eat comes from, and being conscious of whom they include in their meals, and these choices affect who they are as individuals and as families. As Jung says, "Making choices can shape us, our children, and friends, allowing us to develop eating practices that are empowering, delightful, resistant, and hospitable."[71] Choices about how to eat have to be made anyway, but by making them consciously, everyone who participates in the meals can be made aware of the ethical import of those choices.

Gathering

If we are to honor the Christian tradition's elevation of sharing food around a table, we have to find "a deeply satisfying way to eat."[72] This would mean, first of all, sitting down together. Getting this practice right not only provides a context for making just choices but also trains family members in being in community with others. For Jung, "not to share at home constitutes a loss of our mutuality."[73] When families fail to eat together, they practice a problematic kind of individualism where personal tastes and priorities trump the value of community. According to anthropologists, family meals are a primary means of "civilizing children. It's about teaching them to be a member of their culture."[74] Around the table, a family talks about the stories, jokes, and issues that become central to its identity. Here children learn how a conversation is structured, how to ask others about their days, how to respond to questions or to extend a discussion. Moreover, in sharing food that is not always their preference, children and adults learn compromise and tolerance, for "meals together send the message that citizenship in a family entails certain standards beyond individual whims."[75] The practice of eating civilizes and stretches us because it teaches people to participate in something larger than themselves.

Christian families are called to be schools of virtue where communal bonds are forged and the sociality of human beings is taught via experience.[76] When a majority of families do not even sit down together for an evening meal, they lose an opportunity to be schooled in the solidarity implied in the Eucharist. Deciding to eat together even when it may be more convenient to eat separately is a way in which families shape themselves into persons conscious of their social bonds and responsibilities. Not doing so can cause family members to lose their sense of connection to each other and the broader community.[77] Often families place individual needs above communal values. Finding a time to eat is difficult when parents work late or need time to unwind at home, children participate in sports or other activities that overlap with the dinner hour, and teens hold jobs that take them away from home in the evening. Because we now have so many choices and concerns about food, finding food everyone can agree on has become more difficult. It seems easier for everyone to grab the food they want at home or outside it when it is convenient for them. Making a choice to reject these trends means choosing sacrifice and family over individual needs and wants. It is a choice that can school families in the difficult work of being in communion with others.

Beginning a meal with grace is a gathering practice that connects families to God and each other and prepares them for a deeper commitment to social justice. Jung notes the importance of expressing gratitude in blessing: "Gratitude and solidarity may issue in table blessing. Our own bounty must make us conscious of our undeserved situation of privilege. Calling this to mind should make us grateful, mindful eaters."[78] Expressing gratitude is a recognition that the goodness in our lives is not all of our own making. Neither is it all God's blessing. Surely those with abundance do not deserve all that they have anymore than the many who live on less than two dollars a day deserve their lot in life. Paul criticizes the Corinthians for eating their memorials while others go hungry (1 Cor. 11:17–28). He suggests there is something scandalous about eating while ignoring others' hunger.[79] With grace, families can recognize this scandal, express thanks for the privileges that are theirs, and communicate solidarity through prayers with those who are far needier. As McCormick says, we must recognize ourselves as "grateful and unworthy guests."[80] Communal consciousness of undeserved abundance can then become a foundation for growth in solidarity.

Conversations at the table are another important way to gather families together and make them more a part of each other's lives. Discussions at the dinner table are powerful opportunities for valuable formation. Learning to ask about someone else's day and appreciate their stories takes us out of ourselves and our own concerns. Moreover, through listening to the discussions of parents, children can become aware of the world and their responsibilities within it. If conversation centers only on family concerns and interests, children may get the message that what moves their parents is the good of their family alone. What else is the family committed to? Discussions about social issues and how family members approach money, time, charity, politics, and so on can broaden the concerns of both parents and children.[81]

The value of coming together, saying grace, and engaging in conversation should not be understated. "Children," Rebecca Todd Peters insightfully points out, "do not learn simply by listening to what we say; their moral formation is shaped and formed by the actions in which we participate together as a family and as a community."[82] Eating, especially, has formative power because it is a practice families must engage in every single day. Few other practices offer this kind of consistent, ongoing opportunity for cementing a family's identity as Christian community.

Hospitality

Welcoming others to the family table is an essential part of ethical eating practice and a primary way in which families can live more justly. Pope John Paul II provocatively argues that families should exercise their social mission by practicing hospitality, which includes not just inviting friends and families to the table but feeding the hungry and giving drink to the thirsty.[83] David Matzko McCarthy's understanding of the open home speaks to this priority. McCarthy describes a Christian home as incomplete without guests.[84] He knows that middle-class Americans value their privacy but urges them to practice social justice by making a commitment to live in an economically diverse neighborhood where people interrupt each other's lives and feel comfortable in each other's homes.[85] Families, he claims, should depend on others and encourage others to depend on them. This way they can welcome those in need into their homes and receive support in return, instead of having to drive across town to work in a soup kitchen once a month. His vision, though not as radical as Dorothy Day's call to live with the very poor, raises profound questions about where we live and how it affects our eating practice. How are we to welcome the hungry, the poor, and the outcast if we live far away from them and only interact with them by serving them? How does hospitality become more than entertainment of what Dean Brackley provocatively calls our own "middle-class tribe"?[86]

McCarthy suggests that those who want an open home attuned to the requirements of justice will have to make difficult choices. As with other just eating practices, many competing goods are at stake. Choices about where to live may involve concerns about stable neighborhoods, reasonable commuting times for parents, and strong schools for children. Not everyone is called or able to live in a poor neighborhood, but surely all Christian families are called to think about how their table can be a place that is welcoming to people in need, whether they welcome a child who is going through a rough time with parents, a recently divorced friend, or a reclusive neighbor. Hospitality is an eating practice that can powerfully shape children's and adults' sense of what it means to be Christian, especially if hospitality is embraced as an opportunity to extend the table to those in need.

Making Just Food Choices

Christian families have an obligation to think about where the food they eat comes from in order to make their eating practice coherent with their beliefs in justice and solidarity. As Peters suggests, "Attention to what we eat, where and how it is grown, and how it is prepared are central ethical questions for our moral community."[87] Ethical reflection on food is relatively new and involves many competing goods, and thus it is difficult to discern precisely what constitutes just eating.[88] However, justice at least requires that families begin to think about the social systems in which they participate when they choose to buy and eat some foods rather than others. In particular, choices to buy more whole foods, eat less meat, buy more organic produce, and buy more local produce in season seem warranted.

Buying more whole foods is important because much of the energy that goes into producing food is at the processing, packaging, and storing stages. Food writer Mark Bittman argues, "To reduce our impact on the environment, we should depend on foods that require little or no processing, packaging, or transport, and those that efficiently convert energy to calories.[89] More complex calculations by environmental scientists are allowing us to measure this and compare different foods. We now know that whole foods generally have much lower energy costs than processed foods.[90] Packaging and processing alone account for 37 percent of the energy cost of food.[91] For example, producing potato chips take more energy than producing eggs and apple juice and has a higher eco-footprint than milk.[92] Many organic foods are highly processed, packaged, and require refrigeration. Choosing these foods may be healthier than choosing nonorganic frozen dinners but the energy costs may be just as high. The alternative is to buy whole foods such as rice, beans, lentils, pasta, and vegetables that are easy to cook at home.

Eating less meat is crucial to just eating. Americans eat about one-half of one pound of meat per day, or 180–200 pounds per year (Africans consume one ounce per day). Beef consumption has been stable since the 1950s, though chicken and dairy consumption is rising, and meat consumption in the developing world has tripled since the 1970s.[93] Global meat consumption is expected to double within the next forty years.[94] For an increasing number of families around the world, it is difficult to imagine a meal without meat.

However, current consumption levels are unsustainable. Because raising meat places such high demands on land, energy, and water, "It is simply not possible for everyone in the world to eat as much meat as people in the affluent world now eat," according to philosopher Peter Singer.[95] Families should opt to spend most of the portion of their budget devoted to animal protein on chicken, turkey, and eggs. Beef should be an occasional indulgence because its production contributes far more to global warming through the release of methane gas and because it requires thirteen pounds of grain (and corresponding amounts of chemical fertilizers and fossil fuels to grow the grain) to produce one pound of food as compared to three pounds of grain for poultry.[96] Moreover, humanely and sustainably raised chicken and eggs are generally more affordable than pasture-raised beef. If families could aim to cut their weekly meat consumption from the average of three pounds per person to one pound per person, this would bring the industrialized world closer to the developing world's levels. This would constitute a fairer sharing of the world's resources and a more sustainable practice.[97]

Cutting all meat and animal products is not necessary, though some may be called to embrace this level of sacrifice. No doubt meat is a luxury with a large environmental footprint. However, so are many other things we value, including parties, movies, and airplane travel. In the face of environmental crisis, Christians are called to live simply but not to avoid all unnecessary harm to the earth. While we need to cultivate consciousness of the impact of our food choices, we need not let go of all cultural traditions. Like all of the practices recommended in this book, eating less meat and dairy is a reasonable and moderate strategy that most families should be able to embrace. It is possible for all of us to use fewer meat and animal products, lower our impact on the environment, and still make satisfying meals.[98]

Buying more organic produce is an important way to support more sustainable agricultural practices that have a lower impact on the environment. Organic farmers help to maintain soil quality, foster biodiversity, and reduce water pollution, and their methods use 35 percent less energy per unit of crop production than conventionally grown produce.[99] Producing organic fruits and vegetables often requires less energy overall, even when produce must be transported a long distance, so it is not always problematic to buy organic produce that has been transported from other locations.[100] Though large organic producers may not adopt the more radical ethos and labor-intensive practices of small, organic farms "in most cases buying organic means less chemical fertilizer runoff, fewer herbicides and pesticides in the environment, more birds and animals around the farm, better soil conservation, and, in the long run, sustainable productivity."[101] Most food analysts agree that when it comes to the environment, organic matters.[102]

Though many worry that organic produce is too expensive, buying more organic foods is possible for most families. Consider first that the average family spends only 7 percent of its food budget on fresh produce.[103] If they paid twice as much for all that they currently buy, they would not see a major increase in their food budget. Transferring some of the food budget from the snack and fast food categories to the produce category would provide extra money. Beginning with cheaper organic items, such as carrots, potatoes, salad and winter greens, bananas, and root vegetables, could allow families to contribute to increased demand for a more sustainable way of farming.[104]

Some ask whether the money spent on organic produce would be better given to the poor. I would respond first that sustaining the earth's soils and waters benefits all people, but especially the underprivileged, today and in the future.[105] Second, few families actually make this sort of trade-off. Since the 1950s, real incomes have risen but donations to charity as a percentage of income has remained relatively constant.[106] Moreover, the percentage of income given to charity does not vary considerably with income, which suggests that extra income rarely goes to charity.[107] A Christian family should strive to give away a percentage of their income and adjust their food bill so that their choices support better farming methods. By choosing to buy more organic foods, families can resist unjust farming practices and support the growth of alternatives. Given the difficulty of changing the system through legal channels, this practice of resistance seems a viable way of participating in social change from below.[108]

The "gold standard" for some is local, organic produce. However, it is difficult to feed a family all local and organic foods. Buying into a local CSA (community-supported agriculture) is costly and entails working with large quantities of seasonal produce. The sorts of fruits and vegetables that children commonly eat (i.e., bananas, apples, oranges) will rarely be included. During the winter, many areas would be limited to greens and root vegetables. Most families would have to supplement their basket with additional produce from the grocery store. Peters claims that living within the boundaries of what the local area produces may be a legitimate sacrifice, and, in view of the environmental damage agribusiness imposes, buying local and organic produce should be a goal of Christian families.[109] Yet it is more difficult to impose this sacrifice on children, especially considering their need for nutrients and lack of willingness to try new foods. In addition, considerations about how much money a family ought to spend on food are legitimate, especially considering that local organic products can cost several times as much as conventional products or organic produce sold in stores.[110]

Eating more local-seasonal foods is still important, but not as important as eating less meat and dairy, and eating whole foods and organic foods. For families, eating local may be even more challenging than eating organic, as noted. Organic or conventional produce from another state may be a better option anyway. Efficient shipping methods often mean that less fossil fuel is used for transport by big growers than by small farmers who drive their food to multiple local markets and sell to customers who travel long distances and make multiple stops. The transparency that come from knowing farmers and their growing practices is valuable, and it is hard to deny the pleasure involved in patronizing a farmer's market, but, as Singer notes, "not everyone has the time for that, and trust and understanding need not be exclusively local."[111] Moreover, a Christian family's responsibilities extend to the rural poor in developing countries, not just to local farmers.[112]

Perhaps most important, though many sources claim that local farmers are more likely to use sustainable, if not certifiably organic practices, it is not clear that this is always the case. One recent article in the British newspaper the *Guardian* is titled "How the Myth of Food Miles Hurts the Planet."[113] The reporter quotes several sources who have come to believe that food miles are an unhelpful measure that may mislead customers.[114] Citing one study in which researchers found that for people living in Britain, green beans from Kenya had a lower eco-footprint than local beans grown in a greenhouse, she shows that buying local is not always the greener choice. In a 2008, two scientists used a total life-cycle approach to measure energy impact of various food choices, including production, transport, and distribution. They calculated the impact of a family of four switching to all local foods and found that if the family substituted chicken, eggs, or vegetarian protein instead of beef for just one day a week, they would have a much greater impact.[115] Weber and Matthews were criticized by fellow scientists for assuming that the only benefit of local farms was food miles, that is, for failing to assume that local farmers would be much more likely to use organic methods of soil inputs and less likely to use large-scale irrigation, petrochemical inputs, and large machinery.[116] They responded by noting that their critics presented no evidence for their claims, which they could not do because there is little nonanecdotal data proving their contention. While there is local, sustainably grown food that is worth buying, eating lower on the food chain is far more important from an environmental perspective.[117]

In sum, families ought to try to buy local-seasonal produce from farmers committed to sustainable farming, when it is available, and they should make more local produce available by gardening.[118] However, limiting one's shopping to items grown within a one-hundred-mile radius, as some recommend, is not necessary or even optimal for just eating.

Eating justly can be complex because the priorities I have outline can conflict. In addition, families are rightly concerned about buying fair trade products, eating healthfully, and preparing meals that everyone can enjoy. Still, it seems that a family seeking a just eating practice must find a balance of concern for nutrition, sustainable agricultural practices, just wages for workers, cost, and enjoyment. In particular, choices to limit meat consumption, buy more whole foods, buy more organic produce, and more local-seasonable produce seem warranted.[119] Caring for the environment and the world's poor along with our own health will mean trying to eat more simply and saving more environmentally and financially costly foods for special celebrations. In coming together to make these choices, families can strengthen their bonds and work for a more just society from the ground up.

Inclusivity

How can an emphasis on Christian identity and commitment to solidarity necessary to the practices I have advocated be balanced with the radical inclusion that also marked Jesus's eating practice? Christian families can glean from Eucharist a need to come together in community around a meal and a call to conform themselves to Christ and his mission in the world. They are called to become a community of faith and justice with concern for the planet. However, from Jesus's practice of eating with sinners—a practice rooted in solidarity and mercy—they also receive a call to be mercifully inclusive. I argue that honoring the value of inclusivity can be a means of furthering their identity rather than compromising it. Christian families are not called to perfection but to mercy.

Understanding families as domestic churches underscores the importance of their actions as well as their responsibility to witness to the fullness of Christ's message. When families are seen as the smallest Christian communities, their daily practices are acts of Christian discipleship.[120] This suggests that family meals (along with other everyday events) are significant religious acts that say a great deal about a family's identity. McCormick makes it clear that meals are a practice of faith, as he recalls that at meals in his own Christian family, "we were doing more than filling our bellies. We were celebrating and practicing being a family and being schooled in hospitality, friendship, and service."[121] Families discover Christ in the ordinary.

This very statement assumes that families as Christian communities should stand together for something. But, clearly, families do not always stand together; they are not always in agreement about faith or morals. This is why family meals are so painful for so many. In the very place where we should feel the most at home, we can sometimes feel quite alienated. What if a father wants to invite a homeless person home for dinner, and his wife and children do not? What if children want to pray spontaneously, but parents are uncomfortable doing so? What if some in the family are much more committed to sustainable eating practices than others? What if a child hates sitting at the table with a sibling who bullies him? A family, the smallest Christian community, is called first to be a communion of love, yet often such communion is hard to achieve.[122]

Real families are marked by diversity, disagreement, and fragile communion. Like all Christian communities, they struggle with imperfection. Perhaps more than other Christian communities, families have a diversity stemming from their nonintentional foundations. Apart from spouses, relatives are people we do not choose. Families are not more capable of perfection than other human communities and they are somewhat less poised to achieve consensus (at least when children enter later childhood, if not before) than most. Achieving a just and loving practice within families is complex. Any worthwhile analysis of meals must take account of the potential difficulties families face in achieving love and justice at the table. We cannot expect perfection.

Is there ever a time in which a family could justifiably struggle with how inclusive it ought to be? On the one hand, exclusionary behavior seems to violate something at the core of Christian faith. On the other hand, some boundaries seem necessary in order to sustain community. But how is a family to discern when a member or potential guest has moved beyond those boundaries in such a way that the very identity of the community would be threatened by welcome? At what point does exclusion become punitive and unloving, thus distorting a family's identity in other ways? How do families truly recognize the sinfulness of all their members and avoid judging too narrowly or too harshly?

As domestic churches, families are called to follow Jesus, and thus his inclusivity ought to be fundamental to their mission and identity. It ought to mark their treatment of each other and their response to those outside their boundaries. Inclusion and identity can go hand in hand. Moral theologian James Keenan tells about the remarkable personal journey of author James Alison, who found himself having to leave a religious order and teaching position because of disagreement with church teaching on homosexuality. Initially resentful, Alison ultimately found himself over-whelmed by the unconditional love of God and able to forgo "outsiding" those who had rejected him. Alison affirms that the kingdom of God does not rely on the sort of "outsiding" that most people find necessary to af-firm identity. Keenan, echoing this claim, writes, "While the rest of hu-manity finds its identity in excluding, Jesus works for a sense of inclusiveness that defines him and, hopefully, us."[123] Alison's story re-minds us of those who embrace the very families that try to exclude them. Their witness suggests that, more often than not, identity can be main-tained through mercy instead of exclusion.

Moreover, according to Catholic social teaching, families are charged with the duty of solidarity, or uniting in compassion and service with the marginalized in society. This applies inside as well as outside the home. John Paul II has made it abundantly clear that solidarity is not only the responsibility of unattached individuals or nations but a duty of families. He calls families to examine their lifestyles and ask if they are truly show-ing a preferential option for the poor, if they are prioritizing the good of others along with their own good.[124] The pope acknowledges that fami-lies realize their social mission in part by welcoming marginalized people into their homes.[125] Solidarity can also be made evident in the willing-ness of family members to embrace their own lost, to invite inside those who are shunned by others. A troubled teen or struggling single parent, for instance, may need the very sort of forgiveness before repentance that Jesus offered to sinners at his table. A family that prioritizes its own pu-rity or identity over merciful attention to the needs of the most vulnera-ble would be acting against solidarity.

However, there may be times when particularly heinous behavior may justify a limited time of exclusion for the good of the individuals who have sinned, those harmed by the sinful acts, and the good of the family as a whole. An example might be a case of a man who has an affair and leaves the family to remarry.[126] While Christian hope requires an openness to eventual reconciliation on all sides, it seems cruel to deny the need for the father to come to terms with the damaging effects of his behavior, the need of the mother for distance from the one who has hurt her, and the need of the family for time to heal their wounds so that a family meal could hon-estly be a gathering of unity and love.

One could argue that such a gathering should never take place while the father is married to a new woman, out of concern for the father's soul and the family's purity. This would certainly be true to the reasoning of the early church fathers and Paul when arguing for exclusion. However, most of these same authors counseled tolerance in the case of ordinary meals, recognizing that, for instance, if one ate unclean meat with pagans, one's own purity would most likely remain intact.[127] In fact, nearly all of the patristic commentary on table fellowship centers on church meals, which is remarkable given the diversity of early Christian societies and the religious division within many families. In the home, mercy seems to have trumped purity. It ought to today as well, even if temporary exclusion might be justified in rare cases.[128]

As churches in miniature, families have to balance the call to follow Jesus and welcome the lost, including their own lost, with the call to stand united as a Christian community, for certain things and against others. Yet the diversity or messiness of families reveals the difficulty of achieving unity in identity, the persistence of sin in every member of the family, and the need for mercy. Moreover, it seems possible that families may affirm their Christian identity more in forgiving inclusion than in "outsiding." James Keenan claims that practicing the virtue of mercy ("the willingness to enter into the chaos of others so as to answer them in their need") is at the heart of Catholic morality.[129] In the case of family meals, mercy as a rule, along with caution in practicing temporary exclusion, seems warranted. Eating with sinners need not be a sign of moral weakness or an occasion of defilement. It can be, rather, a symbol of a fidelity to Jesus Christ and a recognition that each time the church gathers, it is an occasion of sinners eating with sinners.

Conclusion: The Priority of Mercy

Marcus Borg's interpretation of the prodigal son parable told by Jesus offers a good image of ethical eating practice for Christians. Borg sees the parable as a story about refusing to eat with sinners. In Borg's reading, the elder brother who is not able to rejoice and eat the fatted calf his father has prepared is implicitly contrasted with Jesus, who does eat with sinners. At the end of the parable, the father and younger son go in to the banquet, and readers are left with questions: "Will the elder son join in the festivity? Or will he let his own standard of proper behavior prevent him from joining the celebration? Will the protestors' commitment to the quest for holiness make them adamant that outcasts such as these cannot be part of the people of God?"[130] These same questions are addressed to every Christian family struggling with whether to include sinners or leave them standing outside. The weight of the Christian tradition beckons them toward radical inclusion and mercy.

Other elements of just eating practice are also evident in the parable. Note that the first thing the father does upon the son's return is welcome him to the table. He will become part of the family again by engaging in this most basic of family practices. Moreover, though the ordinary meals of the family were probably simple, when there is cause for celebration, they find it appropriate to kill the fatted calf and have an extraordinary meal. In addition, the context in which Jesus tells the story is a meal—a meal, like so many others in the gospels, that is an occasion for fellowship, conversation, and even conversion—both for those seen by others as sinners and for those who only begin to see themselves as sinners through Jesus's teaching.

Contemporary Christians seeking an ethical eating practice are called to open themselves to gathering with others inside and outside their family, to think about implications of the way they eat for the environment and for the well-being of other human beings, and to practicing open hospitality and inclusivity. The precise shape of an ethical practice is difficult to specify. Details must be hashed out around the table, but surely love, justice, and mercy must be pursued as families work out their own understanding of what it means to be people of faith when they gather to eat.

Notes

1. L. Shannon Jung, *Sharing Food: Christian Practices for Enjoyment* (Minneapolis, MN: Fortress, 2006), 6.
2. "The Magic of the Family Meal," *Time*, June 12, 2006, 52. The CASA study, *National Survey of American Attitudes on Substance Abuse XII: Teens and Parents* is available at www.casacolumbia.org/absolutenm/articlefiles/Importanceof FamilyDinners (accessed September 4, 2009).
3. "Magic of the Family Meal," 53.
4. The low numbers in the teen years cannot be attributed solely to teen defiance. In the CASA study, a majority of teens who ate three or fewer meals with their families wished they had more family meals. *National Survey of American Attitudes on Substance Abuse,* 2. The study also found that Hispanic and black families do better than white families, and less-educated parents do better than their more highly educated peers. "Magic of the Family Meal," 52.

5. Robert D. Putnam, *Bowling Alone: The Collapse and Revival of American Community* (New York: Simon & Schuster, 2000), 100.

6. Ibid., 100.

7. Ibid., 101. Putnam includes vacationing, watching television, attending religious services, and just sitting and talking.

8. Ibid.

9. Ibid., 100–102.

10. Ibid., 101.

11. Ibid., 99.

12. Ibid., 102. Incredibly, even with the growth of coffee shops, the overall number of eating and drinking establishments has decreased since the 1970s.

13. Ibid., 100.

14. Patrick McCormick, *A Banqueter's Guide to the All-Night Soup Kitchen of the Kingdom of God* (Collegeville, MN: Liturgical Press, 2004), 25–26.

15. Ibid., 27.

16. Heaney-Hunter, "Toward a Eucharistic Spirituality of Family," 126.

17. Donald Altman, *Art of the Inner Meal: Eating as Spiritual Path* (San Francisco: Harper, 1999).

18. The limitations of actual eucharistic celebrations cannot be overlooked. Jean-Marc Ela argues that when Africans must rely on foreign priests and use bread instead of native grains, Eucharist "reveals our alienation at the hands of a world that imposes its products on us not only generally, but in the very liturgy that actualizes our redemption." Jean-Marc Ela, *African Cry*, trans. Robert R. Barr (Maryknoll, NY: Orbis, 1986), 5. Diana Fritz Cates notes the alienating potential of eucharistic liturgies dominated by male God language in "Imaging and Speaking of God" in *Practice What You Preach: Virtues, Ethics, and Power in the Lives of Pastoral Ministers and Their Congregations*, ed. James F. Keenan and Joseph Kotva Jr. (Franklin, WI: Sheed & Ward, 1999), 171–76. In the same volume, Margaret A. Farley criticizes the denial of Eucharist to non-Catholics. Margaret A. Farley, "No One Goes Away Hungry from the Table of the Lord," in *Practice What You Preach: Virtues, Ethics, and Power in the Lives of Pastoral Ministers and Their Congregations*, ed. James F. Keenan and Joseph Kotva Jr. (Franklin, WI: Sheed & Ward, 1999), 186–201. Though the meaning of the Eucharist is diminished by these deficiencies, I would argue that it is not lost.

19. David Hollenbach, "A Prophetic Church and the Catholic Sacramental Imagination," in *The Faith That Does Justice*, ed. John C. Haughey (New York: Paulist, 1977), 256.

20. Monika Hellwig, *The Eucharist and the Hunger of the World* (Kansas City, MO: Sheed & Ward, 1992), 64.

21. Ela, *African Cry*, 1.

22. Hellwig, *Eucharist and Hunger*, 72.

23. See James F. Keenan, *The Works of Mercy: The Heart of Catholicism* (Lanham, MD: Sheed & Ward, 2005), 27–28, who calls ignoring the hungry "the great scandal for Christians."

24. On the implications for Eucharist of Jesus's meals with sinners, see David N. Powers, "Eucharistic Justice," *Theological Studies* 67, no. 4 (2006): 856–79.

25. Hellwig, *Eucharist and Hunger*, 75.

26. Power, "Eucharistic Justice," 859.

27. Joachim Jeremias, *New Testament Theology, Part I, The Proclamation of Jesus* (New York: Scribner & Sons, 1971); and Norman Perrin, *Rediscovering the Teaching of Jesus* (New York: Harper & Row, 1967), were two of the first to address the issue. In the past fifteen years, nearly every major New Testament scholar has affirmed the significance of meals with sinners, including John Dominic Crossan, *The Historical Jesus: The Life of a Mediterranean Peasant* (San Francisco: HarperCollins, 1991); John P. Meier, *A Marginal Jew: Rethinking the Historical Jesus*, vol. 2 (New York: Doubleday, 1994); Richard Horsley, *Jesus and the Spiral of Violence: Popular Jewish Resistance in Roman Palestine* (New York: Harper & Row, 1987); E. P. Sanders, "Jesus and the Sinners," *Journal for the Study of the New Testament* 19 (1983): 5–36; Marcus Borg, *Conflict, Holiness, and Politics in the Teachings of Jesus* (Harrisburg, PA: Trinity, 1984), 93–134; Elisabeth Schüssler Fiorenza, *In Memory of Her: A Feminist Theological Construction of Christian Origins* (New York: Crossroad, 1989); and Bruce Chilton, *The Temple of Jesus: His Sacrificial Program within a Cultural History of Sacrifice* (University Park: Pennsylvania State University Press, 1992), 137–54.

28. For a rare contrasting view, see Dennis E. Smith, "The Historical Jesus at the Table," in *Society of Biblical Literature 1989 Seminar Papers*, ed. David J. Lull (New York: SBL, 1989), 466–86. Smith's book *From Symposium to Eucharist: The Banquet as Symbol in the Early Christian World* (Minneapolis, MN: Fortress, 2003), 237, affirms the historicity of the stories of Jesus's table fellowship with outsiders but argues that "tax collectors and sinners" is more likely a literary type indicating the gospel writers' belief that Jesus "was the sort of person who would do such a thing." Though highly skeptical of historicity of most gospel narratives, Smith is convinced that Jesus associated with outcasts and that his followers identified with this aspect of his ministry (277).

29. See works by Crossan, Sanders, and Borg, as cited in note 31, as well as Arthur Just, *The Ongoing Feast: Table Fellowship and Eschatology at Emmaus* (Collegeville, MN: Liturgical Press, 1993), which offers an in-depth discussion of all of the meal scenes in Luke. See also Thorsten Moritz, "Dinner Talk and Ideology in Luke: The Role of Sinners," *European Journal of Theology* 5, no. 1 (1995): 47–69, who convincingly argues that Luke only records and theologizes what seem to have been central reversals in Jesus's thought and practice. Robert Kelley, "Meals with Jesus in Luke's Gospel," *Horizons in Biblical Theology* 17 (1995): 123–31, agrees.

30. Borg, *Conflict, Holiness, and Politics*, 94.

31. Borg points out that "229 of the 341 rabbinic texts attributed to the Pharisaic schools of Shammai and Hillel pertain to table fellowship" (ibid., 95). He argues that Jesus challenged the Pharisaic conception of holiness with his ethic of compassion, exemplified in the inclusive meal tradition, while, like the Pharisees, he paid attention to the moral lives of ordinary believers. However, even Smith, who locates the tension between Jesus and the Pharisees after his death, still sees in stories of meals with Pharisees an early church attempt to contrast Jesus with excluders. See Smith, "Historical Jesus at the Table," 241.

32. See John R. Donahue, "Tax Collectors and Sinners: An Attempt at Identification," *Catholic Biblical Quarterly* 33 (1971): 39–61; or James Dunn, "Pharisees,

Sinners, and Jesus," 264–89, in *The Social World of Formative Christianity and Judaism*, ed. Jacob Neusner and Peder Borgen (Philadelphia: Fortress, 1988).

33. Borg, *Conflict, Holiness, and Politics*, 98–99.

34. Jeremias, *New Testament Theology, Part I*, 109; E. P. Sanders, "Jesus and the Sinners," 8. Sanders disagrees with Jeremias's claim that common people were considered sinners by some Pharisees.

35. Barbara Brown Taylor, "Table Manners," *Christian Century*, March 11, 1998, 257.

36. See Günther Bornkamm, *Jesus of Nazareth*, trans. Irene McLuskey, Fraser McLuskey, and James M. Robinson (New York: Harper & Row, 1960), 83; and John Paul Heil, *The Meal Scenes in Luke–Acts: An Audience-Oriented Approach* (Atlanta: Society of Biblical Literature, 19), 302–10.

37. Sanders, "Jesus and the Sinners," 29.

38. Lisa Sowle Cahill nicely summarizes the research on this subject in *Sex, Gender and Christian Ethics*, 134–37. Smith, "Historical Jesus at the Table," 255, notes that Jesus is portrayed, especially in Luke's gospel, as someone who rejects seating arrangements by ranking that would have been typical in the symposium tradition that served as a basis for early Christian meals.

39. Jerome H. Neyrey, "Ceremonies in Luke–Acts: The Case of Meals and Table Fellowship," in *The Social World of Luke–Acts*, ed. Jerome H. Neyrey (Peabody, MA: Hendrickson, 1991), 378. See also Cahill, *Sex, Gender and Christian Ethics*, 122; and Heil, *Meal Scenes in Luke–Acts*, 162.

40. Crossan, *Historical Jesus*, 338–44. Smith, "Historical Jesus at the Table," 237, who suspects that the meals were literary creations of the gospel writers, nonetheless agrees with Crossan's interpretation of the meal stories as examples of a social egalitarianism the early Christians found significant in Jesus's ministry.

41. John Elliott, "Household and Meals vs. Temple Purity Replication Patterns," *Biblical Theology Bulletin* 21 (Fall 1991): 1–15. There is some disagreement about what the Pharisees believed about purity. See Bruce Chilton, "The Purity of the Kingdom as Conveyed in Jesus' Meals," *Society of Biblical Literature Annual* (Atlanta: Scholars' Press, 1992), 444–59. Of course, households do not always prize mercy over purity, but they are perhaps more likely to do so than larger communities.

42. Borg, *Conflict, Holiness, and Politics*, 134. Borg points out that Jesus's practice is in direct contradiction to that of the Pharisees, for whom purity at table was central. Pharisees could not eat at the home of someone who could not be trusted to prepare clean food or eat with anyone "whose presence might defile the meal." Ibid., 95–96. Moreover, the Pharisees' meals symbolized what was required of all of Israel, "holiness understood as separation." Ibid., 96.

43. Borg notes that neither Jesus nor the Pharisees would deny the importance of holiness or compassion, but their emphases differed. Ibid., 135–55.

44. Schüssler Fiorenza, *In Memory of Her*, 121.

45. Smith, "Historical Jesus at the Table," 271. I found no New Testament writings other than the gospels containing references to the meals with outcasts and sinners and no commentary by early church fathers on the inclusive practice of Jesus.

46. Robert Jewett, "Gospel and Commensality: Social and Theological Implications of Galatians 2:14," in *Gospel in Paul* (Sheffield, Eng.: Sheffield Academic Press, 1994), 241.

47. Ibid., 240.

48. Elliott, "Household and Meals," 106.

49. Ibid. See also Schüssler Fiorenza, *In Memory of Her,* 119.

50. For a contemporary application of this story, see Jeffrey Siker, *Homosexuality in the Church: Both Sides of the Debate* (Louisville, KY: Westminster John Knox Press, 1994), 188.

51. *The New Revised Standard Version Bible* commentary advises comparison with Deuteronomy 17:2–7, where the stoning of immoral people is advocated as a way of purging evil from the community.

52. Roy A. Harrisville, *Augsburg Commentary on the New Testament: I Corinthians* (Minneapolis, MN: Augsburg, 1987), 91. Richard B. Hays similarly claims that "his concern is that the church must truly be a counterculture. . . . [T]able fellowship with nominal Christians living immoral lives would seriously blur the identity of the church as God's holy people." See Hays, *Interpretation: A Bible Commentary for Teaching and Preaching; First Corinthians* (Louisville, KY: Westminster John Knox Press, 1997), 87.

53. Harrisville, *Augsburg Commentary on the New Testament,* 102.

54. Council of Ancyra (314), canons 23–25.

55. Council of Antioch (341), canon 2; Council of Laodicea (3rd–4th c.), canons 32–33. See also Tertullian, "On Modesty," in *The Ante-Nicene Fathers,* vol. 4, ed. Alexander Roberts and James Donaldson (New York: Charles Scribner's Sons, 1913), 94. See also the Apostolic Constitutions, which claims that "one diseased sheep, if not separated from those who are well, infects the rest," quoted in "Discipline, Church," *Oxford Dictionary of the Christian Church,* 3rd ed., ed. E. A. Livingstone (Oxford: Oxford University Press, 1997), 215.

56. Clement of Alexandria, "The Instructor," in *The Ante-Nicene Fathers,* vol. 2, ed. Alexander Roberts and James Donaldson (New York: Charles Scribner's Sons, 1903), 240.

57. Tertullian, quoted in "Discipline, Church," in *Oxford Dictionary of the Christian Church,* 212.

58. Brian S. Rosner, "'Drive Out the Wicked Person': A Biblical Theology of Exclusion," *Evangelical Quarterly* 71.1 (1999): 25–36.

59. Cyprian, quoted in "Discipline, Church," in *Oxford Dictionary of the Christian Church,* 213.

60. Andrew McGowan, *Ascetic Eucharists* (New York: Oxford University Press, 1999), 88.

61. Ibid., 141.

62. McGowan cites from the Psuedo-Clementines, the Apocryphal Acts, and the Acts of Andrew, all of which express concern about eating with pagans. Ibid., 182–91.

63. Miri Rubin, "Whose Eucharist? Eucharistic Identity as Historical Subject," *Modern Theology* 15, no. 2 (1999): 197–208.

64. Cyprian, quoted in "Eucharist," in *Oxford Dictionary of the Christian Church,* 256. Eugene Laverdiere, *The Eucharist in the New Testament and the Early Church* (Collegeville, MD: Liturgical Press, 1996), 163.

65. Smith, "Historical Jesus at the Table," 243–45, emphasizes that Jesus's meals included the unclean and links this invitation to the contrast Jesus makes between rulers who lord their power over others and the one who makes herself the servant of all. He also sees the feeding miracles in Mark as banquet stories that assume inclusivity.

66. Paul Bradshaw, *Early Christian Worship: A Basic Introduction to Ideas and Practice* (Collegeville, MD: Liturgical Press, 1996), 39, 66.

67. Kenneth Hein, *Eucharist and Excommunication: A Study in Early Christian Doctrine and Discipline* (Frankfort: Herbert Lang and Co., 1973), 435–37, 441.

68. Ibid., 441.

69. Smith, "Historical Jesus at the Table," 283.

70. My own earlier work focuses primarily on how meals point beyond the family. See Rubio, *Christian Theology of Marriage and Family*, 196–99. McCormick, *Banqueter's Guide*, 9, too, links justice to feeding the poor outside the home.

71. Jung, *Sharing Food*, 59. For a pastoral resource from the Presbyterian Church USA, see "Just Eating," available at www.pcusa.org/hunger/features/justeating.htm (accessed August 15, 2008).

72. Jung, *Sharing Food*, 6.

73. Ibid., 42.

74. "Magic of the Family Meal," 53.

75. Ibid.

76. *Familiaris consortio*, no. 42.

77. Jung, *Sharing Food*, 42.

78. Ibid., 58.

79. Powers, "Eucharistic Justice," 858–59.

80. McCormick, *Banqueter's Guide*, 7.

81. McCormick suggests thinking about whether the food on the table is harvested by workers being paid unjust wages and is thus "bread leavened with injustice." Ibid., 27.

82. Rebecca Todd Peters, "Supporting Community Farming," in *Justice in a Global Economy: Strategies for Home, Community, and World*, ed. Pamela K. Brubaker, Rebecca Todd Peters, and Laura A. Stivers (Louisville, KY: Westminster John Knox Press, 2006), 25.

83. *Familiaris consortio*, no. 44.

84. David Matzko McCarthy, *The Good Life: Genuine Christianity for the Middle Class* (Grand Rapids, MI: Brazos, 2004), 80.

85. Ibid.

86. Dean Brackley, *Call to Discernment in Troubled Times: New Perspectives on the Transformative Wisdom of Ignatius of Loyola* (New York: Crossroad, 2004), 37.

87. Peters, "Supporting Community Farming," 25.

88. Recent books addressing the ethical dimensions of food include Michael Pollan, *The Omnivore's Dilemma: A Natural History of Four Meals* (New York: Penguin, 2007); Nina Planck, *Real Food: What to Eat and Why* (New York: Bloomsbury, 2007); Marion Nestle, *Food Politics: How the Food Industry Influences Nutrition and Health*, rev. ed. (Berkeley and Los Angeles: University of California Press, 2007); Peter Singer and Jim Mason, *The Way We Eat: Why Our*

Food Choices Matter (Emmaus, PA: Rodale, 2006); and Mark Bittman, *Food Matters: A Conscious Guide to Eating with More Than 75 Recipes* (New York: Simon & Schuster, 2008).

89. Peters, "Supporting Community Farming," 19.
90. James Randerson, "The Eco-diet . . . and It's Not Just about Food Miles," *Guardian*, June 4, 2007. Available at www.guardian.co.uk/uk/ 2007/jun/04/ lifeandhealth.business (accessed May 1, 2009).
91. Bittman, *Food Matters*, 17.
92. Singer and Mason, *Way We Eat*, 237.
93. Bittman, *Food Matters*, 11.
94. Ibid., 9.
95. Singer and Mason, *Way We Eat*, 232.
96. Ibid.
97. Anthony J. McMichael, John W. Powles, Colin D. Butler, and Ricardo Uauy, "Food, Livestock Production, Energy, Climate Change, and Health," *Lancet*, 370, no. 9594 (2007): 1253–63.
98. Bittman, *Food Matters*, 18.
99. Singer and Mason, *Way We Eat*, 202–4.
100. See www.mofga.org for a defense of organic food from a nutritional and environmental perspective (accessed May 15, 2009). Singer and Mason, *Way We Eat*, 201, note the problems with determining what organic means, but insist, "as long as we avoid sweeping generalizations that imply organic farmers can do no wrong, there is no real dispute that, overall, organic farming is better for the environment than conventional farming."
101. Singer and Mason, *Way We Eat*, 277; Peters, "Supporting Community Farming," 18–19.
102. Marion Nestle, quoted in Singer and Mason, *Way We Eat*, 221. See also Bittman, *Food Matters*, 25.
103. Jessie X. Fan et al., "Household Food Expenditure Patterns: A Cluster Analysis," *Monthly Labor Review*, April 2007, 39–51, www.bls.gov/opub/mlr/2007/04/ art3full.pdf (accessed May 20, 2009).
104. This list differs from the so-called dirty dozen (including grapes, peaches, apples, and other fruits with thin skins that are not removed before eating) because my emphasis is on environmental damage. This moral concern outweighs concern for health, as research on the damaging effects of conventionally grown produce is still limited. See Chris Gourlay, "Organic Food Has No Health Benefits, Say Officials," *New York Times*, August 2, 2009, www .timesonline.co.uk/tol/life_and_style/food_and_drink/article6736031.ece (accessed September 4, 2009).
105. The Catholic Climate Change Covenant website offers many resources making the connection between the environment and the poor at http://catholic climatecovenant.org (accessed September 4, 2009).
106. For data on income, see www.econlibrary.org/library/Enc/Distributionof Income.html (accessed November 1, 2008). On charity, see Dean Hoge, Charles Zeck, Patrick McNamara, and Michael J. Donahue, *Money Matters: Personal Giving in American Churches* (Louisville, KY: Westminster John Knox Press, 1996).

107. See "Patterns of Household Charitable Giving by Income Group, 2005," working paper prepared for Google by the Center on Philanthropy at Indiana University, Summer 2007, www.philanthropy.iupui.edu (accessed September 15, 2008).

108. Andrew Szasz, *Shopping Our Way to Safety: How We Changed from Protecting the Environment to Protecting Ourselves* (Minneapolis: University of Minnesota Press, 2009), argues that time-consuming individual practices divert energy from more important work for political change. However, changing the way America farms will be a difficult and long battle. David M. Herszenhorn, "Obama's Farm Subsidy Cuts Meet Stiff Resistance," *New York Times*, April 3, 2009. The potential to reshape markets by shifting demand is real, as is the potential of countercultural practices to influence others, increase political awareness, and encourage political activism. Michael Pollan, "Why Bother?" available at www.michaelpollan.com (accessed November 5, 2009).

109. Peters, "Supporting Community Farming," 26.

110. Nina Planck, *Real Food*, 154, acknowledges the benefits of organic food but argues that the cost is not always justified, especially if it travels far from its origin. She suggests prioritizing food grown locally by farmers using ecological, if not certified organic, methods. Bittman, *Food Matters,* 101–4, emphasizes eating less meat and cooking from scratch.

111. There were more than twice as many farmers' markets in 2004 than 1994. Singer and Mason, *Way We Eat*, 138. Energy costs may be higher if a farmer uses fossil fuel to heat a greenhouse or if a farmer's market is far away from one's home. Ibid., 142. Corporations may find it harder to hide from investigation and organized protest. Ibid., 75. Their choices can effect large-scale change. For example, Whole Foods' sales of organic bananas influenced Dole's decision to make large volumes of its Central America land organic, and increasing demand for organic eggs and dairy led the large Organic Valley cooperative to take on new organic farmers. Ibid., 181.

112. Singer and Mason, *Way We Eat*, 150, 147. Food from developing countries may be less energy intensive, and that may make up for energy used to ship it. Ibid., 277. This is not to deny the need to work for local food security and fair trade in the developing world.

113. Robin McKie, "How the Myth of Food Miles Hurts the Planet," *Guardian*, March 23, 2008, www.guardian.co.uk/environment/2008/mar/23/food.eth icalliving (accessed May 1, 2009).

114. Ibid. This list includes Dr. Adrian Williams of the National Resources Management Centre at Cranfield University, who changed his stance; the British government, which reversed its stance; and Tara Garnett of Food Climate Research Network, who now claims that it is more important to stop eating meat, milk, butter, and cheese; it is not the source but the kind of food you eat that matters most.

115. Christopher L. Weber and H. Scott Matthews, "Food Miles and the Relative Climate Impacts of Food Choices in the United States," *Environmental Science and Technology* 42.10 (2008), http://pubs.acs.org/doi/full/10.1021/es702969f ?cookieSet=1 (accessed May 25, 2009). A totally localized diet would reduce one's carbon footprint, but shifting from meat and dairy to chicken, fish,

eggs, or vegetarian protein for just one day per week would result in a greater reduction.

116. Steven L. Hoop and Joan Dye Gussow, "Comment on 'Food-Miles and the Relative Climate Impacts of Food Choices in the United States,'" *Environmental Science Technology*, April 23, 2009.

117. Weber and Matthews, "Response to Steven L. Hoop and Joan Dye Gussow, 'Comment on "Food-Miles and the Relative Climate Impacts of Food Choices in the United States,'"" *Environmental Science Technology*, April 23, 2009.

118. If families do not have time for a large garden, choosing a few items to grow and trade with neighbors might be possible.

119. For a sensible approach, see Bob Schildgen, "10 Ways to Eat Well," www.sierra club.org/sierra/200611/tenways.asp (accessed October 10, 2009). Pollan, *In Defense of Food*, 1, gives a basic formula, "Eat food. Not too much. Mostly plants," that is helpful in its emphasis on simple, whole foods.

120. United States Conference of Catholic Bishops, *Follow the Way of Love* (Washington, DC: USSC, 1994); Joann Heaney-Hunter, "Living the Baptismal Commitment in Sacramental Marriage," in *Christian Marriage and Family: Contemporary Theological and Pastoral Perspectives*, ed. Michael G. Lawler and William P. Roberts (Collegeville, MN: Liturgical Press, 1996), 60. Florence Caffrey Bourg, "Domestic Churches: Sociological Challenge and Theological Imperative," in *Theology and the Social Sciences* 46, ed. Michael Horace Barnes (Maryknoll, NY: Orbis, 2000): 259–76.

121. McCormick, *Banqueter's Guide*, 40.

122. *Familiaris consortio*, no. 18.

123. James Keenan, *Moral Wisdom: Lessons and Texts from the Catholic Tradition* (Lanham, MD: Sheed & Ward, 2004), 101.

124. *Sollicitudo rei socialis*, no. 47.

125. *Familiaris consortio*, nos. 41, 44, and 45.

126. Abuse is another significant example of a warrant for temporary exclusion.

127. See Clement of Alexandria, "Instructor," 240.

128. An analogue is Martin Luther King's embrace of temporary segregation as a necessary stage for African Americans who needed space apart from whites to build unity and maintain ownership of their own agenda. See James Cone, *Martin and Malcolm in America: A Dream or a Nightmare* (Maryknoll, NY: Orbis, 1991), 232–35. King saw temporary segregation as a "necessary path that blacks had to travel to get to the second road . . . the beloved community." Ibid., 235.

129. Keenan, *Moral Wisdom*, 124.

130. Borg, *Conflict, Holiness, and Politics*, 106.

CHAPTER SIX

How Much Is Enough?

The Practice of Tithing

Are We Rich Yet?

Most American Christian families think of themselves as somewhere in the broad middle on the scale of financial wellness. They know that they are not poor, for they do not struggle to pay for basics like food, clothing, or housing and enjoy certain luxuries. Yet they are also keenly aware that they are not as rich as some people they know, see, or read about, who drive fancy new cars or go on extravagant vacations. Like most Americans, they prefer to think of themselves as middle class. Yet the majority of American families have incomes that place them among the most privileged people in the world.[1] If one were to divide American families into quintiles, the income of the top fifth would average approximately $174,000, the second fifth $100,000, and the third fifth $66,000. In a global context, those in all quintiles are richer than most people and far richer than the 40 percent of people in the world who live on less than two dollars a day.[2] Measuring contemporary family income against earlier generations is also instructive. Though the incomes of middle-class families have been stagnant over the last decade, and many families have seen their incomes drop in the recession of 2008 and 2009, most families have seen their incomes grow in real terms even as the average number of children has dropped.[3] Clearly, the majority of American Christian families have more than most people in the world, more than most families throughout history, and more than enough for themselves.[4] If "rich" is not limited to the "super-rich," then most families can be considered rich.

Most of these families give some of their income away. Charity might be called a common social practice of Christian families. A recent study of American congregations found that on average Catholics give about 1 percent of their income to their church, while Protestants give about 2 percent.[5] Both groups give about another 1 percent to religious and nonreligious charities. Giving to political causes, charities that do not have nonprofit status (such as Catholic Worker houses), and smaller fundraisers is harder to measure because it is not usually reported on tax forms, but this might account for an additional half percent at most. One can then estimate that approximately 3 percent of the income of Christian families is given to churches, the less fortunate, schools, health care, the arts, and to those working for political change. Of this charitable giving, only about one-third goes to serve the needs of the poor.[6]

Is it enough? Anyone who has pondered Jesus's sayings about wealth and has seen the suffering of the poor would probably answer no, but determining what would be enough remains a difficult task. In this chapter I argue that the practice of tithing is an appropriate response for most Christian families seeking to balance care of their own with biblical and traditional understandings of responsibility for the poor. I argue for the practice by reviewing the history of tithing with an emphasis on moral arguments and enduring tensions. Next I suggest how this practice should and could be adapted within a contemporary context. A concluding section shows that renewal of the practice of tithing is a morally significant way to respond to the suffering of the poor given the impact increased tithing could have on middle- and upper-class families, churches, and, most important, those living in poverty.

Foundations: Hebrew and Christian Scriptures

Giving a tithe of 10 percent of a harvest or the spoils of war to a ruler or religious leader was a common practice in many ancient Near Eastern societies.[7] It is this practice that is represented in Genesis 14:18, when Abram brings a tenth of his war spoils to King Melchizedek. Sometimes the tribute was strictly political in nature, while other times tithes were linked to religious rituals. Tithing in the ancient Near East acknowledged the one to whom the tithe was brought as true owner of the land that produced the harvest or as true protector of the warrior.

The Hebrew Bible includes numerous other references to tithes, and though ascertaining how the practice developed is difficult, most scholars see the original offering of the "first fruits" gradually morphing into an offering to religious leaders and the poor accompanied by a feast for all. Leviticus 27:30–33 and Numbers 18:24–28 seem to describe a feast at a local holy site at which those who owned land would bring the first fruits of their harvest and celebrate with their families and friends. What was left over would be given to the local priests and the poor.

When the Israelite faith became centralized in Jerusalem, landowners were asked to travel there to feast and make their offering to the Levites. This is the command of Deuteronomy 14:22–28. If travel with food and animals was too onerous, money could be brought to Jerusalem for the celebration. Every third year, the writer of Deuteronomy asserts, a tithe for the poor was taken up. Commentators assume that different families paid this tithe in different years, so that the storehouse for "the alien, the orphan and the widow" was never empty.[8] The practice of paying three tithes (to priests, Levites, and the poor) is attested to in Tobit 1:7–8. However, it is possible that the different tithes referred to represent different historical stages that are harmonized by later writers.[9] In addition, local practices may have deviated from scriptural norms.[10]

If it is difficult to know exactly what form Israelite tithing may have taken; theological justifications of the practice are clearer and more consistent. First, just as in other ancient societies, a tithe counted as recognition that the landowner was the true owner of the land. In the case of the Israelites, tithing represented a belief that God is the creator and owner of all, and thus all is owed to him.[11] Gratitude is expressed through offering the first fruits or a tithe, and the tither acknowledges that he is not solely responsible for all that his land or toil has yielded. God, sovereign of all, is the giver of all good gifts. Yet, because God does not need the tithe, "the tithe brought to the place is promptly given back to Israel, who is to eat and enjoy the offering it has brought. The tithe owed to YHWH is given over to the joy of Israel. YHWH does not want the produce, but insists on the gesture that acknowledges YHWH's generous sovereignty."[12]

The same tithe that is offered as gratitude for Yahweh's gifts is also needed for those who spend their lives in his service. Priests and Levites do not have the wealth that comes from land or trade, and thus they rely on the people for their support.[13] Tithing enables them to give all of their attention to their ministry "without being distracted by the necessity of providing daily for their own sustenance."[14] They, in turn, are obliged to own no property and to live on what is tithed to them, without asking for more. Given the social reality of the Levites, "the tithe becomes an act of justice towards those who place themselves at the disposition of Israel for the exercise of worship."[15]

Justice is further implicated in the theological understanding of tithing for the disadvantaged. Tithing is a piece of Israel's social ethic of concern for the poor, which also includes the practice of allowing the poor to collect the gleanings from the fields, the prohibition of interest taking, and the proclamation of the Sabbath and jubilee years when debts were to be forgiven.[16] Tithing stems from gratitude to Yahweh for generous giving and is expressed in generous giving to the poor. Walter Bruegemann characterizes it as "a transaction in generosity and gratitude. It can be reduced to parsimonious calculation (as in Matt 23:23–24). But Deuteronomy intends otherwise. Israel gladly contributes a tax to enhance the economy of the community."[17]

The spirit of joyful generosity is also evident in the banquet proscribed in earlier texts on tithing. Rather than just paying a tax, Israelites are enjoined to feast not only with family but with servants, priests, Levites, and the poor. Thus the "obedient reverence" that obligates tithing and feasting "develops in the context of joy and community solidarity."[18] Tithing is linked with feasting, and family boundaries are extended.[19]

In the Hebrew Bible, the practice of tithing is part of an ethic of wealth that assumes "the right of families and clans to own property" and the goodness of abundance but also includes social norms to encourage the sharing of wealth and prevent hording.[20] Wealth and property are not derided, and excessive sacrifice is not held up as a moral norm. Rather, gratitude for God's gifts, respect for priestly ministry, and concern for the vulnerable are linked together so that abundance does not remain an end in itself, but rather becomes a source of solidarity.

New Testament references to tithing are significantly fewer, and it is difficult to find in them a specific Christian obligation to tithe. Some modern theologians, like some early church fathers (see following section), contrast the "Jewish legalistic piety" of tithing with the boundless generosity called for by Christ. It is not that tithing is bad but that it is inadequate, for "Jesus so deepened the problem of having possessions that a positive adoption of the Old Testament commandment of the tithe could not be considered."[21] Yet some churches rely on New Testament passages to enforce tithing. Matthew 23:23 (parallel Luke 11:41–42) reveals the difficulty. Jesus is criticizing some Pharisees for being concerned with tithes on every small thing but neglecting weightier matters such as justice and mercy. Tithing appears to be associated with the poor faith of the Pharisees and is not specifically commanded to Jesus's listeners, yet Jesus tells the Pharisees not to neglect tithing but to also be concerned about justice and mercy. Rather than denigrating tithing as legalistic, it seems more correct to say that, as a Jew, Jesus speaks prophetically to the abuses in the system but does not overturn it.

To his disciples and those who gather to hear him preach, however, Jesus presents a more radical message with regard to money. I cannot deal here with the whole of New Testament teaching on wealth, so I will not attempt to cover all of the relevant passages. However, it should be sufficient to note that the many instances in which Jesus calls someone who wants to follow him to give up possessions (Mark 10:17–31; Luke 14:28–33, 19:1–10), the many parables that uphold giving to the poor (Luke 10:29–37, 16:19–31; Matt. 25:31–46), as well as the many sayings casting doubt on the ability of the rich to be saved (Mark 10:17–22; Luke 18:18–29; Matt. 19:16–22) combine to raise some serious questions about the compatibility of riches with Christianity.

Yet Jesus does not counsel all of his followers to give up their possessions; he is charged with being "a glutton and a drunkard" because he seems to have frequently celebrated at dinner with friends (Matt. 11:19); he rebukes those who questioned a woman who dared to "waste" oil by anointing him, telling them "you always have the poor with you . . . but you will not always have me" (Mark 14:3–7); and his ministry clearly relied on the sustaining wealth of some members (Matt. 8:1–3). While wealth does not appear as clearly in the New Testament as in the Old Testament as God's blessing, it is clearly not a curse. One author even calls Jesus the "Lord of Delight" based on his reputation for feasting with friends.[22] It is important to acknowledge this model of enjoying gifts received without losing sight of the extensive critique of wealth advanced by

Jesus. As Sondra Wheeler deftly points out, wealth in the New Testament is a resource for meeting human needs and an opportunity for charity, but it is also sometimes a stumbling block for those who would be disciples, an idol that competes with God for devotion, and a symptom of economic injustice.[23] Renunciation remains a challenging ideal (a necessity for some who are called to it) while a model of gratitude, delight, and almsgiving is upheld for the many, with few specific instructions.

While the classic description in Acts 2:44–45 of a community wherein all things are held in common suggests a radical unanimity among the early Christians, divergences among the early Christians are apparent. Paul's letters seem unaware or unconcerned with Jesus's more radical teachings on money. His understanding of discipleship does not seem to call for renunciation of wealth, and even almsgiving appears to be optional. In his most extended discussion of alms in Romans 12–13, he does counsel the wealthier members of the church to give to those who are less well-off, put aside conventional notions of honor, and instead be ruled by an ethic of brotherly love (Rom. 12:9–10, 13:8–10).[24] However, his concern is more for the unity of the Christian community and the eternal reward of its members than for the poor themselves.[25] James, in contrast, speaks prophetically against the wealthy, condemning them for storing up treasures while others starve, suggesting that the faith of the wealthy is no faith at all (James 5:1–6).[26]

The New Testament witness on wealth contrasts the goodness of wealth rightly obtained and used to sustain life, welcome guests, and give to those who are needy with wealth achieved by cheating others of right livelihood, horded, and denied to those who stand in need. Almsgiving replaces tithing as an answer to the needs of the poor and the cumber of too many possessions. Though enjoyment of abundance is not ruled out, the model of radical renunciation chosen by a few continues to challenge the rest to share more of what they have and rid themselves of whatever stands in the way of following Christ. Much of the continuing history of the Christian tradition on wealth will attempt to negotiate the tension among these New Testament themes.[27] Though no easy answers can be found either in the New Testament or in the texts of the early tradition, attending to the tensions between moderate and radical solutions to the problem of wealth that animates both periods can help contemporary Christians construct an ethical practice.

Christian Tradition on Wealth and Charity

The early church fathers were mostly unified in denying that tithing was obligatory for Christians. Instead they exhorted their listeners to make voluntary offerings to their bishops and the poor.[28] Tithing was used to shame Christians, as when Augustine writes, "'They gave their tithes' [Luke 8:12]. However, when you give just one percent you boast about it as though you had done something very great."[29] In another sermon, he is even angrier, saying, "The Scribes and Pharisees gave tithes. We should be ashamed, brothers; those for whom Christ had not yet shed his blood gave tithes."[30] Though some of the fathers admitted that tithes would be better than nothing, none claimed that tithing was sufficient to meet the demands of Christian discipleship.

The duty to give in charity was given three main lines of justification: justice, redemption, and the identification of Christ with the poor. Some claimed that money was owed to the poor in justice, whether because the Earth was given to all in Genesis and the poor deserved their portion or because the rich had received all they had from God as a gift and thus should imitate God's justice by giving back to God through others.[31] St. Caesarius (470–543) argues, "Tithes are demanded out of justice; whoever refuses to give them violates another's property. And if he gives no tithes, how many poor will die in his region! For how many murders will he appear responsible before the eternal judge!"[32] Though the claim of justice is not always this explicit in patristic writings, it "is nonetheless certainly at the foundation of virtually every patristic exhortation to do good works."[33]

Redemptive almsgiving was perhaps a more explicit common theme in patristic writings. When early Christian communities were faced with the reality of postbaptismal sin, almsgiving was presented as one way to show love for others and make up for sinfulness.[34] Giving alms would counter greed and thus make living a truly Christian life easier.[35] In addition, the poor who received alms would pray in thanksgiving for the giver to God, and as they were thought to have special influence with God, this was an attractive prospect.[36] The promise of eternal reward made exhortations to give even more forceful.[37]

A less common theme more familiar to modern Christians is the identification of Christ with the poor. The fathers identified Christ with the poor in dramatic ways, often relying on Matthew 25:31–46. Ambrose contended,

"If you have superfluity, give it to the poor and you have dried the feet of the Lord."[38] The most popular story linking Christ with the poor is found in Sulpicius Severus's *Life of Saint Martin,* in which Martin gives half of his cloak to a beggar, and Christ comes to him in a vision, wearing the cloak, saying, "Martin, still only a catechumen, has clothed me in this garment."[39] The connection between faith in Christ and giving in charity is clear.

But how much did the early church fathers expect their listeners to give? Some authors clearly saw the renunciation of all one's goods to be ideal. The worldly life of families was contrasted with the more pure life of monks.[40] Cassian (360–435), for instance, tells the conversion story of Theona, who is told that, "At this stage [i.e., after Christ] it is no longer said: 'You shall offer your tithes and first fruits to your God,' but 'Go, sell what you own and give it to the poor.'" Theona is thus convinced to leave his wife, give all his property away, and become a monk.[41] Still, even if total renunciation was often upheld, because the fathers knew that most of their audience would never attain this ideal, they offered the more moderate alternative of almsgiving. Some modern scholars even argue that the fathers' demands for moderate giving asked far too little of ordinary Christians.[42] However, even if most agreed that Christians need only make moderate sacrifices, they still called all of their listeners to mercy, hospitality, and sharing that would set them apart from their neighbors and in a more equal relationship with the poor. Augustine asks those who would have the poor take care of themselves to "bear one another's burdens. . . . What is the burden of poverty? Not to have. And what is the burden of wealth? To have more than is necessary. He and you alike are burdened. Bear with him who does not have and he will bear with you who have a superfluity, and thus your burdens shall be equal."[43]

Moreover, even if the church fathers did not ask most of their listeners to give up everything, they did not let them off the hook too easily. Speaking to those who believed they had given enough by tithing, Augustine says,

You look at what others have not done rather than at what God commands you to do. . . . You pay no attention to how many poor persons are beneath you; you want only to be above those richer than yourselves. . . . No attention is paid to the hardships of the innumerable mendicants; not a glance is cast on the masses of poor who stand behind but all eyes are cast on the few rich who stand in front. In doing good works, why is there no thought of

Zacchaeus who gave half his possessions to the poor? Instead, we feel compelled to congratulate ourselves for at least following the example of the Pharisee who paid tithes of all he possessed.[44]

The relentless call to change or even renounce affluent lifestyles would be nearly unimaginable today.

The early church period is marked by an ambivalence about wealth that does not easily resolve. Wealth is not demonized but rather legitimized—*if* believers practiced proper detachment, moderation in lifestyle, and high levels of charity. Yet evident in all discourse about money during this period is "constant unease" about how to reconcile ordinary living with gospel teachings. Even when interpreted spiritually as exhortations to increased giving and simplicity of lifestyle, "the fact that this often did not happen at all was testimony to the highly seductive nature of wealth in all its degrees, and also to the power of the human instincts for acquisition, domination, and self-preservation."[45] Negotiating the gap between reality and even a moderate form of the ideal would remain a problem for centuries to come.

During the sixth to the twelfth centuries, a perception among clergy of the declining zeal of their flocks for embracing the challenges of Christian discipleship was met by the reimposition of pointed talk about the moral obligation of tithing along with justification from the Hebrew Bible and penalties of excommunication. A new system was viewed as practically necessary, as "the insufficiency of funds made life more difficult for the clergy."[46] Thus though there is no evidence of a legal or ecclesiastical system for collecting tithes in the patristic period, in the sixth century, both church and secular law would come to be utilized for this purpose.[47]

Ecclesial tithing law began with the Council of Tours in 567 and a subsequent pastoral letter written by four bishops. They exhort all Christians to tithe as Abraham did and warn that dire consequences will follow if payment is not received: "Let him pay his price lest he see himself taken captive by the power of sin. Such a person will find no one to pay his ransom, since in this matter he has resisted the Redeemer."[48] In this early phase of the new era, the obligation to tithe on all possessions is clear, but penalties and collection methods are not given.

Later, as the church solidified and grew in power, both ecclesiastic sanctions (Council of Macon, 585) and juridical sanctions (Council of Rouen,

650) were imposed on those who failed to pay their tithe to local priests, who shared some of it with the poor.[49] Excommunication was imposed after a third warning. Legalism was coming to replace a moral-spiritual understanding of tithing. The spirit of legalism continued with additional legislation at the councils of Ascheim, Arles, Rheims, Autun, and Mainz (755–813).[50] All insisted on the obligatory nature of tithing and imposed penalties. Abuses and attempts to avoid the tithe were widespread.

From as early as the ninth century until the Reformation, as connections between church and state grew, tithing increasingly resembled a tax and corruption increased. At the Council of Mainz in 852, for the first time a king ordered and organized tithing, and "later councils followed this legalistic line of thought with increasing narrowness."[51] Papal legislation through the twelfth century became more and more precise in discussing how to calculate tithes and exemptions.[52] The High Middle Ages were marked by increasing collaboration between church and state, as popes turned tithes over to secular leaders in compensation for protection.[53] In addition, special tithes were imposed for crusades, holy wars, and other papal projects.[54] Eventually, in response to widespread abuses and increasing distrust of the church, tithes were suppressed in most countries.[55]

Theological and moral debates about how much money and property Christians should have continued throughout the medieval and modern periods. Medieval theologians such as Hugh of St. Victor, St. Bonaventure, and Thomas Aquinas all dealt with the question of tithing. Their defenses of tithing as duty are mostly uninspired and include natural law arguments for the responsibility of laypeople to support clergy, highly speculative attempts to spiritualize tithing by focusing on the perfection of the number ten, and casuistic efforts to work out the details of calculating and distributing tithes.

Even Thomas Aquinas, less legalistic and speculative than most, is significantly less challenging than preachers of the patristic era.[56] Thomas deals with tithing in *Summa Theologica* II-II Q. 87 and almsgiving in Q. 32. The former is a practice rooted in obligations to the common good while the latter is "an act of charity through the means of mercy," which becomes more morally necessary as the need of the potential recipient grows. Thomas quotes the more extreme statements of Ambrose and Basil in his discussion of almsgiving, not tithing, though his own discussion is notably tamer than theirs. Still, he admits the possibility of mortal sin if one with "superfluity" fails to aid another in danger of death. Moreover, the demands of one's station (which normally are seen as necessary and thus not eligible for almsgiving) can be set aside in the face of urgent need of a person or community. However, the requirements of station ordinarily serve to limit the obligation to give.[57]

The Catholic Church slowly returned to its prophetic voice with its social teaching on wealth and property beginning with *Rerum novarum* in 1891, in which Pope Leo XIII combined a rigorous defense of the right to private property with a strong call to charity.[58] His teaching on property purports to be an authentic appropriation of Thomas Aquinas on property, but many have convincingly argued since that Leo reads Aquinas through the lens of John Locke and misses both his view that private property is necessary only because of human sinfulness and his distinction between ownership and use of property.[59] However, Leo does seem to match Aquinas in his understanding of what a person is required to give, as both agree that maintaining enough to keep one's station in life is allowed, but charity must come out of what is left over.[60] Neither challenges readers to change their current lifestyle, though Aquinas allows that a stranger in extreme need has a claim beyond a giver's superfluity, and Leo draws attention to the cries of the poor, hoping to call forth greater charity. While Aquinas defends the tithe, Leo avoids the term while separately defending the charitable work of the church and emphasizing the individual's duty to give.

Later popes emphasized the social nature of property more than Leo XIII or Aquinas and developed a weightier right of the poor to the goods needed to sustain life, and this affected the popes' understanding of the obligations of those who have more than enough.[61] In *Mater et magistra*, for instance, Pope John XXIII repeats Leo XIII's assertion that the right to private property is natural but immediately softens it by claiming that "the goods which were created by God for all men should flow to all alike, according to the principles of justice and charity."[62]

With John Paul II, the church came to its most rigorous defense of the freedom of persons to work and flourish in a free market system and its most vigorous challenge to free market systems that ignore the demands of human dignity in the name of freedom. On the one hand, *Centesimus annus* offers an affirmation of private property as a valid part of an economic order that prioritizes freedom and creativity.[63] Yet on the other hand, the former pope orients everything toward the common good, limiting the legitimate accumulation of wealth and the freedom of businesses.[64] The key for John Paul II is the problem of people embracing lifestyles "directed to 'having' rather than 'being,' and [the desire] to have more, not in order to be more but in order to spend life in enjoyment as an end in itself. It is therefore necessary to create lifestyles in which the quest for beauty, goodness and communion with others for the sake of common growth are the factors which determine consumer choices, savings and investments."[65]

Though no specific guidelines are given, the obligation to work toward greater inclusion of those who are not flourishing in the current system is intrinsically related to the duty to give in charity. To live an authentic life means not to lose oneself in "having." The prophetic approach is evident in the earlier encyclical letter *Sollicitudo rei socialis*, when John Paul II claims that private property is "under a 'social mortgage,' which means that it has an intrinsically social function, based on and justified by the principle of the universal destination of goods."[66] It is perhaps most evident in *Ecclesia in America*, in which the pope begins to challenge the lifestyles that make applying the social mortgage concept so difficult. His understanding of conversion is explicitly tied to solidarity made manifest through imitation of Christ in one's way of life.[67] First bishops, and then all Christians, are called to "a genuine identification with the personal style of Jesus Christ, who leads us to simplicity, poverty, responsibility for others and the renunciation of our own advantage."[68]

Despite all the prophetic words about solidarity with the poor through the adoption of a new way of living, specific guidelines such as those regarding tithing have all but been forgotten. Moreover, the debate about how to understand and apply contemporary Catholic social teaching rages on. Conservatives tend to emphasize the church's respect for freedom and property, while liberals highlight the more radical statements on obligations to the common good. Both seem wary of making specific the sacrifices laypersons might be expected to shoulder. But if the church's tradition of respecting property rights, advocating charity to the poor, and provoking adherents to live more simply is to have any effect on the lives of believers, it must be made concrete. The "concretization" of the sixth to the eighteenth centuries is an example of where the church ought not go, but it must go somewhere lest its prophetic words remain unheeded.

Application: Tithing in a Contemporary Christian Context

Why go back to tithing? Admittedly, there are many points against it evident in the foregoing analysis of the history of the practice in the church. It is not clear that the specific ethical demands of the Hebrew Bible necessarily apply today. Jesus did not ask his followers to tithe, but he called at least some to give everything, spoke frequently of the dangers of wealth, and identified himself with the poor, all while depending on and celebrating with some people of means. The early church fathers thought tithing a poor substitute for the radical renunciation the gospel required, and many were more concerned with the effects of almsgiving on the giver rather than the recipient. In the medieval and modern church, the idea of tithing for the poor was overshadowed by the mandate to support clergy, entanglement between church and state led to corruption, and the theological underpinnings of the ethical idea becoming overly spiritualized, leading to a divide between almsgiving and tithing that severely diminished the latter. In recent times, more promising discussions of wealth in Catholic social teaching seem to be moving in the right direction without the potential legalism of tithing.

While these problems can be acknowledged, they are not definitive. One need not make an argument that the Hebrew Bible requires Christians to tithe, but it seems undeniable that tithing was a practice that enabled the Israelite people to concretize the social concern Yahweh demanded of them. Specific interpretations of tithing are no doubt limited by time and culture, but the general idea of putting aside a percentage of one's income for charity may still have a moral claim on believers. Recent attempts to reclaim Sabbath-keeping serve as useful models, as they combine affirmation of the truth of beliefs about the nature of God (creator of the world in which human beings are invited to delight) implied in the theology of the Sabbath, call attention to the importance of having a discipline for reminding people of these beliefs and making them more central in their lives, and offer ideas for bringing the practice into the reality of contemporary living.[69] Similarly, if it is not possible to contend that giving 10 percent of one's income away is obligatory for all Christians, it is useful to uphold tithing broadly defined as a useful discipline that brings compelling, prophetic Christian social teaching to bear upon everyday life.

The practice of tithing allows Christians to live within the complexity of the tradition's wisdom about wealth, enjoying abundance but living with less than they could so that others have a chance for a better life. In the Hebrew Bible, tithing comes from the gratitude due to God for all the gifts of life and the duty of those with more than enough to care for their less fortunate neighbors. The New Testament offers a combination of challenging hard sayings about wealth that distracts followers from the path of discipleship, the witness of Jesus's radically simple lifestyle, and acknowledgment (in meals of celebration, reliance on rich donors, and Jesus's friendships with people who did not renounce all for the kingdom) that wealth, provision for one's family, and even nonnecessary spending are not evil in themselves. Similarly, the early church fathers give believers much to worry about in their reminders that superfluous spending not given to the poor results in the death of innocents and the growing moral indifference of those who fail to give. If the fathers also knew that they dare not ask for mass renunciation, and if Jesus did not require it of everyone, this ought to give most Christians hope without allowing them to sleep too easily. With gratitude, concern for the poor, and acknowledgment of the dangers of wealth, Christians must seek a practice that enables them to delight in abundance, give away enough to keep themselves on the right path, and aid those who cannot provide for themselves.

Applying this general framework to the lives of individual, contemporary Christians is a task of social ethics that requires careful analysis and specificity. The corruption of the tithe in church history clearly points to a need to rethink application and justification but does not take away the need for some sort of discipline. While recent moral exhortations in Christian social teaching point the way by reflecting on right use of wealth, they do not provide a way of discerning how to put these teachings into practice, and this results in their marginalization in the church. The best theological arguments for tithing (i.e., the recognition of God's sovereignty and the gift of creation, the responsibility of believers to support a religious community, the need to respond to the suffering of fellow human beings, the duty to serve Christ in the poor, and the spiritual effects of giving on believers universally tempted to put their needs and those of their families above all others) remain cogent and in need of application.

How might tithing be retrieved in a contemporary context? Some churches (e.g., Assemblies of God) have very successful tithing programs that inspire a large majority of congregants to give nearly 10 percent.[70] Most mainline Protestant and Catholic churches avoid discussion of tithing, preferring the language of stewardship or contribution to parish programs.[71] Typically, theological justifications for tithing advanced in contemporary tithing churches center on recognition of God's sovereignty and links between believers' tithing and their salvation; concern for the poor and discussion of the effects of the excesses of consumerist lifestyles on believers are rare.[72] There are serious theological problems with tying salvation to tithing and ignoring the dangers of wealth for Christians. Moreover, in an era in which few churches give even 10 percent of their own resources to the poor, it is difficult to call for reinstating traditional tithing practice of giving 10 percent to one's religious community.[73] Whereas the Hebrew Bible describes a practice that provided a minimum level of support of religious leaders and kept the poor of the local community from going hungry, giving solely to one's church today would not serve the same purposes.

A contemporary tithe would seek new ways to make concrete Christian obligations to aid the less fortunate and support one's local church. Thus a more nuanced and flexible notion of tithing is needed. A tithe of 10 percent could include a percentage given to one's church—2 percent might be a reasonable goal, especially if a program to encourage increased church giving were accompanied by initiatives to increase church services for the poor, which would help churches live their mission in a more profound way. Perhaps some families would feel called to give more to their church, especially if its needs were great and it served an economically mixed congregation. The rest of their giving, in keeping with historical understandings of the tithe, should be directed to other programs to aid the less fortunate. Currently, less than 15 percent of all money given to charity in the United States goes directly to the poor.[74] Families should assess their giving, discerning how needs for medical research, education, and the arts (areas that receive much more funding) compare to the needs of development programs such the One campaign, Oxfam, Bread for the World, Catholic Relief Services, and other development/aid groups.[75] Flexibility is important, as tithing could function best as a common practice with different, context-appropriate manifestations.

Even given necessary flexibility, the concept of a percentage remains helpful. A recent large-scale study of church giving found that those who give a percentage give more than those who give a set amount and much more than those who spontaneously give what they can.[76] A percentage challenges families to make tithing a regular part of their budget, like a car payment or a 401K plan, and it ensures that their giving will increase as their income grows. Figuring out how to compute 10 percent is complicated. Some advocates of tithing take 10 percent of gross income, while others use net (after-tax) income and exempt money going directly to retirement accounts, reasoning that this money will come to them later and be tithed then.[77] This latter approach seems appropriate, given that money paid in taxes is theoretically directed to the common good, even if this goal is realized in imperfect ways.

For some, 10 percent may not be enough. Ron Sider proposes a graduated tithing scheme, in which families give 10 percent of the amount needed to live in basic comfort and then increase their tithe an additional 5 percent for each additional thousand dollars earned.[78] This proposal is certainly faithful to the more radical strains of the Christian tradition and involves a more thorough questioning of American middle-class lifestyles. I would hold it out as an ideal for some, while maintaining that standard tithing is true to the mainstream of the tradition and a challenging but realistic standard most Christians should be able to meet. Christianity, which has included people of means from the earliest days of its existence, does not seem to require radical renunciation. It does, however, challenge everyone to question contemporary living standards, support the church, and come to the aid of the poor. It seems that 10 percent is a reasonable level of sacrifice, given the abundance most in our society enjoy and the manifold needs of the poor around the globe, though the wealthiest of families should be encouraged to give even more.[79]

Why, then, do more families not tithe already? The difficulties of tithing in a consumerist society are considerable. One need not be unduly or uniformly gloomy about contemporary society to see the problem. A market economy is committed to growth and needs increasing consumption to thrive. Buying and having more seem unquestionable individual and social goods. In such a system, personal and social temperance is dismantled, so it becomes almost impossible to feel as though one has enough.[80] So when families are asked in Catholic social teaching to give out of their excess, most feel they have little to give—"the category of 'surplus' or of 'superfluous goods,' which one is obliged to distribute to the needy neighbor, effectively drops out."[81] Every time income goes up, perceived needs go up as well via what Christine Hinze calls "reference group upscaling"; thus "amid unprecedented material abundance, people are afflicted by a pervasive sense of insufficiency."[82] A sense of never having enough makes it all but impossible to give very much away.

Even though most acknowledge that they have too many things and care that many others go without, they feel powerless to act. Vincent Miller illustrates this problem through a provocative discussion of the case of a Chinese worker who died on the factory floor after working from 8 AM to midnight for sixty days straight.[83] He rightly points out that while all those in the first world bear some responsibility for global injustice, it is unfair to blame American consumers for this woman's death, for "if faced with the choice, absolutely no one would demand Chunmei's sacrifice for their ability to buy more cheap toys than they could ever enjoy."[84] The problem is that people would like to live in such a way that deaths such as Chunmei's did not happen but do not know how. Despite concern for the poor and stands against injustice, in the face of criticism against materialism they understand and accept, most people are unable to take religious values seriously by living and acting for a better world. In Miller's view, if the church wants to take on consumer culture, it cannot rely solely on inspiring counternarratives to the consumer way of life. "It can do so only by engaging consumer culture on the level of practices and structures rather than meanings and beliefs."[85]

Tithing is a practice with the power to check consumer culture. Certainly, it does not require embracing voluntary poverty and rejecting all unnecessary goods. However, for most families, giving 10 percent or more of their income will mean reversing "reference group upscaling" by living more simply than those around them. The majority would find the practice to be a serious challenge. Advice on downscaling from those who manage to give more away has common themes. Families tend to trim their food bills, shop less with more information and forethought, buy some things secondhand, reduce entertainment costs, decrease their use of utilities, resist the impulse to update clothes and home décor for the sake of fashion, do themselves what others pay to have done for them, and take care of what they have so that it lasts.[86] Giving 10 percent or more does not require radical change, but it does require making some sacrifices.

Those who advocate simple living almost always speak more often of the joys than the difficulties.[87] Still, there are significant costs of maintaining a simpler lifestyle in order to tithe. One parent profiled in Sider's book speaks of how his family had become "more 'materialistic'" in that they examine their material choices with great care.[88] This kind of detailed analysis of economic choices can be distracting and draining, as can the extra work needed to live without conveniences that cost money. Other stresses are laid out even by those who would not make different choices: "It has not been easy to discern where to draw lines, how much is enough, and when it makes sense to spend more time in order to use less resources. Our lifestyle has meant a lot of extra work, less leisure time to do the things we want and less individual independence."[89] Another says, "I cannot claim we have felt the freedom and exhilaration some talk about. For us, it is often a struggle. Decisions are constantly facing us that I wish would go away."[90]

This realism is important to acknowledge, along with the freedom that is more commonly claimed. Greater freedom and greater struggle coexist when all economic choices become moral choices, especially in a family where members are bound to disagree about what constitutes simplicity or even whether simplicity is worth pursuing at all. Unlike Dorothy Day or Mother Theresa, who lived in intentional communities, families have to decide together how to live without the benefit of having voluntarily chosen their commitments. Yet one hopes the struggle is ultimately worthwhile, as the mother quoted earlier follows her realistic appraisal of the hardships of simplicity with the following affirmation, "We have gained as a family, if not exhilaration, then a deep sense of joy in sharing with our whole lives in God's kingdom work. We have known a greater communion with those who live simply not because they choose to, but because they must."[91] As the early church fathers affirmed, tithing offers benefits for the spiritual lives of givers as well as the physical lives of receivers.

The difference for families who are able to make significant sacrifices and those who struggle and often give in seems to be community. Many advocates speak of the support they receive from like-minded families in church or other intentional community as crucial. In a consumer culture in which it is so hard to see alternatives to what appears to be the only normal way to live, forming communities within churches of people committed to living differently, but are not sure how, may be necessary. If tithing is a practice worthy of preserving, families who attempt it may find in committed communities precisely the challenge, support, and accountability they need.[92]

Families struggling to tithe ought not lose sight of the delight in the goods of creation the God of the scriptures so clearly desires for humanity. John R. Schneider rightly questions Ron Sider's sometimes harsh judgments about spending beyond one's needs, claiming that according to both Hebrew and Christian scriptures, "There are a good many things that we do not really need, it seems, that indeed enrich human life and bring it nearer what God envisions it to be."[93] Knowing that God enjoins feasting along with tithing in the Hebrew Bible and that Jesus indulged in festive meals with outcasts and friends allows people with means to enjoy some of the luxuries to which they have access. However, Schneider's conclusion that rich Christians owe those mired in poverty only "a spirit of compassion, full of respect" falls short, for true compassion can only mean desiring God's fullness for all and committing to some level of sacrifice to bring about shared celebration.[94] Feasting when others are dying of hunger surely is not God's will or any compassionate person's desire, and if tithing can move the world toward a day when this sort of tragic juxtaposition is not the norm, Christians ought to reembrace it without regret.

Conclusion: Why Tithing Matters

The significance of widespread tithing has the power to contribute to social change in the church, in families, and in poor communities. For the church, an extra 1 percent that would be generated if Catholics tithed as much as their Protestant neighbors would yield an additional $7 billion a year or about $400,000 for an average parish.[95] If even half of that money were directed to social ministry, many more congregations would be able to do service together as a church—a valuable formative practice.

For families, a commitment to tithe would mean taking up the challenges of budgeting and doing without. Ideally, the discernment on decisions about what to give up and where to send money would be shared in the context of formal or informal family meetings. Sharing a budget with children allows for more transparency about family financial decisions and perhaps more understanding and ownership of those decisions. Including children in decisions about where to give allows them to see that their small sacrifices are going to help specific communities and gives them the chance to be generous as givers of aid. Their commitment to live with less will help them avoid the problems of wealth to which the early church fathers point; they will be less likely to forget humility and kindness. Families committed to tithing have to come together both to save and to give. Investing in something beyond themselves gives their domestic church a mission and links them to the mission of the larger church.[96] A simple, moderate practice, tithing nonetheless requires enough sacrifice and outward focus to change family life in small but profound ways.[97]

For the poor, the tithing of Christian families could be extremely significant. In 1971, Sider estimated that a tithe from most Christians would mean about $13 billion more for the poor. Today it would be considerably more, perhaps as much as $56 billion.[98] If that money was earmarked for relief and development, as Sider suggests, organizations directed to these ends would be tremendously more effective. Though some argue that money would be better directed to capital investment via our own spending, Sider contends that giving to development organizations "does not mean you have no understanding of the need for capital investment to increase productivity. It simply means that you invest among the poor."[99] One hopeful study found that if Christians would simply tithe, global poverty could be eliminated.[100] Of course, this study calculates financial need and does not take into account political, cultural, and structural barriers. Yet, however complicated the problem of poverty, there is new hope for those seeking structural change.[101] The initial success of the Bill and Melinda Gates Foundation shows that, when large amounts of capital are directed intelligently at the global health problems associated with poverty, change can occur.[102] The possibilities for dramatically decreasing poverty are unprecedented.

Unlike the early Christians who never believed that they could make a dent in poverty, let alone contribute to social change, today's Christians do legitimately hold that hope. The choice of Christian families to practice resistance to poverty and overconsumption by tithing could have an enormous impact on the world. The problems of poverty and cumber are immensely complicated, and tithing alone cannot solve them. Nonetheless, it is a key part of a Christian ethic that recognizes abundance as a gift to be shared, links belief in Christ with attention to the least, and sees the potential of everyday practices to transform believers and the sinful social structures that inevitably distort that delight in the goods of creation that God enjoins upon all creatures.

Notes

1. See www.census.gov/hhes/www/income/histinc/histinctb.html for data on family income. I rely on family data rather than household data because my subject is families consisting of at least two persons while households can consist of just one person.
2. Kent A. Van Til, *Less Than Two Dollars a Day: A Christian View of World Poverty* (Grand Rapids, MI: Eerdmans, 2007), 2.
3. See www.econlibrary.org/library/Enc/DistributionofIncome.html (accessed November 11, 2008). Families in the lowest quintile average $2,000 more in 2004 than 1969, in the second quintile $8,000 more, in the third $17,000 more, in the fourth $35,000 more, and in the fifth $27,000 more. Growth was rapid in the post–World War II era and has been slower since the 1970s. Income growth in recent years is linked to the presence of more family members in the workforce.
4. While it is true that middle-class families perceive themselves to be struggling, even a casual glance at previous generations of middle-class families (who had smaller homes, fewer cars, fewer extracurricular pursuits, less technology in the home, and lower entertainment and travel budgets) reveals that rising expectations deserve most of the blame for middle-class stress.
5. Hoge et al., *Money Matters*, 49. Other studies are similar, finding that Americans give 1.6–2.2 percent of their income away to all charities, with Christians averaging 2.4 percent. Cited in Craig L. Blomberg, *Neither Poverty nor Riches: A Biblical Theology of Material Possessions* (Grand Rapids, MI: Eerdmans, 1999), 20. Charles E. Zech, "Population Shifts Pose Problems, Opportunities for Church Finance," *National Catholic Reporter*, August 12, 2005, 6a, notes that the 1–2 percent finding is well established.
6. "Patterns of Household Charitable Giving by Income Group, 2005," working paper prepared for Google by the Center on Philanthropy at Indiana University, Summer 2007, www.philanthropy.iupui.edu (accessed September 15, 2008). The study counted both charities specifically directed to meet the basic needs of the poor and money given to organizations for broader purposes (health care or education, for example) that directly aids the poor.
7. See Terzo Natalini, *A Historical Essay on Tithes: A Collection of Sources and Texts* (Washington, DC: National Catholic Stewardship Council, 1973), 3–9, who gives attention to tithing in Egypt, the Orient, Greece, and Rome.
8. Anthony Phillips, *Deuteronomy* (Cambridge: Cambridge University Press), 1973.
9. Lukas Vischer, *Tithing in the Early Church*, trans. Robert C. Schultz (Philadelphia: Fortress, 1966), 8–9. See also Joseph Reider, *Deuteronomy with Commentary* (Philadelphia: Jewish Publication Society of America, 1937), 145.
10. Vischer, *Tithing in the Early Church*, 9.
11. Natalini, *Historical Essay on Tithing*, 11.
12. Walter Bruegemann, *Deuteronomy* (Nashville, TN: Abingdon, 2001), 161.
13. Ibid. Support for the Levites in Jerusalem was more important after the Exile, when religious practice or cult was being centralized in Jerusalem. Richard D. Nelson, *Deuteronomy: A Commentary* (Louisville, KY: Westminster John Knox Press, 2002), 183.

14. Natalini, *Historical Essay on Tithing*, 14.

15. Ibid.

16. Ibid., 47. See also Nelson, *Deuteronomy*, 183. It is not clear whether these laws were observed; nonetheless, they retain significance as God's commands.

17. Bruegemann, *Deuteronomy*, 163.

18. Nelson, *Deuteronomy*, 185. See also Natalini, *Historical Essay on Tithing*, 18.

19. It is also appropriate to point out, as John R. Schneider does, that the Hebrew Bible affirms feasting and abundance in contexts in which money could be given to the poor instead. See *The Good of Affluence: Seeking God in a Culture of Wealth* (Grand Rapids, MI: Eerdmans, 2002), 179. This suggests that not all "superfluous" enjoyment of one's goods is problematic but nonetheless leaves us with a problem: How much enjoyment is compatible with prophetic calls to care for the poor?

20. Blomberg, *Neither Poverty nor Riches*, 55, 84, 49.

21. Vischer, *Tithing in the Early Church*, 9, 11.

22. Schneider, *Good of Affluence*, 160.

23. Sondra Wheeler, *Wealth as Peril and Obligation: The New Testament on Possessions* (Grand Rapids, MI: Eerdmans, 1995), 127–33.

24. Roman Garrison, *Redemptive Almsgiving in Early Christianity* (Sheffield: Journal for the Study of the New Testament, 1993), 137.

25. Peter H. Davids, "James and Peter: The Literary Evidence," in *The Missions of James, Peter, and Paul*, ed. Bruce Chilton and Craig Evans (Boston: Brill, 2005), 383. Davids emphasizes that, for Paul, almsgiving should be voluntary. Regie M. Kidd, *Wealth and Beneficence in the Pastoral Epistles: A Bourgeois Form of Early Christianity?* (Atlanta: Scholars Press, 1990), 200, argues that, in advocating unity despite inequality and denying rich Christians the honor and deference to which they were accustomed, Paul was radical in his own way.

26. Davids, "James and Peter," 383.

27. My argument here is that those looking for a simple principle (i.e., it would be just to live at x level with y kinds of possessions, giving z amount away) will not find it in the New Testament. Discerning what an authentic economic practice is means acknowledging the tension in affirming the goodness of abundance, the obligation of charity, and the dangers of wealth.

28. Natalini, *Historical Essay on Tithing*, 34–37.

29. Augustine, *Sermon 9*, quoted in Vischer, *Tithing in the Early Church*, 16.

30. Augustine, *Sermon 85*, quoted in Natalini, *Historical Essay on Tithing*, 51.

31. Boniface Ramsey, "Almsgiving in the Latin Church: The Late Fourth and Early Fifth Centuries," in *Studies in Early Christianity: A Collection of Scholarly Essays*, ed. Everett Ferguson (New York: Garland, 1993), 287–88, speaking especially of Ambrose, Ambrosiaster, Paulinus, Jerome, and Augustine.

32. St. Caesarius, *Sermo*, quoted in Natalini, *Historical Essay on Tithing*, 53. In the same volume, similar themes occur in St. Ambrose (49) and St. Gregory Nazianzen (43). One can certainly question whether a failure to give to the dying can be equated with murder, but at least St. Caesarius perceives the import of economic choices.

33. Ramsey, "Almsgiving in the Latin Church," 287.

34. Garrison, *Redemptive Almsgiving*, 140.

35. Ramsey, "Almsgiving in the Latin Church," 291–92.
36. L. William Countryman, *The Rich Christian in the Church of the Early Empire: Contradictions and Accommodations* (New York: Edward Mellen Press, 1980).
37. Ramsey, "Almsgiving in the Latin Church," 298. See also Susan R. Holman, *The Hungry Are Dying: Beggars and Bishops in Roman Cappadocia* (Oxford: Oxford University Press, 2001), 109, who shows how Basil of Caesarea and Gregory of Nazianzus both threatened the rich but also promised them joy in the world to come in return for alms.
38. *Tract in Ioann*, quoted in Ramsey, "Almsgiving in the Latin Church," 278. Ramsey cites similar statements in other fathers.
39. Ramsey, "Almsgiving in the Latin Church," 278. Also concepts of "pious usury," or lending money to Christ via the poor, and leaving one's inheritance to Christ through the poor are common. Ibid., 279.
40. Vischer, *Tithing in the Early Church*, 23.
41. Cassian, *Collat. 21, Abbatis Theonae*, quoted in Natalini, *Historical Essay on Tithing*, 45.
42. Countryman, *Rich Christian*, 117.
43. Augustine, *Sermon 164*, quoted in Ramsey, "Almsgiving in the Latin Church," 307.
44. Augustine, *De decem chordis*, quoted in Natalini, *Historical Essay on Tithing*, 50.
45. J. A. McGuckin, "The Vine and the Elm Tree: The Patristic Interpretation of Jesus' Teachings on Wealth," in *The Church and Wealth*, ed. W. J. Sheils and Diana Wood (New York: Basil Blackwell, 1987), 13, 14.
46. Natalini, *Historical Essay on Tithing*, 60.
47. Ibid., 58–59.
48. Ibid., 61.
49. Ibid., 62–63.
50. Ibid., 64.
51. Ibid., 66.
52. Ibid., 68–69.
53. Ibid., 92.
54. Ibid., 93–98.
55. Ibid., 105–7.
56. Ibid., 117.
57. See Stephen J. Pope, "Aquinas on Almsgiving," *Heythrop Journal* 32 (1991): 167–91.
58. The social gospel movement provides a similar trajectory in the Protestant tradition. See Walter Rauschenbusch, *A Theology for the Social Gospel* (Louisville, KY: Westminster John Knox Press, 1997).
59. Curran, *Catholic Social Teaching*, 175–77, writing about *Rerum novarum* nos. 8–9, reprinted in Michael Walsh and Brian Davies, eds., *Proclaiming Justice and Peace: Papal Documents from Rerum Novarum through Centesimus Annus* (Mystic, CT: Twenty-third, 1991).
60. Aquinas, *Summa Theologica* II-II Q. 31. While Aquinas does allow for the possibility of "legitimate theft" in the case of dire need (Q. 67), his discussion of charity does not seem to allow for the claim that "the strict right to private property is limited by the more generic intention that the goods of creation serve the needs of all," except in extreme circumstances. Curran, *Catholic Social*

Teaching, 177. Otherwise, charity is counseled, but the recipient does not have a claim on the giver's excess.

61. See *Quadragesimo anno,* no. 48; *Mater et magistra,* no. 43; *Gaudium et spes,* no. 69; and *Populorum progressio,* nos. 22–23, all in Walsh and Davies, *Proclaiming Justice and Peace.* See also Curran, *Catholic Social Teaching,* 179–81.

62. *Mater et magistra,* no. 43. See also no. 121.

63. See *Centesimus annus,* no. 13, in Walsh and Davies, *Proclaiming Justice and Peace:* "A person who is deprived of something he can call 'his own,' and of the possibility of earning a living of his own initiative, comes to depend on the social machine and on those who control it. This makes it more difficult for him to recognize his dignity as a person, and hinders progress towards the building up of an authentic human community."

64. Ibid., nos. 31–34.

65. Ibid., no. 36. In no. 40 he explains further that the market is limited by human needs that are not well served by the market and in no. 43 notes that "the obligation to earn one's bread by the sweat of one's brow presumes the right to do so." Clearly, obligations exist to persons who are left out of the new market economy, and the potential of those who enjoy its fruits to neglect higher goods is a very real concern.

66. *Sollicitudo rei socialis,* no. 42.

67. *Ecclesia in America,* nos. 28–30. The pope is clear that not only bishops and pastors but also laypeople (and even families, no. 46) are called to renunciation, prayer, and charity. Holiness is defined as extending Christ's love in history to the poor, sick, and needy.

68. Ibid., no. 28, speaks of bishops. This is followed by an extension of the ethical framework to the laity: "The proposal of a new style of life applies not only to Pastors, but to all Christians." Ibid., no. 29.

69. See, for instance, Belden Lane, "Holy Silence: An Invitation to Sabbath," *Christian Century,* October 24, 2001, 27–31; or Wayne Muller, *Sabbath: Finding Rest, Renewal and Delight in Our Busy Lives* (New York: Bantam, 2000).

70. Hoge et al., *Money Matters,* 15–17.

71. Ibid., 36–39.

72. Ibid., 36.

73. Ibid., 34. Churches in Hoge's study reported devoting between 10 and 16 percent of their budget to "mission work, diocesan offices, denominational offices and social programs" combined.

74. Giving USA provides the most comprehensive annual survey of charitable giving in America. In 2005, they report that 5 percent was contributed in the broad "public-society benefit" category, and 10 percent fell into the "human services" category. In contrast, Americans gave 15 percent of their charity dollars to education and 36 percent to churches. Significant amounts also went to health care, animals, and the environment. See www.aafrc.org/about _aafrc/index.cfm?pg=chart2.cfm&ID=gusa1 (accessed September 15, 2008).

75. Political contributions could also be included in the tithe, if the alleviation of poverty were central to candidates or causes.

76. Dean R. Hoge, Charles Zech, Patrick McNamara, and Michael J. Donahue, "Giving in Five Denominations," in *Financing American Religion,* ed. Mark

Chaves and Sharon L. Miller (Walnut Creek, CA: Alta Mira Press, 1999), 8–9.

77. John K. Brackett, *On the Pilgrim's Way: Christian Stewardship and the Tithe*, rev. ed. (Harrisburg, PA: Morehouse, 1996), 94–95.

78. Ronald J. Sider, *Rich Christians in an Age of Hunger: A Biblical Study* (Downers Grove, IL: Intervarsity Press, 1977), 168. Blomberg, *Neither Poverty nor Riches*, 248, uses a version of this concept and is able to tithe 30 percent per year. I know of families in St. Louis who embrace voluntary poverty and give away 40 percent of their small incomes.

79. Even Sider, *Rich Christians in an Age of Hunger*, 168, allows that some situations, such as the need to save for college tuition, would alter the duty to tithe. I would add to this very low income, health problems, child care expenses, and elder care responsibilities. Not everyone will be able to tithe all of the time. Still, it is a reasonable goal for most American families. Conversely, the very rich (i.e., those in the top 10 percent of American families) should be in a position to give more than 10 percent.

80. Christine Hinze, "What Is Enough? Catholic Social Thought, Consumption, and Material Sufficiency," in *Having: Property and Possession in Religious and Social Life*, ed. William Schweiker and Charles Matthewes (Grand Rapids, MI: Eerdmans, 2004), 164.

81. Ibid., 169.

82. Ibid., 187, 186.

83. Vincent J. Miller, *Consuming Religion: Christian Faith and Practice in a Consumer Culture* (New York: Continuum, 2005), 16.

84. Ibid., 17.

85. Ibid., 180.

86. See testimonials in Ron J. Sider, ed., *Living More Simply: Biblical Principles and Practical Models* (Downers Grove, IL: Intervarsity Press, 1980), 59–107.

87. Ibid.

88. Ibid., 75.

89. Ibid., 102.

90. Ibid., 106.

91. Ibid.

92. Intentional communities and Catholic Worker houses are good and oft-cited options. Miller, *Consuming Religion*, 219. However, tithing does not usually require going this far. Parish-based discussion groups with service commitments in the model of the Christian Family Movement or Cursillo are alternatives for those who are working toward simplicity rather than voluntary poverty.

93. Schneider, *Good of Affluence*, 170.

94. Ibid., 219. Blomberg's summary and conclusions are a helpful rejoinder: He reads scripture as describing material possessions not only as a gift from God meant to be enjoyed but also as revealing wealth as a primary means by which people turn away from God, extremes of wealth and poverty as intolerable, and almsgiving as a sign of a redeemed life. Blomberg, *Neither Poverty nor Riches*, 243–45. The cries of the poor cannot be answered with sympathy alone.

95. Zech, "Population Shifts," 6a. If an extra 1 percent of Catholic incomes would yield $7 billion, then an extra 8 percent (given 2 percent to churches in my

model) would yield $56 billion. Sider, *Living More Simply*, 108–44, presents helpful case studies of churches choosing to live more simply and engage in more service.

96. See Rubio, *Christian Theology of Marriage and Family*, 183–99; and Bourg, *Where Two or Three Are Gathered*, 136–56. Children who are taught to give of themselves may grow up to be less self-centered and more socially conscious.

97. Tithing would be a natural choice for a practice to counteract the consumerism that Vince Miller so powerful examines in *Consuming Religion*. Miller advocates "developing structures in daily life that can support the ideas, values, and practices that contemporary spiritual practitioners appropriate." Ibid., 143.

98. Sider, *Rich Christians in an Age of Hunger*, 176.

99. Ibid., 169.

100. John Ronsavalle and Sylvia Ronsavalle, "Facts Related to U.S. Wealth from a Global Christian Perspective," in *The Midas Trap*, ed. David Neff (Wheaton, IL: Victor, 1990), 151–61.

101. Some evangelical writers worry that the Bible does not seem to call Christians to work for structural change. Catholic social teaching, while maintaining its advocacy for charity, affirms developmental and political efforts to aid the poor. Solidarity, in modern Catholic teaching, requires not only charity but justice enacted through changing sinful structures. *Sollicitudo rei socialis*, no. 39. Similar themes are central to modern Protestant social thought. See Walter Wink, *The Powers That Be: Theology for a New Millennium* (New York: Doubleday, 1998).

102. "From Riches to Rages," *Time*, December 26, 2005, 1–10. Sider, *Rich Christians in an Age of Hunger*, 174–76, notes the importance of giving a large percentage of the tithe to organizations focusing on development. There are, of course, problems with development models that do not include input from and empowerment of aid recipients. However, there are plentiful models of development projects that avoid those mistakes. See, e.g., www.crs.org.

CHAPTER SEVEN

Serving

Reimagining a Central Practice of Middle-Class Family Life

Contemporary Catholic Family Life: A Rough Sketch

Very few Catholic parents are in need of something more to do. When they meet each other, it is on the sidelines of soccer games, dance classes, and baseball diamonds; working booths at parish festivals; helping with school parties; buying birthday treats for a child's class; borrowing chairs for an extended family gathering in their home; chaperoning a field trip; rushing to parent-teacher conferences; slipping into a hardware store to pick up a forgotten item for a home-repair project; gratefully sinking down in the pews at Mass, hoping this time they will not have to struggle with restless children who would rather be elsewhere. Their conversations center on the details of their busy lives and concerns about the well-being of their children. These are not frivolous people whose energy is consumed with fashion, self-promotion, or entertainment. For the most part, middle-class American Catholics are hardworking, family centered, and devoted to the common good of their communities. They are engaged in plenty of service—to their children, their parents, and their parishes, as well as their children's schools, teams, and extracurricular groups.

It seems difficult to say of them, using John Kavanaugh's well-known categories, that their lives have more in common with the commodity form rather than the personal form.[1] Even though they live in a consumer society, their willingness to give to their families and communities can be seen as a way of "perceiving and valuing men and women as irreplaceable persons whose fundamental identities are fulfilled in covenantal relationships."[2] Surely they do not see persons "as replaceable objects whose goal and value are dependent upon how much we market, produce, and consume."[3] Their gift of self to the persons they love is made concrete in hours at work to support their households and in the hundreds of small tasks, from laundry to coaching to carpooling, that fill their days. Though they have a great many more things than most people in the world, I would hesitate to say that they have lives consumed with having rather than being.[4] The strongly negative characterizations of the literature on consumerism seem a poor fit.

And yet one can hear in the conversations of middle-class adults a certain dissatisfaction with this way of life, a yearning for a slower pace, deeper friendships, and more time to simply be with their spouses and their children. They are conscious of their relative privilege and of the waste of resources that middle-class life entails. They know their children do not really need more things and more activities. They wish they had more time to do something for the poor. They would like to spend more time in prayer or meditation. There is a certain emptiness that is evident amid the "fullness" of middle-class American suburban life, a suspicion that busyness does not allow us to live below the surface, a sense that this life is less than it ought to be. People are generally satisfied with their families and communities, but they know at some level that there is something missing.[5]

This emptiness in busyness is, I argue, paradoxically connected to low expectations for marriage. Middle-class families expect suburban comfort, friendly local communities, and loving families, but the modern Catholic vision for marriage and family developed by John Paul II asks for much more than what most families would dare to imagine. As I pointed out in chapter 1, in *Familiaris consortio* the late pope speaks of relationships between husbands and wives using the term "communion," suggesting a certain depth in both physical and emotional connection.[6] He asks families to serve life by welcoming children, honoring life in all its forms, and creating an environment where the countercultural values of the Christian tradition can flourish. He gives families a mission to serve society, working to transform its unjust structures and soften its hard edges with works of charity, mercy, and hospitality. He calls families to own their identity as domestic churches in prayer, witness, and service. This vision of John Paul II is lofty and inspiring. But given the heavy load most married people are carrying in trying to achieve a middle-class vision of happiness, it seems all but impossible.

However, I have suggested thus far that the work to which the pope calls families, the very work that seems as if it would burden families, is in reality the work of communion and solidarity that will fulfill them. When husbands and wives take time to nurture their intimate relationships, they are nurturing communion that can flow out into solidarity. When families take time to eat together, choose just eating practices, and offer hospitality without judgment, they are building communion and solidarity. When a family makes an intentional decision to live more simply so that they can tithe on their income, they are extending communion and solidarity. By resisting the emptiness of "normal" middle-class family life, Christian families can find something far better. In this chapter I argue that, when families participate in service that involves opening themselves to being in relationship with those who are needy, this too is the nurturing, building, and extending of family communion and solidarity. This practice of resistance, a requirement for Christian families whose responsibilities to society do not, according to John Paul II, end with birthing and rearing children, is a way out of emptiness to fullness.[7]

Why are most middle- and upper-middle-class Catholic families unaware of what is asked of them and/or unready to embrace this way of life? An obvious place to turn is the parish, for if American middle-class culture is at odds with the Catholic vision for families, parishes should be places of refuge where an alternative way of life is nurtured. Two-thirds of all Catholics are registered parishioners and most attend their local parish.[8] Another 16 percent attend one parish more than any other but are not registered, while only 16 percent are not affiliated at all.[9] Parishes are the communities that most Catholics call home. They are ideally placed to form families in Christian family values. However, as much as I want to believe that if the culture is working against families the church is building them up, I am concerned that this is only rarely the case. In fact, my research on

Catholic parishes suggests that most are not supportive of the kind of family lives Catholics have been called to live in the post–Vatican II context.

This chapter addresses the problem in four parts. The first part describes how American parishes functioned to sustain families in the early twentieth century. The second part discusses changes in the late twentieth century and their impact on families. The third part offers suggestions for transforming parish culture so that families are more able to engage in service. The fourth and final part argues that service with the poor is an essential practice of Christian life for families that can be transformative for them and for others. The "givens" of middle-class life—including parish life—already structure so much of family time and energy that this sort of alternative practice is unlikely to flourish if families attempt it on their own.[10] Families will need parishes if they are to break out of the sort of service they are currently doing and break into another way of life. If parishes are to support families that are distinctively Catholic in their striving for communion and to help them overcome the problem of emptiness, they will have to question much that they have taken on as they have traveled from the margins to the center of middle-class American life. Only then will families be able to ask similar questions about their own lives and practice resistance by engaging in service together.

Pre–Vatican II American Parishes

Most American Catholic families lived in urban settings from the 1880s well until the 1950s, and they were deeply loyal to the ethnic parish neighborhoods that were the center of their existence.[11] The number of Catholics in America expanded as immigrants from southern and eastern Europe flooded into American cities. From the late 1800s until the mid-1960s, Catholics were underrepresented in the upper class, somewhat overrepresented in the middle class, and very overrepresented in the lower classes.[12] Marginalized by ethnicity, class, and religion, they remained to a large extent outside the mainstream of American society. Parishes functioned as indispensable subcultures for these immigrant Catholics, providing social services, education, social life, and moral boundaries. Historians of this period speak of a "unified family-based parish as the source of internalized Catholic identity."[13] Even today, the generation of pre–Vatican II Catholics is more strongly identified with the church than younger generations.

Ninety percent say being Roman Catholic is an important part of who they are, 85 percent say it is important that the younger generation in their family grow up Catholic, 66 percent say the church is the most important part of their lives, and 57 percent attend Mass weekly.[14] Catholics tied to pre–Vatican II neighborhood parishes strongly identified with the church and its core teachings and rituals. Those parishes commanded their loyalty in a way that few parishes today do.

Parishes during this period provided a wide variety of activities and services to respond to the needs of their congregations. Social services such as food pantries, orphanages, soup kitchens, building and loan associations, and dues-paying societies that paid out benefits when family members got sick or died were necessary to meet the needs of those struggling to make a living.[15] Social life was rich and varied and included sports clubs, social clubs, dances, picnics, carnivals, and variety shows.[16] Small parishes could support a wide range of activities because they served as the central gathering place for parishioners who were united not only by faith but by ethnicity, class, proximity, and family ties. There were also a range of lay groups that offered parishioners opportunities to deepen their spiritual life in the company of friends and neighbors, such as the Legion of Mary, St. Vincent de Paul, Young Catholic Students, Young Catholic Workers, the Altar Society, the Holy Name Society, and the Christian Life Community.[17]

Parish-based groups such as these acculturated people into their faith, but so did the whole of parish life. As one theologian puts it, "The living tradition must be passed on at least in part . . . through festivity, that is, through the live interaction of the community engaged in celebrating its own life."[18] Ethnic urban parishes drew people to the tradition by gathering them not only for Sunday Mass but for spiritual associations, novenas, Saturday confession, Mass on holy days, parish missions, processions and festivals honoring saints, Lenten suppers, and other spiritual-social celebrations that formed Catholics in a life centered around the church, and this helped them sustain families that were countercultural in faith and practice if not intent.

Parish life in the early 1900s differed from parish life in post–World War II society. As the century progressed, Catholics gained in economic and social status, and parishes were no longer needed to sustain families economically. Nonetheless, through midcentury, social life in urban and ethnic parishes remained vibrant, regular mass attendance rose to a high of 75 percent, families remained stable, and a majority of Catholics strongly identified with the church.[19] In many ways, the late 1960s were the peak time for Catholics in America, when schools, parishes, and the structures of the Catholic subculture were thriving.

If ethnic Catholic subcultures formed Catholics into tightly knit communities, they did not necessarily prepare families to live a countercultural life. Families in these times may not have been more able or willing to live out the sort of mission contemporary Catholics were given by John Paul II. Marriages in this era were longer lasting, but it is hard to determine if they were also rooted in total self-giving and directed to communion. Families were larger and welcomed more of the marginalized because Catholics themselves were on the margins of American culture, but married couples may not have engaged in service of life as defined by John Paul II. They were probably less able to serve society by engaging in hospitality and work for justice, as so many were still struggling themselves. If the domestic church was actualized in ritual practices in the home, it was not necessarily realized in depth of faith. Clearly, traditional practices alone do not ensure communion or solidarity. Catholic identity can be more cultural than religious, and strong identity does not guarantee radical commitment.

Nonetheless, the parishes of an earlier era could count on things that few contemporary parishes can, because they were at the center of families' lives. Family, extended family, neighborhood, parish, school, and social network were one, and that integration produced a kind of Catholic identity and commitment that is uncommon today.

American Catholics cannot go back in time and should not discount the good things about contemporary Catholic life. We rightly celebrate the economic stability of contemporary American Catholic families, their multilayered identities and overlapping commitments, and their willingness to question and adapt the tradition rather than simply accepting it as given. In fact, one Catholic historian suggests that because we now have to ask what it means to be Catholic, we have a new "opportunity for building a Catholic community based not on ethnicity or on defense, but on religion."[20] Still, we would do well to consider how parishes have changed in order to better understand where we are. Then we will be better able to see what reforms might be necessary to strengthen Catholic identity and community in the contemporary context when we can no longer assume that parishes are strengthened by ethnic, class, and neighborhood ties.

The Changing Shape of Parish Life

Several aspects of contemporary parish life impede the realization of Catholic hopes for marriage and family life, most notably upward mobility, a middle-class approach to social justice, and overinvestment in activities unrelated to distinctive Catholic concerns. Aspects of parish life generally understood as positive and progressive must be questioned if the contemporary Catholic vision of family as a faith community working toward communion and solidarity at home and in the world is to have a chance of capturing the hearts and minds, let alone shaping the lives, of ordinary families.

First, the upward mobility of American Catholics in the last fifty years has been extraordinary, and it has loosened their identification with their local parishes. As James Davidson shows using a number of key indicators, "Catholics are now firmly planted in the nation's upper middle class."[21] After World War II, Catholics, like many Americans, left factory jobs to become employees in white collar companies, moved from urban neighborhoods to suburbs, sent more of their own to college, and saw their family incomes rise.[22] Ethnic conclaves became less necessary as Catholics felt more at home in the multiethnic mix of American society.[23] No longer segregated in Catholic-only neighborhoods, Catholics begin to live next to, go to school with, work with, befriend, and marry more people of other faiths than ever before.[24] With upward mobility came integration into American middle-class society and a loss of a certain kind of distinctive Catholic identity. Says Catholic historian James Fisher, "By the 1990s it appeared that Catholics truly were 'like everyone else' in the U.S., but it was not entirely clear just what made them Catholic."[25] If Dorothy Day was once attracted to the Catholic Church because she saw in it working-class and poor believers devoted to their church, today she would see a very different reality.[26]

It is not only parishioners who have changed; parishes themselves have also become upwardly mobile. Despite the low levels of tithing described in chapter 5, only 7 percent of parishes have financial problems; the great majority are financially stable.[27] Many parishes have added new buildings to accommodate a growing range of activities, gyms for extensive sports programs, and professional staff to do what used to be done by priests, nuns, or volunteers.[28] Suburban parishes, which are growing, tend to be bigger than urban parishes that are closing in large numbers. Though about one-fourth of parishes are still small, that is having fewer than 450 members, the average parish today has 3,097 members.[29] Upwardly mobile parishioners are now congregating in larger churches where they are not necessarily widely known or personally invested.

Parishes of today are serving middle-class suburbanites for whom the parish is one of many loyalties. Pastors tend to report that their congregations are vibrant and alive, though only a minority say that "providing people with a place to belong" is a key priority.[30] Conversely, most families do not see their parish as their primary source of community, but they are not disturbed by this.[31] They are more invested elsewhere, and parishes are not providing a compelling alternative. Upward mobility in the parish has disrupted the bonds of community, leaving individuals and families more isolated in their quest to live a Christian life.

Changing parish demographics have resulted in the second major change: a restructuring of the way local churches approach social justice. Parish social justice efforts were once centered in the local community and in the lives of parish families, but today they are external and largely marginal to parish life. In the early twentieth century, Catholics often were poor or working class, and their parishes helped meet their needs and brought together a network of families who could share resources and responsibilities. People in parishes needed each other for social and spiritual support; they suffered no illusions about their independence. They knew firsthand the struggle of poverty and could have identified with the struggles of the poor masses identified in Catholic social documents of the time, though they were much more likely to work on those struggles in the labor movement or various incarnations of Catholic Action than to read or learn about them in the classroom.[32]

When Catholics moved into the middle classes, social justice became something removed from everyday life. Most no longer come to a parish seeking social support. Although the majority of Catholics still stay in their neighborhood parishes, they do not feel compelled to by either tradition, ethnicity, class, or need. Financially comfortable younger Catholics today shop around and choose the parish they like, one that will help in their quest for greater spiritual growth and their desire to do something for others—others who probably do not live in their neighborhood.[33] Half of all parishes do engage in at least some direct social ministry and one-third engage in some advocacy, and Catholics generally support this.[34] In fact, younger Catholics are even more likely than older Catholics to say that the church's teaching on helping the poor is very important to them.[35] However, middle-class parishes tend to focus their energy on low-commitment social service activities such as food baskets delivered at holidays rather than ongoing, direct community service.[36] Though parishes do offer some higher level service opportunities, few parishioners are involved in these efforts in a significant way. Moreover, nearly half believe that one can be a good Catholic without doing anything for the poor.[37] More people know about and are sympathetic to the social teachings of the church: 82 percent say charity is important, and 71 percent agree that God is present in the poor in a special way.[38] They are proud that their church takes prophetic stands on social issues. Yet working for social justice seems to be an option for some Catholics, one possible way to live out one's faith rather than an essential part of life in an interdependent community.

Moreover, most Catholics make decisions about how to spend their time and money—the key social justice decisions of their lives—without much guidance from their parishes, because their parishes are not their primary communities. Contemporary Catholics are largely satisfied with their parishes and rate them high on friendliness, average on meeting their spiritual needs, but lowest on helping them with ethical questions related to their daily lives at home and work.[39] However, "though parishes are becoming increasingly large and complex, most Catholics do not believe that they are too large and impersonal."[40] Parishes provide spiritual nourishment and social interaction but do not ask much of lay Catholics or play a central role in their lives, and most are comfortable with this arrangement.

In truth, the structure of middle-class American life does not allow for very much direct involvement in parish social justice efforts. More families are balancing two careers (or one career and one parent), and multiple schools more likely to be farther from home than the neighborhood parish, where only a small minority attend school anymore.[41] There are more children's activities that require more volunteer time and more driving, and hours at home are more hectic because chores, homework, family time, and extra work from professional jobs have to be squeezed into a very small time frame each day. All of this leaves very little time for committing to a parish community and living out the service to which John Paul II calls families.

In this new situation, parishes have a difficult task. Parishioners are sympathetic but unable to commit. They are willing to be members of the church but not willing to place the church at the center of their lives. Although 81 percent of Catholics still say that being Catholic is an important part of who they are, only 44 percent say the church is most important, and only 37 percent attend Mass weekly.[42] Among the youngest generation, the millennial Catholics, only 40 percent say religion is important in their daily lives, and fewer than 30 percent attend weekly Mass.[43] The decline in identity and participation in parish life appears to be not stabilizing but accelerating.

For most, the parish experience is something that fits into middle-class culture rather than challenging its terms. That is why most laypeople are satisfied with it, even though it has little effect on how they live. According to sociologists of religion, Vatican II–era parents and religious leaders who influenced the current generation of Catholics "have stressed the view of the Church as a means of meeting members' social and spiritual needs. Today's young Catholics have learned that the Church is meaningful insofar as it helps them establish relationships with other like-minded people and contributes to their personal relationship with God. Thus, it should be no surprise that younger generations of Catholics are less committed to the Church. They do not see it as an entity to which they should commit themselves. Instead, they see it as only one of many possible means to help them meet their own needs."[44]

Catholics are sympathetic to the church's social message and willing to contribute to good causes, but the work of charity and advocacy remains distant from the lives of most. Parishes are but one of many communities to which they are committed, and their choices about work and money are not greatly influenced either by these communities or by the social teachings to which they adhere in theory.

A third problem in contemporary parishes is directly related to economic mobility and the de-centering of social justice: Parishes themselves tend to overinvest in activities that keep parishioners from doing the work they are called to do. Parishes offer plenty for families to do, but much of it offers little help to married couples trying to realize a distinctive Christian vision of marriage.[45] It is not that these ministries are bad in themselves. Catholic sports programs provide a values-centered recreation experience for kids, but in some parishes they consume too large a portion of families' free time.[46] Teen activities can be a means of spiritual growth but can also serve to isolate teens from the needs of their communities.[47] Men's and women's groups provide opportunities to socialize but rarely engage parishioners in challenging conversations about their faith.[48] Religious education programs for children benefit from the generosity of committed teachers who try their best to pass on the faith they love but are far from adequate substitutes for the full parish life that used to form the characters of Catholic children.[49] Service opportunities to collect food, clothes, or money for the needy are valuable but marginal to the life of most parishes.[50] Moreover, in nearly all parish programs, spouses are separated from each other, parents are separated from children, siblings are drawn apart. While some separate activities are no doubt beneficial, it is disturbing that few programs exist to bring spouses or families together to deepen their personal communion or to live out their familial vocation to be disciples of Christ in the world. Outside of Mass, it is difficult for married couples or families to find places to pray or serve together.

Parish activities in the middle-class American parish are also are more likely to contradict the church's call to families to live more simply out of solidarity with the oppressed. Social events require large investments of parishioners' time and, increasingly, their money.[51] Fundraisers such as auctions, carnivals, trivia nights, and golf tournaments raise money for good causes but are costly to put on and attend. It is not clear how central they are to forming Christian community and Christian families, as they seem to mimic the culture rather than help families construct an alternative to it. John Paul II claims that a commitment to live simply is part of a family's mission to serve life.[52] However, his countercultural plea is unlikely to be heard when parishes themselves ask for more money from their parishioners and seem to encourage high-end entertainment. In addition, time spent on social activities takes away from time that could be spent in faith formation and service. Most parish families spend their weekends in pursuit of the goods of middle-class life, but very few include service to those who are truly needy or engagement with Christian faith. It is not at all clear that middle-class parishes truly build up Christian marriages and families.

Some claim that they do. Andrew and Mary Greeley write with great appreciation of contemporary parish life, with affection for sports teams, open gyms, dances, youth clubs, shows, golf and bowling leagues, card groups, tennis clubs, and socials offered by parishes. They assert that "people will better appreciate the sacramentality of all their experiences when they learn to appreciate the sacramental possibilities of playing."[53] Surely the Greeleys are right to remind us that "discover[ing] the supernatural in the midst of the natural" is a central part of being Catholic. Yet parishes today do not command the loyalty or build the community that they did in previous generations. Moreover, Christian families are called to do more than socialize with other Christians. The task of being Christian in a secular, postmodern world is difficult, and if parishes offer more of what the culture provides and fail to challenge parishioners to shape their lives differently from their neighbors', few Christian families will be able to tackle this on their own.

There are, of course, parish activities that do push adult Catholics. They are groups that help people see the connection between their faith and their work, such as Christian Life Communities, Focolare, the Community of Sant'Egidio, and JustFaith.[54] There are bible study groups, prayer groups, and small faith communities of various kinds. But the best estimates indicate that only about 5 percent of Catholics are involved in these kinds of groups.[55] Some shy away from this kind of high level commitment, while others do not find it offered in their parishes, but how many might be drawn to it if their lives were not so consumed by other activities far less essential to living out their faith? Something in parish culture allows most Catholics to assume that they need not take up this challenge, to believe that their efforts in sports, youth ministry, and social events are central to being Catholic, but engaging in a small community that provides support and challenge as they discern how to live together is not.

In sum, even as they ask too much of Catholic families in some ways, Catholic parishes that are steeped in upward mobility and more invested in social activities than social justice, discernment, and prayer ask far too little of families in others. They unwittingly help sustain a culture in which upward mobility remains unquestioned, social justice is accepted as a good cause but plays a marginal role in the daily lives of most families, wrestling with ethical decisions in the context of Christian faith is rare, and spiritual life outside of Sunday liturgy is thin. It should not be surprising that sustaining communion and solidarity inside and outside the family seems beyond the capacities of most Catholic families.

Reshaping Parish Life to Support Christian Families

In the church, valuing families has to be about much more than trying to keep middle-class families strong and happy. It must also be about sustaining marriages and families that are Christ centered and directed toward personal and social communion. Michael Warren writes with frustration about middle- and upper-class parishes that ignore the Jesus who stood with the poor and emphasize a Jesus who offers self-affirmation and self-aggrandizement: "We end up with a Jesus who affirms our culturally conditioned aspirations, not the Jesus who embraced the lepers and who was condemned and eventually criminalized for healing the blind on the Sabbath. All of us . . . need to embrace, not just any Jesus but Him who calls us to the hard choices of discipleship in our day."[56]

Warren's remarks about the vague Christian faith preached in most middle-class parishes merit consideration. One of the most important things parishes can do for married couples is to help them to live out their marriage as Christian calling. This will not mean downplaying the significance of marriage and family but striving to transform them in light of contemporary Catholic theology. John Kavanaugh writes that "the entire life of Christ, is a testimony received in faith that we are redeemed by a God-made-vulnerable in loving creation, and that we are fulfilled only in our irreplaceably unique self-donation."[57] Following Kavanaugh, I have argued that Christian life involves pursuing strong relationships in the home and fulfilling responsibilities to others through practices of resistance. Parishes can make resistance more difficult, but they can also play a crucial role in making Christian life more possible for the majority of Catholics.

Parishes should begin by actively encouraging upwardly mobile Catholic spouses to critically reflect on the pace of their lives so that they have time to form strong relationships among themselves. All who work in the home or outside the home need space to think about the place of work in their lives. Parents need to be in conversation with other parents about how much extracurricular and social activity is too much. If communion in marriages and families is to be sustained, time to be together without hurry is crucial. The communion between the spouses that John Paul II seeks cannot come about when spouses are too busy, both outside the home and in it, to pay attention to the other. Parents and children need to be encouraged to spend time in conversation and play. Churches have a responsibility to help their members let go of certain middle-class assumptions about what makes a good life and remember the virtues of home. The notion of Christianity as a countercultural faith requiring a different way of life should be central to parish culture.[58] It can be brought forward in homilies, speaker series, and short-term, small-group experiences designed to encourage reflection on the pace of middle-class family life and discernment about how to resist it.

In addition, parishes and pastors should be encouraged to develop ties that bind parishioners more closely in community. Without strong community, Catholics lack a place to be nourished and challenged in ways that will help them stand apart from the excesses of American middle-class life. Central to parish life should be the development of small faith-sharing groups where singles, single parents, and married couples can reflect on the struggles of creating countercultural households, pray, and serve the poor together.[59] Without such explicit reflection in community, it is unlikely that Christian marriages or families will look much different from any others. Perhaps during the pre–Vatican II era such groups were unnecessary because the whole of parish life communicated a distinctive message. Today, when commitments are most diffuse and the culture is in many ways more at odds with Christian life, intentional community building and reflection is more important than ever for sustaining Christian marriages. In addition, instead of offering activities that focus solely on entertainment, parishes might encourage parishioners to share tools and skills, start babysitting or food co-ops, plant community gardens, exchange used clothing, care for the sick or elderly in their neighborhoods, or mentor young married couples. These sorts of activities encourage interdependence, simple living, and questioning of middle-class norms. David Matzko McCarthy writes that a wedding binds a couple closer together and binds the two more closely together in the church.[60] Through encouraging different activities directed to a higher purpose, parishes can bind couples together and bind them to other Christians in friendship. These sorts of friendships are unlikely to develop if parishioners only see each other at dances, carnivals, and progressive dinners. Social events play an essential role in forming relationships, but parishioners also need ways to serve each other and come together around common interests more significant than their own good. It is through these kinds of efforts that their sense of community will grow.

With a foundation of shared reflection and community, service can be placed at the center of parish life, and parishes can help families grow in solidarity with those in need. A majority of parishes today do not provide service on site, but more parishes should consider starting programs offering food, legal help, employment assistance, or mentoring or adopting particular sites where families can engage in service together. If parishioners' energies are not tapped out from more mundane social activities, they may be more available for substantial service—not just a once or twice a year delivery of food baskets or presents—but ongoing commitments to people in need. While other ministries are also important, Christian parishes are particularly obligated to orient families to this essential practice.

Service as Family Practice

In *Ecclesia in America*, John Paul II makes perhaps his strongest argument for direct service to the poor. The pope places encounter with Christ at the heart of Christian life and identifies three sources of that encounter: scripture, prayer, and the poor.[61] He believes that encountering Christ will reveal the truth of human interconnectedness and lead to genuine solidarity with the needy.[62] Convinced that only encounter leads to true conversion, he returns again and again to the theme of finding Christ in the poor, whose suffering reminds us of Christ's suffering.[63] Like the early church fathers before him, John Paul II directs his listeners to go to those to whom they would rather not go, assuring them that the practice of direct service is not the calling of a few, but essential to Christian life.

Service is enjoined upon Christians as an "imperative of faith" in the central narratives of the Christian tradition and in the person of Jesus.[64] The story of the Last Judgment (Matt. 25:31–46) tells us not only that service to the poor is the criterion by which we will be judged but that Christ so identifies with the poor that in feeding them we are feeding him.[65] In John 13:14–15, right before the Passion begins, Jesus enacts the service he enjoins, washing his disciples' feet in a shocking reversal of roles and an unambiguous illustration of what it means to be human.[66] No other commandment is given the privileged place of love of neighbor, nor is any other linked so closely to love of God. Jesus teaches that to be holy is to give our lives for others (John 15:13).[67] It is difficult to imagine how service could be more central to Christian faith.

Service to the poor is important not just because it is commanded but because it is needed. When people close to our homes are hungry, suffering from violence, without shelter, or in need of jobs, of all the things we choose to do on a free evening or Saturday afternoon, service should have priority. As Kavanaugh says, "Social action is not the preserve of some special-interest group . . . because there are social conditions which minimize the very possibility of experiencing love, hope, and faith. Destitution, degrading prisons, world hunger, and armament are affairs of spirituality. The human spirit is at stake, not 'just' the body."[68] Those who are less needy can give hope to those who may have lost all hope.[69] Service has the potential to transform broken lives, and thus it should command our energies.

Somehow, despite the imperatives from scripture, tradition, and the reality of human need, families have often been excused from service. Perhaps children are asked to bring canned food to school, adults put together food baskets for Thanksgiving, or parents adopt a family for Christmas, but most of year, most of the time, the service families engage in is directed toward their own families, schools, and parishes. Because those groups are more and more homogeneous, the needy remain untouched on the other side of town. Families, it is thought, cannot be asked to bear another burden, and generally they are not asked to do so.

Kavanaugh challenges this norm by asking laypeople to tithe their time to the needy, making an example of a mother of three. He insists that, in addition to serving her family, "it will be valuable for her to have some kind of continuing and regular contact with the very poor, the dying, the lonely, the handicapped. I mean by this not only organizational or support work, but immediate contact."[70] When asked what Americans could do to help the poor in her native Brazil, a poor woman named Maria da Silva Miguel, interviewed by the late photojournalist Mev Puleo, echoed Kavanaugh's plea: "God isn't responsible for the suffering here. People are responsible—the powerful, the rich people who want to be richer. They forget about the poor, who are becoming more and more poor. . . . So I ask God to open their hearts. I ask God to make the powerful have compassion on the poor."[71]

Direct service works like nothing else to increase compassion, in part through encouraging a recognition of privilege. Maria da Silva Miguel points out that the people in a position to help her are rich, but most are unable to see this without encountering people like her. Safe within the confines of middle- and upper-class neighborhoods, it is easy to feel as though everyone has as much or more than we do. Everyone we know is struggling to keep up with bills for tuition, extracurricular activities, clothes, home repair and remodeling, the modest yearly vacation, mortgage, utilities, and so forth. But walking into a shelter or soup kitchen throws our privilege into sharp relief: our shoes, haircuts, and jeans are of a different quality. Our cars look out of place. We are suddenly conscious of the value of our purses, wallets, or cellphones. Encountering those who are truly struggling enables us to think differently. Toinha Lima Barros, interviewed by Mev Puleo in 1987, identified herself as poor because she supported her family of five on forty-two dollars a month, but she still devoted huge reserves of energy to helping those poorer than herself.[72] Talking to people who live on very little makes middle-class privilege much clearer.

Working directly with the poor reveals not only the privilege of the rich but also the poverty of the rich. Liberation for the poor is liberation for the rich as well. Barros claims, "I believe that with the liberation of the poor, the rich person will lose his or her fear. We have to convince the rich that we're struggling for liberation, not for the misery of the rich. We don't want to see rich people begging in the streets! . . . Equality for all people—this is liberation from fear!"[73] This is why Kavanaugh says that service is not so much about what the rich can give the poor but about how the poor allow the rich to see their own neediness. Those who are wounded, he says, "have an unequalled power to educate us to our pretenses, our fears, and the rejection of our humanity. . . . They bear the wounds of humanity, visible before all, reminding us of our most dependent, fragile beginnings, of our diminishment and our dying, of our ultimate inability to manage and control either our bodies or our world."[74] In coming to know their poverty we recognize both our gifts and our needs.

The connection between service and growth in other areas of family life cannot be overestimated, for care for others, especially the poor, encourages an awareness of neediness that is fundamental. Stronger faith "emerges out of the conviction of one's own poverty and connectedness to that of others."[75] It is precisely the recognition of human vulnerability or incompleteness that comes in service to the marginalized that makes possible growth in communion.[76] Thus, as families serve together, they may find themselves more able to approach relationships inside the family with humility and a willingness to sacrifice, more ready to risk intimacy, more able to endure small sacrifices to eat more justly, more willing to welcome sinners like themselves to the table, more joyful about spending less in order to give more money away, and more conscious of their need for prayer and worship. Direct service is practice in love, a school of virtue with the potential to transform those who make it an essential part of their lives.

Some may argue that intelligent and diligent work for structural change at higher levels is more necessary than ongoing personal contact with the needy. Those who are gifted with skills that can contribute to such change, it may be argued, would be better off spending their time organizing big projects rather than engaging in direct service. The need for great minds to work on the problem of poverty is undeniable. Clearly, much more can be done at the global and national levels that would greatly help people in need. However, finding solutions to poverty is long-term work that requires knowledge of poverty from below. Dean Brackley, who has lived and worked with the poor in Brooklyn and San Salvador, suggests that the prospects for top-down political change are bleak if reform proceeds from afar. Rather, he says, "the world needs a critical mass of people who will respond to suffering, who are ready for long-term commitment, and who will make wise choices along the way. Without such 'new human beings,' I doubt that any amount of money, sophisticated strategies, or even structural change will make our world much more human."[77] For the sake of the world and those who suffer, Brackley believes the willingness to serve—or better, to suffer with—is necessary.

Yet direct service is important not only for the sake of the poor but for the sake of those Brackley calls members of his "middle class tribe," for they need contact with those who struggle daily to survive in order to realize how the comforts of middle-class society "induce in us a chronic low-grade confusion about what is really important in life: namely, life itself and love."[78] The poor teach us not only about poverty but also about how to live with gratitude and joy despite suffering.[79] The emphasis on joy is a necessary correction to Kavanaugh's focus on how the poor teach us of our emptiness. When we see through regular contact with the poor that those with so much less than we have laugh, sing, dance, celebrate, and hope more than we are able to despite all our gifts, a new gratitude and joy can take root in us. This too can overflow in communion inside the family, in intimacy, in a willingness to sacrifice time and resources for others that is born of the sure knowledge that our lives are very good.

The recognition that the poor have at least as much to give us as we have to give them eventually transforms service into accompaniment. In a book devoted to hearing the stories of North Americans who have spent time with the poor of El Salvador, Laetitia Bordes defines accompaniment as keeping company, being with, or walking with people in need.[80] She notes that North Americans went to El Salvador to accompany Salvadorans in the 1980s as a way of recognizing the evil committed in their name by the United States, but often "they discovered that it was the poor who accompanied them and led them to a greater depth in their heart, a depth that lay unexplored, to find there treasures they never dreamed existed."[81] They speak with gratitude of being unconditionally accepted and forgiven by people who had been victimized by the policies of the United States and of how that forgiving love freed them to become more loving in their own lives.[82] In their accompaniment, they find meaning and communion that the middle class tribe often lacks. One volunteer in El Salvador writes, "I feel an exuberance in being alive and being where I am. I feel like I am just being born, that there is new life in me. And it is related to feeling a part of the struggle for life here, of feeling connected to others because we are putting our energy towards a broader vision beyond just our individual selves."[83] Shared struggle can bring meaning to the lives of Christian families, as they give their energy to something more than their own success.

Conclusion: Community, Practice, and Service

Integrating the practice of service into Christian family life can only happen if parishes can sustain a culture in which Christian discipleship is imbued and absorbed. Michael Warren insightfully points out that today's Catholic parishes count on religious education programs to pass on the faith. However, one hour a week of religious education is far from sufficient when "not integral to the lived life of actual communities. . . . The main formative agent is the believing community, and, its verbal declarations notwithstanding, its communal or corporate commitments and way of viewing reality are, for better or worse, the key formative factors."[84] What a Christian community does with its time, people, and money says much about the people who make up the community. The Christian tradition must be practiced in a rich variety of ways if it is to shape the families of contemporary believers. The most profound challenge facing parishes is finding new ways to help parishioners live out a tradition in which many if not most have not been enculturated. If parishes take up this challenge and strive to become places of serious transformation, Christian families will have a fighting chance of becoming what they are called to be.

Direct service ought to be a central practice of Christian family life, a key way of resisting depersonalization in the home and outside it. Tithing time may be a helpful rule for individuals, but it is less easily applied to families. I suggest instead that the practice of direct service, along with the practices of sex, eating, and tithing, should be a regular part of family life.[85] Married couples should make service a priority from the beginning of their life to-gether. When children arrive, the practice may have to be adapted, but it should not be wholly dropped in favor of service to middle-class commu-nities. Rather, families should strive to make service to the marginalized an ongoing part of their lives together. Service cannot be left to single Chris-tians, even if single Christians have unique opportunities to serve. Families need to move beyond their comfortable isolation to encounter those on the margins of life, those "who bear the wounds of humanity, visible before all, reminding us of our most dependent fragile-beginnings, of our diminish-ment and dying, of our ultimate inability to manage and control either our bodies or our world."[86] Being with those who have little and give much breaks through the numbness that is the sickness of our middle-class tribe, allowing joy, sadness, and passion to seep in. If families commit to this practice, they will find an anecdote to "emptiness in busyness" in commu-nion—in richer relationships at home, in community with fellow believers, in service to and friendship with those in need, and in a deeper sense of gratitude and connection to the God who made us all.

Notes

This chapter is based in part on two earlier works: Julie Hanlon Rubio, "Sustaining Marriage in the Post–Vatican II Catholic Parish," in *Sustaining Marriage*, ed. Cynthia Doeski (Chestnut Ridge, NY: Crossroad, 2008); and "A Familial Vocation beyond the Home," *CTSA Proceedings* 63 (2008): 71–83.

1. Kavanaugh, *Following Christ in a Consumer Society*, 126.
2. Ibid., 75.
3. Ibid., 64.
4. *Sollicitudo rei socialis*, no. 28.
5. Anecdotally, I hear familiar laments that friendships with depth are no longer a possibility and constant references to busyness. On the flip side, interest in spirituality and flexible work arrangements that allow more time with family is high.
6. *Familiaris consortio*.
7. Ibid., no. 44.
8. Paul Wilkes, *Excellent Catholic Parishes: The Guide to the Best Places and Practices* (New York: Paulist, 2001), xii.
9. James D. Davidson, *Catholicism in Motion: The Church in American Society* (Liguori, MO: Liguori, 2005), 15.
10. Among the "givens," consider the following: elaborate children's birthday par-ties, sports games and practices with accompanying parental responsibilities, school holiday parties, extended family gatherings and gift-giving traditions,

parent involvement in school and parish fundraisers including sales, auctions, and carnivals, and so on.

11. James T. Fisher, *Catholics in America* (New York: Oxford University Press, 2000), 121. Not all parishes were dominated by one ethnic group. When parishes first developed in the late 1800s, some were territorial and others were national or ethnic. Still, ethnic and religious cultures were often intertwined and mutually supporting. See Gerald P. Fogarty, "The Parish and Community in American Catholic History," reprinted in *Building the American Catholic City*, ed. Brian C. Mitchell (New York: Garland, 1988), 1–25.

12. John Kosa, "The Emergence of a Catholic Middle Class," in *Catholics/U.S.A.: Perspectives on Social Change*, ed. William T. Liu and Nathaniel J. Pallone (New York: John Wiley and Sons, 1970), 16.

13. George A. Kelly, *The Second Spring of the Church in America* (South Bend, IN: St. Augustine's Press, 2001), 7.

14. Davidson, *Catholicism in Motion*, 136.

15. Fogarty, "Parish and Community," 9.

16. Andrew M. Greeley and Mary Greeley, "The Parish as Organic Community," in *How to Save the Catholic Church*, ed. Mary Greeley Durkin (New York: Viking, 1984), 173.

17. Ibid., 169. See also Philip Murnion, "The Catholic Parish in the Public Square," in *American Catholics and Civic Engagement: A Distinctive Voice*, ed. Margaret O'Brien Steinfels (Lanham, MD: Sheed & Ward, 2004), 76.

18. Michael Warren, *Faith, Culture, and the Worshipping Community: Shaping the Practice of the Local Church*, rev. ed. (Washington, DC: Pastoral Press, 1993), 40.

19. William V. D'Antonio, James D. Davidson, Dean R. Hoge, and Mary L. Gautier, *American Catholics Today: New Realities of Their Faith and Their Church* (Lanham, MD: Sheed & Ward, 2007). The authors show changes in Mass attendance (55) and Catholic identity (41) over time. Catholic practice and identity peeked in the mid-1960s.

20. Fogarty, "Parish and Community," 25.

21. Davidson, *Catholicism in Motion*, 12.

22. Ibid. See also Kosa, "Emergence of a Catholic Middle Class," 24, who predicts problems that would arise from Catholics' new position in American society in 1962.

23. Integration is incomplete. Even in 1994, Catholics were still highly concentrated in the urban Northeast and upper Midwest. Fisher, *Catholics in America*, 163. In addition, new immigrants (Mexican, Filipino, Polish, Dominican Republican, and Vietnamese) continue to provide a fresh influx of Catholics who are poorer, less educated, more closely tied to ethnic parishes, and less assimilated. Davidson, *Catholics in Motion*, 19. Still, general trends are clear.

24. William V. D'Antonio, James D. Davidson, Dean R. Hoge, and Ruth A. Wallace, *Laity: American and Catholic; Transforming the Church* (Kansas City, MO: Sheed & Ward, 1996), 10.

25. Fisher, *Catholics in America*, 162.

26. Day writes that she chose the Catholic Church because it "held the allegiance of the masses of people in all the cities where I had lived. They poured in and

out of her doors on Sundays and holy days, for novenas and missions." *The Long Loneliness: The Autobiography of Dorothy Day* (San Francisco: Harper & Row, 1952), 139.

27. James D. Davidson and Suzanne C. Fournier, "Recent Research on Catholic Parishes: A Research Note," *Review of Religious Research* 48, no. 1 (2006): 74.

28. D'Antonio et al., *Laity*, 127. See also Mary Beth Celio, "Celebrating Catholic Parishes," March 7, 2001 (Seattle, WA: Catholic Archdiocese of Seattle), 15, who reports that the size of the average parish staff is now 5.4, and more than three-fourths of parishes have difficulty recruiting volunteers.

29. Davidson and Fournier, "Recent Research on Catholic Parishes," 72. The average parish size increased from 1,881 in 1959 to 3,097 in 2000.

30. See Celio, "Celebrating Catholic Parishes," 2, who lists vibrant parish life and major contributions to the welfare of communities as "Reassuring FACT findings." In "Recent Research on Catholic Parishes," Davidson and Fournier note the problem that many surveys (such as the one upon which Celio relies) target pastors rather than laypeople.

31. David C. Leege, "The American Catholic Parish," in *American Catholic Identity: Essays in an Age of Change,* ed. Francis J. Butler (Kansas City, MO: Sheed & Ward, 1994), 78.

32. See Mich, *Catholic Social Teaching and Movements,* 30–75, who describes American Catholic social movements in the early twentieth century.

33. Kelly, *Second Spring,* 7.

34. Murnion, "Catholic Parish in the Public Square," 84. Poor parishes have much more to offer in this area. Ibid., 85.

35. D'Antonio et al., *American Catholics Today,* 93. This is the only teaching that is more important to millennials than to other generations of Catholics, though the percentage gap (91–84%) is not wide.

36. Celio, "Celebrating Catholic Parishes," 10. Celio notes that the average parish supports 6.1 ongoing programs, but this figure includes teen activities, altar guild, prayer groups, and so forth. The majority of ongoing service opportunities (averaging 4.1) that are provided are to the elderly and sick, with a significant number of parishes also providing cash or vouchers for people in need. The percentage of parishes offering ongoing service involving contact with the poor is much lower. Ibid., 11.

37. D'Antonio et al., *American Catholics Today,* 27.

38. Davidson, *American Catholics in Motion,* 135.

39. Ibid., 68.

40. D'Antonio et al., *American Catholics Today,* 121.

41. In the 1950s, more than half of Catholic children attended parish schools. Today the figure is closer to 15 percent. See National Catholic Educational Association, *United States Catholic Elementary and Secondary Schools, 2006–2007: The Annual Statistical Report on Schools, Enrollment, and Staffing* (Washington, DC: National Catholic Education Association, 2007).

42. Davidson, *American Catholics in Motion,* 134.

43. Ibid., 182.

44. D'Antonio et al., *American Catholics Today,* 149.

45. A recent survey found that parishes offer an average of four organized ministries, though many offer more. See Murnion, "Catholic Church in the Public Square," 73.
46. CYO or CYC sports programs are offered by 50 percent of parishes. Celio, "Celebrating Catholic Parishes," 11. In my neighborhood parish, games are scheduled from Friday night until Sunday night, and children commonly play one or two sports each season. For families with multiple children, this means most weekends are spent driving to and watching games.
47. Teen activities are the most common program offered in Catholic parishes, followed by Altar Guild and Knight of Columbus. Celio, "Celebrating Catholic Parishes," 10. Most of these groups do not have extensive service components.
48. A recent men's club advertisement at a local parish exemplifies this problem and points to the related issue of social mobility. The parish men invite people to an annual sports trivia night with no observable connection to Christian faith. Tickets divide parishioners into four groups according to how much money they have to spend. Twenty dollars buys dinner, an open wine and beer bar, and unlimited peanuts and popcorn. However, those willing to give seventy-five dollars receive "premium padded chair seating," a "personal waiter," "complimentary top shelf liquor," and "VIP treatment."
49. See Peter Steinfels, *A People Adrift: The Crisis of the Roman Catholic Church* (New York: Simon & Schuster, 2003), 203–52.
50. The most common social services offered by parishes are ministry in nursing homes or hospitals, but there are no good figures as to how many parishioners participate in these off-site ministries. Next are cash or voucher assistance and food pantries, programs that may be run by pastors and parish staff. Participation in direct service to the poor such as prison ministry and substance abuse counseling is far less common. Celio, "Celebrating Catholic Parishes," 11.
51. Last spring, my local parish bulletin included an advertisement in the form of a letter from a child begging her parents to buy her a ride bracelet for $25 so that she could ride all day at the parish carnival. This is a high price for a day of entertainment, especially for families with more than one child.
52. *Familiaris consortio*, no. 37.
53. Greeley and Greeley, "Parish as Organic Community," 173.
54. Murnion, "Catholic Church in the Public Square," 81. Murnion notes that these groups deal with Catholic social teaching less by engaging in work for political change and more in encouraging changes in family life and work places, thus attesting to their focus on the shape of everyday life. Ibid., 82. For a broader view of the effects of small communities, see Bernard J. Lee, *The Catholic Experience of Small Christian Communities* (Mahwah, NJ: Paulist, 2000).
55. Davidson, *Catholics in Motion*, 138.
56. Warren, *Faith, Culture, and the Worshipping Community*, 118.
57. Kavanaugh, *Following Christ in a Consumer Society*, 122.
58. The Ekklesia Project aims to grow countercultural churches from below. See www.ekklesiaproject.org.
59. A good model is the Christian Family Movement, www.cfm.org. However, small communities that include households of all kinds can also be good vehicles for critical analysis of culture, spiritual support, and communal action.

60. McCarthy, "Becoming One Flesh," 276.
61. *Ecclesia in America*, no. 12.
62. Ibid., no. 52.
63. Ibid., no. 12.
64. Kavanaugh, *Following Christ in a Consumer Society*, 136.
65. *Ecclesia in America*, no. 18.
66. Foster, *Challenge of the Disciplined Life*, 228.
67. *Ecclesia in America*, no. 30. The pope defines holiness as carrying on Christ's work of love, "especially towards the poor, the sick, the needy (cf. Lk. 10:25ff.)."
68. Kavanaugh, *Following Christ in a Consumer Society*, 136.
69. *Ecclesia in America*, no. 18.
70. Kavanaugh, *Following Christ in a Consumer Society*, 189.
71. Maria da Silva Miguel, quoted in Mev Puleo, *The Struggle Is One: Voices and Visions of Liberation* (Albany, NY: SUNY, 1994), 18.
72. Puleo, *Struggle Is One*, 59–60.
73. Ibid., 71.
74. Kavanaugh, *Following Christ in a Consumer Society*, 189.
75. Warren, *Faith, Culture, and the Worshipping Community*, 66.
76. Kavanaugh, *Following Christ in a Consumer Society*, 204. Knowing the truth of our humanity—our incompleteness—allows us to be vulnerable and radically open to relationships with God and others, according to Kavanaugh.
77. Brackley, *Call to Discernment in Troubled Times*, 3.
78. Ibid., 37.
79. Ibid. Brackley speaks of the joy (201) and gratitude (214) he has learned from the poor.
80. Laetitia Bordes, ed., *Our Hearts Were Broken: A Spirituality of Accompaniment* (Oakland, CA: Red Star Black Rose, 2000), 62.
81. Ibid.
82. Ibid., 76–77.
83. Ibid., 145. Christine Reesor is quoting from her own journal entry on December 9, 1988.
84. Warren, *Faith, Culture, and the Worshipping Community*, 66.
85. An example of regular service would be an ongoing weekly commitment to a Catholic Worker house that might evolve over the years as children's abilities grow and change to include cooking meals, tutoring or playing with children, and mentoring men or women.
86. Kavanaugh, *Following Christ in a Consumer Society*, 189.

CHAPTER EIGHT

Family Prayer as Practice of Resistance

Prayer: Beyond Platitudes

Praying is perhaps the most important practice for Christian families. Yet addressing family prayer adequately is more difficult than it may first appear. One does not have to read far into any Christian text on prayer to find the affirmation, "The family that prays together stays together." Stanley Hauerwas questions the appropriateness of this aphorism, pointing out how an overemphasis on family stability can displace the fundamental role of the church and misconstrue the point of prayer. He asserts that "if we have not first learned what it means to be faithful to self and other in the church, then we have precious little chance of learning it at home."[1] Character, Hauerwas says, is formed in Christian community and through Christian tradition. When people say, "the family that prays together stays together," they suggest that family is more significant than church or that prayer is good simply because it strengthens family ties. Instead, Hauerwas suggests that the church as first family of Christian believers provides the primary foundation for ordinary families.[2] While the role of the Christian community is important, families, I have argued throughout this book, play a key role in forming believers in the faith. Thus prayer ought to be a practice of the home as well as the church. Family prayer is a good practice for families because it has the potential to draw spouses and their children closer together, connect them with God, and strengthen them in their common struggle to live a more meaningful person-centered life in and outside the home.

However, coming together to pray is not necessarily easy for modern families. Many give up on it altogether. The busyness of modern family life leaves little time for constructing meaningful family rituals, little energy for bible study, and little patience for quiet reflection. Morning and evening prayer become more difficult when family members rise and eat breakfast at different times before going off to multiple job sites and/or schools; when working parents bear the burden of getting everyone out of the house in the morning and taking charge of chores and meal preparation in the evening; when children are shuttled to an increasing number of practices and lessons; when TV, computer, and cellphone are poised to interrupt at any time of the day; and when spirituality is more likely to be sought in private than in community with others.[3] Bonnie Miller-McLemore notes that even the best-intentioned people of faith often end up giving up on family devotions because of time pressures.[4] She calls for thinking less about traditional practices and more about being attentive to the presence of God in everyday life.[5] Such attentiveness is a good thing to cultivate. Still, though the practice of prayer is no doubt difficult to sustain in the context of modern living, it is crucial if parents and children want to see the rest of life through the eyes of faith and practice resistance to more typical forms of middle-class family life.

Yet the experience of contemporary families does not sit well with the advice from typical Christian prayer books.[6] For the most part, these books assume uniform Christian belief between husband and wife and among children, and they imply that if families were sufficiently motivated to put aside the time and overcome feelings of discomfort, prayer would come to be a joyful practice rather than a continuing problem. However, if my discussions with students in fourteen years of teaching courses in marriage and family at Catholic universities are a reliable indicator, prayer is not a common practice in Christian homes. Only the most committed couples pray during engagement or in the early years of marriage. Even after children arrive, very few Christian families consistently practice anything but grace before meals. Bible reading, rosaries, and other intentional practices are even rarer among post–Vatican II Catholic families.[7] Sustaining a vision of one's family as a Christian community seems to be an extremely difficult task.[8]

An important contributing factor to the neglect of prayer may be that a unity of belief is not as pervasive as one would think. At least 40 percent of Catholics today marry a spouse of a different Christian faith or a different religion, and this number continues to rise.[9] The substantive differences between spouses of different faiths can no longer be ignored or discussed as rare exceptions. In addition, different levels of commitment to faith are even more common. Even if they are able to pray with young children, parents may do so without a strong foundation between the two of them, and if so it is unlikely that the experience will carry them through later stages of marriage marked by adolescent doubt and rebellion, let alone an empty nest. Moreover, though prayer books blithely assume parents can take up their appointed roles as leaders in the domestic church, many parents are less certain in their faith and less consistent in their practice than they would like to be. Recognizing parental differences and limitations is crucial to approaching the practice of prayer realistically. Children, too, are more complex than the family prayer literature allows. Although many accept the faith of their parents without question, most of today's Catholic children grow up outside the comfort and certainty of ethnic enclaves described in chapter 7, and they are far less likely to sustain strong faith in adulthood.[10]

The image of family as domestic church that is brought forward by John Paul II and many lay theologians seems, then, somewhat ill-suited for the reality of Christian family life.[11] For theologians who write about the domestic church, the problem is often how to adequately recognize and celebrate the sacred in the home. However, if parents and children differ in religious inclination and harbor doubt along with faith, joint religious practice becomes more complicated, more like the dilemmas of interreligious families that are treated in this literature—if at all—as exceptions.[12] We must discern just what sort of churches today's religiously diverse families can be.

This chapter is an attempt to deal honestly with the problems of prayer in contemporary Christian families, that is to ask, "In a world where uniformity of belief and shared devotion are increasingly rare, what sort of family spiritual practice is appropriately sought?" In answer, it first briefly reviews the history of Christian thinking on parental religious responsibilities. Second, it examines data on interfaith marriages and the spiritual development of children in order to understand the religious diversity of contemporary families. Finally, it suggests a practice of prayer for contemporary families who seek a way to "be church" together—despite considerable difficulties—in order to better know themselves, deepen their communion with each other, and grow in solidarity and compassion for others.

A Brief History of Christian Thought on Parental Religious Duties

Why would Christian families want to pray together? Despite all the developments of the last forty years that make belief less obvious and more difficult to pass on, most parents continue to seek some exposure to religion for their children. They believe children should be raised in a faith tradition rather than being left to choose their own path from all available options.[13] Most Catholic parents see that their children receive the sacraments, attend religious education classes, go to Mass at least some of the time, and understand that there is a God who loves them. Yet many parents perceive that their duty to pass on the faith requires more of them, so they turn to prayer. In seeing the seriousness of their parental obligation to form their children in Christian faith, they are on solid historical ground.

A major emphasis of historical Christian theology on children is the parental duty to nurture and rear offspring. The New Testament offers only a few references to child rearing, but those texts express similar concerns with rearing obedient and believing children.[14] In the second century, portions of the *Didache, The Letter of Barnabas,* and Polycarp's *Letter to the Philippians* instruct parents to teach children to fear God, using force if necessary.[15] Only in the third century does a whole chapter devoted to children appear in the *Didascalia.* In it parents are warned that neglecting religious formation may result in their children's adopting the morals of pagans.[16] Their responsibility for their children's salvation is quite clear. The later fourth-century *Apostolic Constitutions* goes even further, with assurances that parents will be punished for their children's sins.[17]

The fourth-century father John Chrysostom wrote two key texts on child rearing, both more substantive than anything else that had appeared thus far but agreeing with earlier wisdom. He roots parental obligations in the special, biological connection between parents and children and calls parents to tend to their moral and religious rearing duties. Like many earlier writers, Chrysostom puts the souls of children in parents' hands, claiming that "whether a child inherits the kingdom of heaven relies upon the care he or she receives from parents."[18] This strong sense of parents' ultimate responsibility comes from Chrysostom's belief that a child is more intimately linked to her parents than to anyone else. He says, in *On Marriage and Family*, "The child is a bridge connecting mother to father, so the three become one flesh. . . . And here the bridge is formed from the substance of each! Just as the head and the body are one, so it is with the child. That is why Scripture does not say, 'They shall be one flesh.' But they shall be joined together into one flesh, namely the child."[19]

The Christian tradition sees religious formation as the most significant responsibility of Christian parents so closely connected to offspring, yet throughout Church history theologians have complained that parents' efforts are less than adequate. In his "Address on Vainglory and the Right Way for Parents to Bring Up Their Children," Chrysostom criticizes his culture, mourning the emphasis parents put on giving a new child new clothes and wealth, when they could be focusing on teaching virginity, sobriety, discipline, and contempt of wealth and fame. Instead, he exhorts them, "Raise up an athlete for Christ."[20] Chrysostom seems to want parents to think of a child differently in order that they might reconceive their own duties. Parents are for him artists or sculptors, shaping their children's character. He urges them to be conscious that "when we teach our children to be good, to be gentle, to be forgiving . . . we instill virtue in their souls, and reveal the image of God within them."[21] The parent's role is to be a co-creator whose "work" is a reflection of God.

This ideal is shared by many other Christian thinkers. Martin Luther calls parents "apostles to children" and advocates the teaching of the catechism at home as well as at church and school.[22] John Calvin, too, emphasized instruction in piety and stated that the primary duty of parents is to teach godliness and the submission of worldly desires to the common good.[23] Although Menno Simons (along with the Mennonite martyrs) believed that faith could call parents to leave children in extreme circumstances, he held that when parents were able to remain with children, their most important task was to nurture their children's faith and character and help them work out their salvation.[24] Horace Bushnell, author of the popular nineteenth-century work *Christian Nurture,* counseled parents that nurture was a long process involving specific practices and emphasized the importance of parental role in faith formation, saying, "Religion never thoroughly penetrates life until it becomes domestic."[25] This strong sense that parents have a crucial role in faith formation is a consistent theme in the Christian tradition, which continues in the present day in frequent references to parents as primary educators of their children in all things religious.[26]

However, in the writings of most Christian theologians, even when moral and spiritual nurture is given the highest priority, parents are not the only ones seen as capable of that nurture. Nor is it the case that parents hold no other significant obligations. From the beginning of the Christian tradition, discipleship to Christ is the primary obligation of all Christians and cannot be overridden by the demands of parenthood. In fact, no historical Christian author gives parents full responsibility for moral or spiritual formation of their children. Rather, most theologians assume that parents share the task of rearing with churches, schools, and communities. One need not speak only of Calvin's Geneva to drive home this point, though his experiment is surely a primary example of corearing.[27] One might also look to the Mennonites' sense of communal responsibility for children, especially (but not only) in times of persecution, or to Luther, who glorified the day to day duties of child rearing by parents and called parents "apostles" to their children, while holding that parents shared the responsibility to catechize with the schools and the church.[28] Even when Jesus tells his listeners not to lead a child astray, he speaks to his disciples, not specifically to parents.[29] Indeed, though Jesus strongly upholds lifelong marriage (Mark 10:6–9), there is no record of his addressing parental responsibility for children. In short, religious formation is at the center of historical Christian discourse on children, with parents viewed as the primary, but by no means exclusive, shapers of their children.

The extent to which this weighty but not exclusive parental responsibility was carried out is difficult to ascertain. In the pre–Vatican II U.S. Catholic community, the parish and school played central roles in the religious formation of children.[30] In the home, rosaries, devotions, and prayers at mealtimes and before bed were typical of family piety, and Mass attendance and reception of the major sacraments were assumed.[31] Mary Reed Newland's well-read 1954 book, *We and Our Children: Molding the Child in Christian Living,* offered parents guidance as they sought to aid their children's struggle for holiness in a dangerous world. In this unified Catholic subculture, "mutually reinforcing home and church influences sought to equip young Catholics for the fight, furnishing children's imaginations with luminous images of saints, angels, and the devil, and of heaven, hell, and purgatory."[32]

In the post–Vatican II Catholic world, as many Catholics moved out of ethnic and religious enclaves into the suburbs, the role of the parish and school declined.[33] It was up to parents to protect children from the excesses of the culture and train them in the home to accept faith. Lay Catholic organizations such as the Christian Family Movement emphasized the need to build family spirituality so that families could transform the world around them. There was more scholarly attention to family among theologians who saw potential in the revived imagery of the "domestic church," but most families who were not connected to movements were unaware of their new lofty mission.[34] Family Mass attendance declined, and "structured, individually focused devotions such as the rosary gave way somewhat to free-form, interpersonal practices like spontaneous group prayers before meals or bedtime, or prayer groups rather than Altar and Rosary Guilds."[35] In the 1970s and 1980s, in response to revived interest in the domestic church, numerous books encouraged families to "add a spiritual dimension to family life" with a combination of traditional and spontaneous prayers and home-based rituals such as name day celebrations and family reconciliation services.[36] References to parental responsibility for the souls of their children have been tempered by a recognition that parents have limited control over their children and a widely shared sense that it is counterproductive to force children to take part in family practices they find meaningless.[37] But the belief in a primary (though shared) parental responsibility to shape the children they have brought into the world with God's help is constant. Moreover, the dominant assumption of most texts, whether popular or academic, is that children will come to appreciate the opportunity to practice their faith with their parents, if only their parents will answer the demands of their calling. The reality of diversity in faith within families remains unacknowledged and unexplored.

Interfaith Families as Models

Interfaith families (in which spouses who practice different religions or different Christian faiths are united) are the most obvious example of diversity in faith, and they are becoming more and more numerous. Before Vatican II, intermarriage between Catholics and Protestant spouses was all but impossible inside the church, and most Catholics avoided it. Today, however, 40 percent of Catholics are in interchurch or interreligious marriages, and official Catholic teaching recognizes the validity of their unions.[38] In their marriage patterns, Catholics mix with those of other faiths almost as much as other Americans do.[39] Changes in liturgical rules and greater openness to other faiths, both hallmarks of Vatican II, contributed to the new situation, as did the growing integration of Catholics into a pluralistic American society.

Yet Catholic theological writers on marriage and children rarely allude to the possibility of mixed marriage and certainly do not assume that nearly half their audience is in this situation. Existing brief discussions in the work of theologians are limited to general assertions of the need for understanding and dialogue.[40] This failure to recognize and respond to diversity is unfortunate, for those advocating various beliefs and practices present arguments that assume unified families when in fact fewer and fewer of such families exist.

There is a need to address this problem and examine its relevance to all couples, for interfaith couples are not so different from same-faith couples. No doubt, interfaith marriages have greater challenges, and the differences between same-church and interfaith marriage should not be overlooked, but often the gap between the two groups is overstated. For instance, in a large Creighton University study, researchers found that 78 percent of same-church couples reported no differences in ideas about how much emphasis to place on the religious aspect of child rearing, while 63 percent of interchurch couples reported a similar like-mindedness.[41] Note on the one hand that the gap of 15 percent is not overly wide and that the majority in both groups attests to a great deal of like-mindedness. On the other hand, it seems likely that both groups could be overreporting conformity in the context of a general question. As noted earlier, there are many kinds of religious differences that can affect married couples, as no one's faith is just like another's. To cite just one example, a recent worldwide comparative study found that "in most families the mother is the primary figure in the children's religiosity."[42] Popular works on Christian prayer reflect this situation when they allude to the difficulty of getting fathers involved in family spiritual practice.[43] The pervasiveness of this gap shows that there are real differences between many spouses about how much to emphasize religion in child rearing, in that most women are more committed to religious child rearing than their husbands. Thus some plurality of views about faith and how to practice and teach it exists even in same-church families, and this situation must complicate the idea of engaging in shared spiritual practices. In this respect, those in interfaith marriages experience in an explicit way what many same-church families also encounter.

Religious differences in mixed marriages can destabilize marriage in a number of unique ways. Interchurch couples are at greater risk for marital difficulties.[44] Religious affiliation is a predictor of marital stability, and interchurch couples are less religious as a rule, so they are at greater risk right from the beginning.[45] In addition, religious differences limit opportunities for joint religious activities that nurture shared identity and purpose.[46] Interchurch couples are also "most at risk for drift from church belonging and practice."[47] All of these factors contribute to marital instability and make sustaining a common faith life more difficult for couples of different faiths.

Children in interfaith marriages are less likely to remain people of faith in adulthood. Key predictors of religious inheritance include parental religiosity, quality of family relationships, and family structure.[48] The lower religiosity in interchurch families contributes to the diminished possibilities for religious inheritance.[49] In addition, interfaith couples are less likely to emphasize religion in childrearing. Williams and Lawler think it "likely that developing a joint religious life requires a greater effort for interchurch couples."[50] Moreover, though the non-Catholic spouse in a Catholic interfaith marriage is no longer required to promise to raise children to be Catholic, the Catholic spouse must promise to do all in her power to share faith with her children via baptism and child rearing (though religious education remains the responsibility of both parents).[51] Serious obstacles exist for faith formation in interfaith families, and these ought not be overlooked.

R. R. Reno offers a rare glimpse of the pain of interfaith marriage through an analysis of his own experience in an Episcopal-Jewish household. Reno clearly knows the joys of intermarriage, but he also knows the pain and darkness, or what he calls the "blows" of intermarriage. Belying the simple piety of "we're in love so it will all work out," he acknowledges that choosing and practicing different faiths means separation. Reflecting on his daughter's bat mitzvah, he provocatively writes, "My daughter loves me very much, but she is very conscious that this day of her bat mitzvah is also a hating of her father."[52] Choosing to be a Jew, like her mother, means leaving her father outside, renouncing the faith that is everything to him. He can deeply respect and admire her commitment, but he cannot follow her, nor can he deny the sadness her choice brings to both him and his daughter. The pain will not simply dissolve with time.

Yet this is not to say that there is nothing to be gained from interfaith marriage. Reno eloquently describes the way that seeing those he loves embrace another tradition forces him to question his own. As he ponders the significance of a Jewish faith that asks for circumcision for his son and keeping kosher in his kitchen, he wonders if his faith is too spiritual: "Christ was in my heart and on my lips, but was I unmarked in my flesh, unchanged in the brute reality of my life?"[53] The questioning is fruitful, for as Reno admires his wife's dedication—"She was nailing her spiritual journey to the concrete reality of life"—he is led to a deeper appreciation of his own tradition's attempts to link the spiritual to the physical.[54] His unrelentingly honest portrait of the joy and pain of unity in difference illustrates how difficult achieving such unity in practice can be.

Spouses of different faiths who want to build a life together are advised "to strive to understand and respect each other's faith as fully as possible."[55] This does not come naturally for most, and time will be needed if couples are to achieve "mutual respect, mutual appreciation, mutual trust, mutual love, and mutual unity in diversity."[56] John Paul II's words to interchurch couples in 1982—"You live in your marriages the hopes and difficulties of the path to Christian unity"—are instructive, for though we can now better see that these couples prophetically "mark out the path by which divided churches can reach their goal," it is crucial not to overlook the painful and difficult nature of the path itself.[57]

Interchurch couples are models not only for ecumenical dialogue but for all families who seek shared religious practice in spite of differences that could pull them apart. Few couples are totally unified in belief and commitment. One spouse might be more religious while another struggles with her faith. One might be drawn to traditional faith practices while another finds God more easily outside the organized religion to which he belongs. One might be very comfortable as a lifelong adherent of the faith of his childhood, while another practices more cautiously, having converted before marriage. Perhaps the convert's zeal is not matched by the faith of the cradle Catholic. Spouses—even same-church spouses—do not always agree on matters of faith and may find faith to be a source of tension as often as a source of unity. If they are to have any hope of experiencing spiritual unity, they, like interfaith couples, will need to acknowledge the painfulness of holding different beliefs and desiring different practices, explore their differences, and find common ground upon which to build a practice consistent with their respective faiths.

Spouses grounded in their own interfaith spiritual practice should be more ready to take their children's diverse religious needs, beliefs, and doubts seriously, for children only extend the interreligiosity of most families. If good family practice in prayer must respect what moves and grounds both parents, it makes sense that children's distinct faith experiences should also be respected. Adults and children alike approach the prayer table from some point on their individual journey of faith.

Children in contemporary Christian homes are more likely to question the faith of their parents because they encounter on their streets, in their classrooms, among their friends and relatives, and in their own parents people of different faiths and no faith at all. Early on they realize that some people do not go to church every Sunday, many do not adopt Lenten sacrifices, and, certainly, most do not engage in daily family prayer. Millennial Catholics (those born after 1983) are the least likely of all Catholics to claim strong Catholic identity and practice.[58] Thus, although America remains unique among developing countries in its relatively high levels of belief, even here religion becomes a question much earlier and doubt and resistance are more likely to surface.[59] A recent study by the Pew Forum on Religion and Public Life found that 44 percent of Americans have changed their faith affiliation. Sixteen percent of Americans now count themselves as "unaffiliated," more than double the percentage who were raised that way. Moreover, Catholics have suffered the biggest losses in recent years, as 31 percent of Americans were raised Catholic, but only 24 percent now consider themselves Catholic, and even this number reflects the high number of immigrants who are Catholic. Clearly, common faith in families can no longer be taken for granted.[60] Along with the literature on interfaith families, recent research on children's spiritual development provides the basis for a new direction in family prayer. The practice defended in this chapter is rooted in a recognition that children may bring to prayer questions with which adults struggle and doubts adults share.[61]

Understanding more about how children's faith develops is crucial. James Fowler's theory of faith development helpfully shows both children's initial religious capacity and growth in faith over time. Fowler distinguishes four stages: primal (birth to age two), during which parental attachment is crucial to trust formation; intuitive-projective (early childhood), when children are drawn to symbols and stories of good and evil; mythic-literal (middle childhood), when most children see God as a caring, just, distant ruler (though some that he calls "11 year old atheists" see that life is not always fair and "give up believing in a God built along the lines of simple cosmic retribution"); and synthetic-conventional (adolescence), during which identity is the key concern and beliefs are formed via interaction with significant role models.[62] Three later stages are found among adults, though few reach the final stage and some remain stuck in stage four.[63] Fowler shows that children's faith in a personal God develops along with their attachments to parents and friends, personal identity, intellect, and a diversity of experiences that lead them to increasingly complex understandings of faith and ever-broadening social concern. This model, confirmed by ongoing research, affirms that most children have some sort of faith from a fairly young age but need time and experience to progress toward a broader, more mature religious understanding.[64]

However, it is also important to acknowledge that children can have unique spiritual insights. Maria Montessori found that, when given structured freedom and meaningful tasks, children can do much more than adults might imagine. Sofia Cavaletti applied Montessori's insights to create the Catechesis of the Good Shepherd, a program of religious education for young children that assumes children's inherent spirituality.[65] The program moves progressively, honoring Fowler's basic insight that children's faith develops over time, while recognizing the sometimes prophetic voices of children. In praying, singing, and talking together about God, students and teachers grow in faith together. The program continues at home via the prayer table, a nightly ritual in which children's spiritual insights and needs are given a central place.[66]

This emphasis in Catechesis of the Good Shepherd points back to Jesus's radical statement in the gospels that his disciples must become like little children in order to enter the kingdom of God (Matt. 18:1–5; cf. Mark 9:33–37). This insight has not been fully explored in the Christian tradition until recently. Dawn DeVries recalls Friedrich Schleiermacher's relatively unknown, eloquent (if overly enthusiastic) celebration of children's vitality, spontaneity, and purity.[67] Schleiermacher holds up children as models for adults. Instead of telling parents how to break their children's wills or shape their characters, he follows Jesus's lead by putting the child at the center and asking adults to imitate her. In his story "The Celebration of Christmas," one character expresses the sentiment that Schleiermacher hopes will eventually come to all of his readers: "I can only laugh and exult like a child. Today all people are children to me, and are dear to me just for that reason. Smoothed of serious furrow, the years and worries for once are no longer written on their brows. Eyes sparkle and live again, the presentiment of a beautiful and grace-filled existence within. Also, I myself am become entirely a child again, luckily for me."[68]

Perhaps both developmentalists such as Fowler and those who honor the faith of children such as Schleiermacher can agree that children, like adults, are on a spiritual journey. Harvard psychologist Robert Coles, who spent many hours interviewing children about their spiritual lives, was deeply impressed by "the abiding interest they have in reflecting about human nature, about the reasons people behave as they do, about the mysteries of the universe as evidenced in the earth, the sun, the moon, the stars."[69] He uses a model of pilgrimage to describe their religious ideas and concerns, noting that the pilgrimage begins early: "How young we are when we start wondering about it all, the nature of the journey and of the final destination."[70]

This is not to say that all children are naturally spiritual, but only to allow that most think about the big questions of life. Coles calls some children secular seekers, saying, "Pascal's dilemma is the dilemma of many of the children I have met, who seek faith with all their heart, all their might, yet also know much of the honest self-confrontation of twentieth century secular soul-searching." Children, religious and secular, are, like adults, all "on the edge," Coles claims, seeking and doubting all at once.[71] Coles's pilgrimage model captures more of the diversity of faith that exists in children and adults alike without losing the insight that children may have unique spiritual insights and questions.[72]

In comparison with this complex picture of children's spirituality, theologies assuming the immaturity or purity of children's faith seem just as unsuited to the reality of family life as theologies assuming strong belief or perfect unity between parents. Children, like adults, grow in faith (and continued to be plagued by doubt) over time. Religious formation in the home, whether technically interfaith or not, must not assume same-faith parents equally committed to forming their eager children. Rather, it should encourage the mutual sanctification of children and adults through practices that meet both where they are. Doing so means embracing a contemporary vision of family as domestic church.

Praying as Church in Contemporary Families

In contemporary Catholic theology, families are called domestic churches.[73] John Paul II claims that a family shares in the mission of the church, "placing itself in what it is and what it does as an 'intimate community of life and love' at the service of the church and of society."[74] The family has a rich spirituality in the home but is also directed outward to live for Christ and for others. Concretely, as priests of the domestic church, parents are given responsibility not just for teaching prayers and formally instructing children in the faith but for building a Christian ethos in their home by "constantly review[ing] the family's environment and atmosphere, lifestyle and priorities . . . so that the whole life of the home [will] be suffused with the values and perspectives of Christian faith."[75] Children can also minister to their parents, for "parents not only communicate the Gospel to their children, but from their children they can themselves receive the same Gospel as deeply lived by them."[76] As domestic churches, families are to deepen their faith and take it out into the world.[77]

Research suggests that children from families that engage in intentional faith-based practices with their families are more likely to have strong faith later in life, perhaps because practices "helped form the narrative structure of religious meaning" in their home.[78] For better and for worse, homes are the locus of most of our significant encounters with (and doubts about) the existence of the holy. Christian families ought to own their calling to be a church because it is within families that people are loved, fail to love, sin, are forgiven, and have any number of other experiences that communicate to them something about God's presence or absence. Failing to place these experiences in the context of faith would be overlooking a major resource in the lives of most Christians. Moreover, accepting the alternative of avoiding church language by speaking simply of the vocation of parents would mean giving up the potentially radical idea that in the family, all are church together. In the domestic church, it is not only parents who have vocations; the family as a Christian community is called to discipleship.

Yet, because families in a world of religious pluralism are significantly different from those in a tightly unified Catholic subculture, being a domestic church today must mean acknowledging the faith struggles and differences of both adults and children. Parents must acknowledge their responsibility for the souls of their children, but children must also accept responsibility for their own spiritual lives, as well as their potential to be prophets to their parents. The formation that the church has traditionally placed in the hands of parents would become a shared mission as families seek to be a church together.

Church leaders today call parents "first educators" of their children, and ask them to adopt traditional religious practices in their homes. John Paul II insists that parents have a responsibility to pray with their children because nothing else will shape them as profoundly. "Only by praying together with their children," he claims, "can a father and mother—exercising their royal priesthood—penetrate the innermost depths of their children's hearts and leave an impression that the future events in their lives will not be able to efface."[79] He especially commends the divine office, popular devotions, and the rosary.[80] The U.S. bishops expand the possibilities for spiritual practice, telling families that whether they are celebrating family birthdays, lighting Advent candles, or blessing a new house, they are being church together.[81] The church tells families that through practices like these they become stronger, more of a community, because they are focused on something more important than meeting daily needs.[82] They hope that this vision of Christian prayer and ritual will become normative in ordinary Christian homes.

However, since many find traditional forms of prayer and ritual unfulfilling, some theologians argue that the daily life of families provides plentiful opportunities for spiritual growth. Bonnie Miller-McLemore claims that faith is not only acted out in prayer and ritual but "*is* what we do in time and space, with our bodies and through our movements . . . playing with children after school, interacting around dinner, greeting and parting, attending and pondering—these practices are formative of faith. They train our eyes to see God amid change and time."[83] Just in attending to each other, members of families engage in spiritual disciplines. Christian families, some writers suggest, should focus on cultivating an awareness of the presence of grace in the ordinary.

However, as important as it is to seize opportunities as they arise in family life, intentional spiritual practices are also crucial parts of cultivating resistance to the excesses of modern culture because they encourage growth in virtues that this culture tends to stifle.[84] It is good to make more room for seeing God in the ordinary. Faith can be found in unexpected places, applied to the smallest of acts, and related to a family's way of being. However, prayer can make a profound contribution to the formation of imagination and emotion, as it inculcates gratitude, reverence, and love of God.[85] Placing one's needs before God is an acknowledgment of one's own limits. Without this kind of formation, it will be difficult to stand against the tide of a culture that directs family members to avoid communion and focus solely on their own desires. The practice of prayer has the potential to transform a family's understanding of what its life together is all about. Prayer is also a uniquely solid foundation for social justice. Expressing gratitude, admitting sin, and asking for help remind human beings of their insufficiency and link them with others in their city, nation, and world who are similarly flawed and seeking compassion.[86]

Prayer can be a practice of resistance for the domestic church if it is approached with knowledge of potential difficulties. In the theology of John Paul, prayer is central to a family's life together as church, a crucial part of their efforts to become more a community of love, and a solid foundation for their service to society.[87] This is a positive and prophetic vision. However, it is important to consider the possibility that family members may differ among themselves about faith and how it ought to be practiced. What if children question the existence of God or lack interest in spirituality? What if parents are troubled by doubts about the divinity of Christ or the holiness of the church? What if a child or spouse objects to shared prayer or religious ritual? What if spouses disagree about the kinds of practices they ought to embrace? Fissures like these mark contemporary families and disrupt their attempts at unified practice. Being domestic church is a high expectation for families any time, but it is even harder for families living in a world where unity of belief cannot be taken for granted.

The prayer of the contemporary domestic church should not run from or smooth over the struggle to sustain faith and be in community with people who may differ in belief and practice. Spouses need to confront their own spiritual differences and take seriously children's religious needs, desires, doubts, and beliefs. A good family practice would respect what moves and grounds all family members. The key would be recognizing that adults and children alike approach the table from some point on their journey of faith. Their prayer should be directed to binding them together and giving them the strength they need to share a journey—as much and as well as they can.

This practice of prayer would be a practice of both internal and external resistance. On the one hand, if the practice honestly respects the differing faith journeys of all members and asks of them joint responsibility for spiritual growth, it could open families to communion in ways that profoundly challenge stereotypes and hierarchies implicit in much of Christian thinking about family. On the other hand, by refusing to give in and abandon the practice despite the difficulties, by persisting in prayer while honestly acknowledging differences and doubts, families can strengthen their compassion for others. Key elements of prayer as resistance might be silence, gratitude, immersion, reflection, and petition.

Silence

Knowing oneself requires carving out a time of silence in a world where it is in short supply. With the TV, computer, and cellphones turned off, members of a family can find a place to be quiet and engage in contemplation, defined by Dean Brackley as "paying close attention to reality and allowing the truth to sink in, penetrate us, and stir our feelings and thoughts."[88] The aim of silent contemplation is to disengage from unreflective living in order to engage "the Holy Mystery at the heart of reality, a personal Mystery that addresses us and invites a response."[89] When children are young, a time of shared silence may be especially helpful, as it is difficult for most children to be silent for long or to understand the object of silence. Later, when children are older, family members may want to seek quiet time on their own, while reminding each other to take some time for silence before going off to school, work, or bed. Given the difficulties many have adhering to regular spiritual practice, however, there is an argument for taking this time together. Moreover, if silence is a way to finding one's center through engaging the holy, being silent together may help families center themselves as a community of faith committed to deepening their relationships with one another. Together, they can appreciate their connectedness in a quest for the holy, however they conceive it.

If some have trouble finding God in the silence, the pain of this difficulty can be eased with the knowledge that others in the family are there for support. Mother Theresa sought God but did not experience the consolation of divine presence through much of her life, but she continued in fidelity to the cross.[90] Even when we seek God's presence but experience "the dark night," silence can reorient us to God's project in history. Still, it is important to keep striving to hear God, who is constantly speaking a word of love to us.[91]

This way of practicing "interiority" can be a foundation for resisting the culture of consumerism and its accompanying lack of regard for covenantal relationships and compassion for others. As Brackley puts it, "Our frailty and our fears block our way to serious commitment. To respond with love to a world which seems to have gone wrong in fundamental ways, a broken world, we must get free to love."[92] In this sense, it makes sense to call the silent seeking of God "a social and political act."[93]

Gratitude

A family's practice of prayer should include a time for giving thanks for whatever brings them joy. Mark Chmiel tells how his late wife, the photojournalist Mev Puleo, used rosary beads to say her "gratitudes" before going to sleep.[94] A simple practice, she found that it made her less prideful and more peaceful. By remembering the events of the day as blessings, she was able to de-center herself and move beyond her own worries to study and photograph marginalized peoples and bring their plight to the attention of the affluent. The practice of giving thanks allowed her to appreciate the important people in her life and maintain her commitment to social justice. Without gratitude, worry and self-centeredness may have limited her, as it limits so many others.[95] By speaking individual "gratitudes" aloud, family members can cultivate a sense of abundance that can open up space for compassion for others.

Immersion

A practice of prayer ought to include some form of getting out of one's own head and orienting oneself in Christian faith. Ordinarily this is done through reading scripture, spiritual texts, or stories of saints. Listening to Christian music or looking at holy objects can also help to engage the imagination through the senses. Immersing ourselves in the narratives of holy men and women and the Bible seems a particularly important way to dislodge dominant cultural narratives and think about our lives in terms of the

Christian story. James Keating and David McCarthy write, "By entering into communion with Christ, we discover who we are. . . . This is the mystery of the saints: they have not grasped the fullness of our good end and the possibilities of human life, as much as they have been gripped by Christ."[96] More accessible than many formal prayers, stories can engage the mind and the heart.

The difficulty here is that readings or music that some experience as spiritual may not be inspiring for others. Finding sources that are inspiring, challenging, and transformative for all will require a shift in thinking. Spouses will have to listen hard to and open themselves to what moves the other. Children may present an even greater challenge. Werner Jeanrond asks, "Are we afraid of the forms of expression of our children's belief in God, which may differ from ours? Do we allow only our 'adult' expression of faith a place in the church or do we give space, time and language to the new and possibly different experiences of faith that our children have?"[97] Jeanrond's call to listen to what children want can be seen as analogous to John Wall's understanding of a childist ethic. Wall argues that paying attention to children means confronting both their radical otherness and our deep responsibilities to other human beings. He calls for a de-centering moment in which "children's experiences must be allowed to disrupt and constantly open up even the interpretive assumption adults bring to them."[98]

This notion of openness to the potential disruption of children ought to be applied, with appropriate limits, to families as well. Family religious practice should be "a mutual process in which those involved learn from each other . . . a reversal of the usual situation of teaching and learning; before God children, teenagers and grown-ups are linked in a common situation of learning."[99] This may seem hard to imagine, but trying it is necessary if parents are to honestly take up Wall's challenge to answer the dilemma of the child with a "responsiveness and self-critique" appropriate to adherents of a tradition that "trace[s] a transformed world to the possibilities incarnated in an infant's birth."[100]

Concretely, responding to children means incorporating sources that are spiritual to them. This might mean reading stories of children's heroes along with Christian saints, listening to Christian rock or other music that children find moving, or finding objects that, while not specifically religious, evoke spiritual feeling in some members of the family. The dangers in being so open are the possibility of losing the distinctive character of the

tradition and giving into the self-centered spirituality of consumer culture.[101] However, the greater danger is that, by limiting the holy, parents will
fail to engage children at all. Those family members who are stronger in
their belief should attempt to make the tradition live for others but should
also make known their willingness to find wisdom in other texts, stories,
and songs.

Reflection

Families need to make room in their spiritual practice for reflection,
questioning, exploration, and explanation. Children, especially, have questions about why rituals are done a certain way, about the strange stories of
Jesus and the saints, about belief itself. Opening oneself to conversation is
necessary, even though it places parents in a vulnerable position. Are we
afraid of children's unbelief, of questions for which we have no good answers? Do we worry about their boredom with our ideas about God and our
ways of expressing deeply held beliefs? Just as Jeanrond calls the church to
give up the idea of religion as a comfort and accept it as a challenge that
may lead to unexpected places, families ought to embrace the challenge of
honest religious conversation, for without it, all members are left with less
understanding of themselves, each other, and their faith.[102]

Religious practice in families ought to be similar to the best of modern
catechesis, which, instead of attempting to transmit faith to those with none,
accepts differences and seeks growth in holiness for all. The goal cannot be
just conversion for the neophytes, for "each person is confronted by the
Gospel."[103] In religious families, "the reciprocal dynamic in conversation allows parents and children to co-construct meaning."[104] This does not mean
forgetting children's vulnerability or desire for direction, but it does mean
acknowledging a need for parents and children to reflect and grow together.

Petition

Kathleen and Jim McGinnis claim that if parents "want these two
worlds—prayer and action—to come together in a single, faith-full life," it
makes sense "to include the needs of others in our family prayers."[105] They
suggest beginning with petitions for friends and family and expanding to
include people who family members have read about or encountered in
service work. Asking for God's mercy and justice is a way to express concern for others that children can understand. It is an easy way for those

uncomfortable with prayer to participate in spiritual practice, connecting faith and compassion.

Dean Brackley radicalizes the idea of petition by defining it as asking God to "intensify God's own activity within us."[106] He notes that in the Lord's Prayer we "don't ask for just anything . . . but that God's reign come, with its justice, peace, and abundant life. All petitions should fit under that umbrella."[107] And though God can work miracles or bring about "disproportionate surprises" in our lives, because God works in and through human beings, ordinarily we ask for God to help us to bring about God's kingdom. Mev Puleo's prayer in 1991 in the midst of the first Iraq war provides a powerful example: "God have mercy. God, empower us to strive and struggle with integrity, love and humility for a better world, to strive and struggle courageously, willing to risk, willing to be inaccomodated, placing our freedom on behalf of others' unfreedom—empower and inspire us to act creatively and justly and lovingly and disruptingly. Life as usual cannot go on, as it grinds the poor into the dust and sand—sick, sick, sick. God, heal this sick world and let us be your hands."[108]

In a practice of prayer involving silence, gratitude, immersion, reflection, and petition, Christian families can nurture their resistance to everything in our culture that diminishes persons. In their willingness to be vulnerable in shared prayer, they can bind themselves to God and each other and bring the energy of that relatedness to the world. This more humble theological understanding of the spiritual duties of Christian families takes seriously the insights of children and the responsibilities of parents to form their children in the faith, but it also requires attentiveness to religious diversity and the reality of human finitude. On this journey, parents and children have much to offer each other.

Conclusion: Practices of Resistance as Ordinary Morality

To acknowledge the diversity and difficulty of faith as I have done in this chapter complicates the discussion of prayer and of Christian family ethics in general. It would be far easier to assume strong, shared commitment. However, not to acknowledge it would be to step around a very real part of contemporary family life. It is better to begin with the actual situation and seek new ways of adapting the tradition, not abandoning practices of faith, but continuing to work through them. If this sort of honesty and commitment is difficult for individuals or married couples, it is even more so for families with children who strive not only to love each other but also to contribute to the cause of justice in the world. Prayer is not the easiest Christian family practice but rather the most challenging. Yet it is, as Brackley claims, necessary if families want to be free to love.

Notes

This chapter is based in part on Julie Hanlon Rubio, "Praying in Contemporary Christian Families," in *Children's Voices: Children's Perspectives in Ethics, Theology, and Religious Education*, ed. Annemie Dillen and Didier Pollefeyt (Leuven, Belgium: BETL, Peeters-Publishers, 2009).

1. Stanley Hauerwas, "The Family as a School for Character," in *Perspectives on Marriage: A Reader*, ed. Kieran Scott and Michael Warren (Oxford: Oxford University Press, 1993), 152.
2. Ibid., 148. Theologian Jeff Astley criticizes Hauerwas's emphasis on the church, arguing that families do form character while many churches are incapable of doing so. See Astley, "The Role of Family in the Formation and Criticism of Faith," in *The Family in Theological Perspective*, ed. Stephen C. Barton (Edinburgh: T & T Clark, 1996), 187–202.
3. Kieran Scott, "A Spirituality of Resistance for Marriage," in *Perspectives on Marriage: A Reader*, ed. Kieran Scott and Michael Warren (Oxford: Oxford University Press, 1993), 400.
4. Bonnie Miller-McLemore, *In the Midst of Chaos: Caring for Children as Spiritual Practice* (San Francisco: Jossey-Bass, 2007), 57.
5. Ibid.
6. See, for instance, Dolores Curran, *Family Prayer* (West Mystic, CT: Twenty-third, 1978); Robert E. Webber, *The Book of Family Prayer* (Peabody, MA: Hendrickson, 1996); Jacquelyn Lindsey, *Catholic Family Prayer Book* (Huntington, IN: Our Sunday Visitor, 2001); Christopher Anderson, Susan Gleason Anderson, and Lavonne Neff, *A Prayer Book for Catholic Families* (Chicago: Loyola Press, 2000).
7. Christine Firer Hinze, "Catholic: Family Unity and Diversity within the Body of Christ," in *Faith Traditions and the Family*, ed. Phyllis D. Airhart and Margaret Lamberts Bendroth (Louisville, KY: Westminster John Knox Press, 1996), 53–72.
8. Ibid., 64. Most families in the post–Vatican II church were, Hinze asserts, unaware "of the lofty and provocative mission that their leaders had begun to propose for them." Only participation in the sacraments and personal prayer increased during this period. Ibid., 65.
9. Michael G. Lawler, Gail Risch, and Lisa Riley, "Church Experience of Interchurch and Same-Sex Couples," *Family Ministry* 13.4 (1999): 36.

10. See Portier, "Here Come the Evangelical Catholics," 48–50. Although Portier concentrates his attention on the minority of postsubculture Catholics who are very committed to Catholic identity, he acknowledges that the majority of young adult Catholics are "loosely affiliated." Ibid., 51.

11. *Familiaris consortio*, nos. 51–63. Bourg, *Where Two or Three Are Gathered*, is the most important theological treatment of the concept.

12. Nearly all adults who identify themselves as religious question aspects of their religious traditions, but many also experience doubt or find it difficult to keep believing everything they profess during church services in the face of questions they cannot answer. An articulate defense of a faith never fully beyond doubt is Andrew Sullivan, "My Problem with Christianity," www.time.com/time/magazine/article/0,9171,1191826,00.html (accessed December 15, 2008). Developmental models of faith are inadequate to the lived experience of many adults.

13. Chris J. Boyatzis, David C. Dollahite, and Loren D. Marks, "The Family as a Context for Religious and Spiritual Development in Children and Youth," in *The Handbook of Spiritual Development in Childhood and Adolescence*, ed. Eugene C. Roehlkepartain (Thousand Oaks, CA: Sage, 2006), 297. The authors report that 90 percent of parents in the United States want their children to have religious training of some kind.

14. O. M. Bakke, *When Children Became People: The Birth of Childhood in Early Christianity*, trans. Brian McNeil (Minneapolis, MN: Fortress Press, 2005), 153–54. See esp. Ephesians 6:1, 6:4; Colossians 3:20; Titus 2:4, 1:6–9; 1 Timothy 3:4.

15. Ibid., 157.

16. Ibid., 158–89.

17. Ibid., 160.

18. Vigen Guroian, "The Ecclesial Family: John Chrysostom on Parenthood and Children," in *The Child in Christian Thought*, ed. Marcia J. Bunge (Grand Rapids, MI: Eerdmans, 2001), 69.

19. John Chrysostom, "Homily 12 on Colossians 4:18," in *On Marriage and Family Life* (Crestwood, NY: St. Vladimir's Press, 1986), 76.

20. John Chrysostom, "An Address on the Vainglory and the Right Way for Parents to Bring Up Their Children," in *Christianity and Pagan Culture in the Later Roman Empire*, trans. M. L. W. Laistner (Ithaca, NY: Cornell University Press, 1951), 93.

21. Chrysostom, *On Marriage and Family Life*, 44.

22. Jane E. Strohl, "The Child in Luther's Theology: 'For What Purpose Do We Older Folks Exist, Other Than to Care for . . . the Young?'" in *The Child in Christian Thought*, ed. Marcia J. Bunge (Grand Rapids, MI: Eerdmans, 2001), 140, 146.

23. Barbara Pitkin, "'The Heritage of the Lord': Children in the Theology of John Calvin," in *The Child in Christian Thought*, ed. Marcia J. Bunge (Grand Rapids, MI: Eerdmans, 2001), 174.

24. Keith Graber Miller, "Complex Innocence, Obligatory Nurturance, and Parental Vigilance: 'The Child' in the Work of Menno Simons," in *The Child in Christian Thought*, ed. Marcia J. Bunge (Grand Rapids, MI: Eerdmans, 2001), 207–8.

25. Horace Bushnell, *Christian Nurture,* quoted in Margaret Bendroth, "Horace Bushnell's *Christian Nurture,*" in *The Child in Christian Thought,* ed. Marcia J. Bunge (Grand Rapids, MI: Eerdmans, 2001), 356. Others who emphasized the family's role as domestic church include Chrysostom, Gregory of Nazianzus, and St. Augustine. See Florence Caffrey Bourg, "Domestic Church: A New Frontier in Ecclesiology," *Horizons* 29.1 (2002): 42–63, for a fuller discussion.

26. *Familiaris consortio,* no. 38.

27. Barbara Pitkin claims, "In Calvin's view, it was society's duty to provide the right conditions for raising children to be godly." "Heritage of the Lord," 174.

28. Miller, "Complex Innocence," 219–22. Miller offers a contemporary example of a Mennonite dedication service for infants that includes a congregation's promise "to share in your child's nurture and well-being." Ibid., 225. Strohl, "Child in Luther's Theology," 146.

29. Judith M. Gundry-Volf, "The Least and the Greatest: Children in the New Testament," in *The Child in Christian Thought,* ed. Marcia J. Bunge (Grand Rapids, MI: Eerdmans, 2001), 44.

30. Hinze, "Catholic," 55–56.

31. Ibid., 57.

32. Ibid., 58.

33. Ibid., 61.

34. Ibid., 64.

35. Ibid., 65.

36. Curran, *Family Prayer,* 32.

37. Ibid., 32. See also McGinnis and McGinnis, *Parenting for Peace and Justice,* 141–43, who offer a less rosy view of trying to pray with teens.

38. *Familiaris consortio,* nos. 68 and 77.

39. Lee M. Williams and Michael G. Lawler attest to the growing numbers of intermarried Catholics in "Marital Satisfaction and Religious Heterogamy: A Comparison of Interchurch and Same-Church Individuals," *Journal of Family Issues* 24 (2003): 465. Marsha Wiggins Frame reports that more than 50 percent of American marriages are mixed in "The Challenge of Intercultural Marriage: Strategies for Pastoral Care," *Pastoral Psychology* 52.3 (2004): 219. Protestants intermarry at even higher rates (Williams and Lawler, "Marital Satisfaction and Religious Heterogamy," 465). I will use the term *interfaith* to describe marriages between a Christian and a person of another religion and between two Christians of different denominations.

40. Bruce T. Morrill, "Music, Liturgy, and Religious Formation," in *Religious Education of Boys and Girls,* ed. Werner G. Jeanrond and Lisa Sowle Cahill (London: SCM Press, 2002), 104. On the pastoral side, some suggest that couples work on forming a combination religious identity by blending their backgrounds, with little understanding of the theological difficulties involved. Frame, "Challenge of Intercultural Marriage," 228.

41. Williams and Lawler, "Marital Satisfaction and Religious Heterogamy," 474.

42. Boyatzis, Dollahite, and Marks, "Family as a Context," 302. This is so for interreligious families as well, in which children most often are reared in the mother's faith tradition. Around the world, women are more religious, attend

services more often, pray more, and have more conversations about religion with their children.

43. Curran, *Family Prayer*, 41–42.
44. Lawler, *Marriage and the Catholic Church*, 131.
45. Ibid.
46. Ibid., 132.
47. Center for Marriage and Family, Creighton University, *Marriage Preparation in the Catholic Church: Getting It Right*, November 1995, 35. Still, much depends on the couple's religiosity at engagement. See Williams and Lawler, "Marital Satisfaction and Religious Heterogamy," 476.
48. Williams and Lawler, "Marital Satisfaction and Religious Heterogamy," 466.
49. Ibid., 475. This is consistent with other studies, the authors report.
50. Ibid., 476.
51. Lawler, *Marriage and the Catholic Church*, 134.
52. R. R. Reno, "Interreligious Marriage: A Personal Reflection," in *Marriage in the Christian Tradition*, ed. Todd A. Salzman, Thomas M. Kelly, and John O'Keefe (New York: Crossroad, 2004), 248.
53. Ibid., 244.
54. Ibid. He "despaired of an invisible Christianity," 245.
55. Lawler, *Disputed Questions*, 134.
56. Ibid., 136.
57. Ibid.
58. In "Generations of American Catholics," *CTSA Proceedings* 53 (2008): 1–17, James Davidson reports that only 35 percent of millennials say they would never leave the church (versus 69% of the pre–Vatican II generation), and even lower percentages attend Mass weekly or worry about disagreeing with the magisterium on moral issues. The generational effect is much more significant than age.
59. See Laura H. Lippman and Julie Dombrowski Kieth, "The Demographics of Spirituality among Youth: International Perspectives," in *The Handbook of Spiritual Development in Childhood and Adolescence*, ed. Eugene C. Roehlkepartain (Thousand Oaks, CA: Sage, 2006), 109–23. Eighty-four percent of American youths age thirteen to seventeen believe in God, and about half report that religion is very important to them. Ibid., 118.
60. See "U.S. Religious Landscape Survey," http://pewforum.org/reports (accessed November 15, 2008). The survey of thirty-five thousand adults was completed in 2007.
61. This reality is acknowledged in most parish sacramental preparation programs, in which the opportunity to catechize parents is often seized in the form of a required information class. Many adults struggle to explain the beauty of the Eucharist or the need for Reconciliation to their children. Some send their children to religious education and see that they receive the sacraments of initiation but rarely attend Mass as a family.
62. James Fowler, "A Gradual Introduction into the Faith," in *Transmission of Faith to the Next Generation*, ed. Norbert Greinacher and Virgil Elizondo (Edinburgh: T and T Clark, 1984), 51–52. See also James W. Fowler and Mary Lynn Dell, "Stages of Faith from Infancy to Adolescence: Reflections on Three Decades of

Faith Development Theory," in *The Handbook of Spiritual Development in Childhood and Adolescence*, ed. Eugene C. Roehlkepartain (Thousand Oaks, CA: Sage, 2006), 34–45. Fowler reviews decades of critical commentary and reasserts the validity of the model but acknowledges that it will need to be tested with a broader range of faith traditions.

63. Fowler, "Gradual Introduction," 41–44.

64. Fowler's initial research was based on interviews completed in the 1970s. Since that time, the results have been replicated into the 1990s. Fowler and Dell, "Stages of Faith," 35, 44.

65. See Sofia Cavaletti, "The Child as Parable," *Occasional Papers from the Center for Theology and Children* 1, no. 3 (2000): 1–12.

66. See Ann M. Garrido, *Mustard Seed Preaching* (Chicago: Archdiocese of Chicago, 2004). Miller-McLemore also notes that faith development does not necessarily accompany maturation and points out that faith may be "as likely to be lost in adolescence and adulthood as to grow." *In the Midst of Chaos*, 68–69. She wants to honor the capacity of children for wonder as possibly superior to that of adults.

67. Dawn DeVries, "'Be Converted and Become as Little Children': Friedrich Schleiermacher on the Religious Significance of Childhood," in *The Child in Christian Thought*, ed. Marcia J. Bunge (Grand Rapids, MI: Eerdmans, 2001), 337–39.

68. Quoted in DeVries, "'Be Converted and Become as Little Children,'" 338.

69. Robert Coles, *The Spiritual Life of Children* (Boston: Houghton Mifflin, 1990), 332.

70. Ibid., 355.

71. Ibid., 301.

72. In addition to Coles, see Gerhard Buttner, "Where Do Children Get Their Theology?" and Elaine Champagne, "Children's Inner Voice: Exploring Children's Contribution to Spirituality," both in *Children's Voices: Children's Perspectives in Ethics, Theology and Religious Education*, ed. Annemie Dillen and Didier Pollefeyt (Leuven, Belg.: BETL Peeters Press, 2009), both of which analyze children's conversations about spiritual things and reveal children struggling to make sense of faith. John Wall's insight that romantic views of children neglect children's unique dependent status as beings who stand in need of adult guidance is also an important corrective. Wall, "Childhood Studies, Hermeneutics, and Theological Ethics," *Journal of Religion* 86, no. 4 (2006): 531.

73. See Bourg's survey of the literature in *Where Two of Three Are Gathered*, 9–22.

74. *Familiaris consortio*, no. 50.

75. Thomas H. Groome, "Total Catechetical Education," in *Religious Education of Boys and Girls*, ed. Werner G. Jeanrond and Lisa Sowle Cahill (London: SCM Press, 2002), 84.

76. *Familiaris consortio*, no. 52.

77. Matthew Sherman offers a rich comparison of family theology in the pre- and post–Vatican II eras and the age of John Paul II and shows that the late pope fruitfully brought together pre–Vatican II family piety with post–Vatican II social consciousness. *"Become What You Receive": A Transformative, Eucharistic Vision of Family and Prayer* (PhD diss., Boston College, 2009).

78. Boyatzis, Dollahite, and Marks, " Family as a Context," 298. Many studies show a connection between family religious practice and the continuing faith of children. For an overview of the literature, see also Leif Kehrwald, "Families and Christian Practice," *Family Ministry* 13, no. 4 (1999): 54–57.

79. *Familiaris consortio*, no. 60.

80. Ibid., no. 61.

81. U.S. Bishops, *Follow the Way of Love*, 9–10.

82. Julie Hanlon Rubio, "Does Family Conflict with Community," *Theological Studies* 58 (December 1997): 615–17.

83. Miller-McLemore, *In the Midst of Chaos*, 57 (emphasis mine).

84. Fowler, "Gradual Introduction into the Faith," 51.

85. Ibid., 52.

86. Kavanaugh, *Following Christ in a Consumer Society*, 179–80, speaks of the centering power of prayer that makes it easier to avoid becoming so lost in the particulars of one's life that one cannot see the significance of the ordinary. He also claims, "Laboring for justice demands the support of a culture-transcending faith." Ibid., xii.

87. *Familiaris consortio*, no. 64.

88. Brackley, *Call to Discernment*, 225.

89. Ibid.

90. See John F. Kavanaugh, "Godforsakenness: 'Finding One's Heart's Desire,'" *America*, October 1, 2007, 8.

91. Cooke calls this "uncreated grace." "Christian Marriage," 48.

92. Brackley, *Call to Discernment*, 10.

93. Kavanaugh, *Following Christ in a Consumer Society*, 152. McGinnis and McGinnis, quoting Elise Boulding, reflect on the power of silence to encourage peacefulness in *Parenting for Peace and Justice*, 119.

94. Mark J. Chmiel, *The Book of Mev* (Bloomington, IN: Xlibris, 2005), 41.

95. See Ed Vacek, "Gifts, God, Generosity and Gratitude," in *Spirituality and Moral Theology*, ed. James Keating (New York: Paulist, 2000), 81–125.

96. Keating and McCarthy, "Moral Theology with the Saints," 205.

97. Werner G. Jeanrond, "Faith, Formation, and Freedom: Categories of Religious Education in the Church," in *Religious Education of Boys and Girls*, ed. Werner G. Jeanrond and Lisa Sowle Cahill (London: SCM Press, 2002), 67.

98. Wall, "Childhood Studies," 537. Later he notes that confronting the child calls for creative responsibility in adults who, in relation to children, are face to face with their responsibility for others. Ibid., 543.

99. Norbert Mette, "The Christian Community's Task in Religious Education," in *Transmission of Faith to the Next Generation*, ed. Norbert Greinacher and Virgil Elizondo (Edinburgh: T and T Clark, 1984), 74. This can be so even if adults bring greater theological knowledge and faith experience to the table.

100. Wall, "Childhood Studies," 548.

101. See Scott's critique of popular spirituality, "Spirituality of Resistance," 398–402.

102. Jeanrond, "Faith, Formation, and Freedom," 70.

103. Gerard Vogelisen, "Catechesis: Handing on the Faith Today," in *Transmission of Faith to the Next Generation*, ed. Norbert Greinacher and Virgil Elizondo (Edinburgh: T and T Clark, 1984), 26.

104. Boyatzis, Dollahite, and Marks, "Family as a Context," 300.
105. McGinnis and McGinnis, *Parenting for Peace and Justice*, 121.
106. Brackley, quoting Xavier Zubiri, in *Call to Discernment*, 231.
107. Ibid., 230.
108. Quoted in Chmiel, *Book of Mev*, 372.

Conclusion

Practices of Resistance as Ordinary Morality

I began this book by talking about the marginalization of ordinary life in Christian ethics. The gap between issues taken up in theology journals and those discussed at dinner tables, coffeehouses, and parish socials is overly wide. When families struggle to decide how to allocate their time, where to buy a house, or what job to take, they are on their own, because few theologians have addressed these sorts of concerns. These mundane choices seem too minor to merit theological analysis.

However, I have argued that ordinary moral dilemmas are worthy of sustained ethical reflection. Decisions about how to spend time, money, and energy are the most fundamental moral decisions most of us make. These choices provide the framework within which we enter into relationship with God, engage the world around us, pursue friendship and intimacy, raise children, and respond or fail to respond to the suffering of other human beings. Through our everyday choices, we construct our lives. We choose worthy and unworthy pursuits. We make time for the people we love or continue to find ourselves too busy. We contribute or fail to contribute to social change.

It is important to know where we stand on complex issues such as end-of-life care, torture, abortion, humanitarian intervention, globalization, and capital punishment. But thinking through the implications of our smaller, daily choices is, I submit, our primary ethical responsibility, because it is with these choices that we will have our largest impact on both those nearest to us and society as a whole. Each decision may seem minor when considered in itself, but when repeated over and over, decisions form significant patterns. Through the life patterns of millions of individuals and families, society itself takes shape. When couples choose to take time for intimacy, they build their relationship. When they eat together at a table where all are welcome, they extend their communion to their children and others around them. When they buy sustainably grown food, they help to slow environmental destruction. When they give a portion of their income away, they limit consumerism and create new opportunities for those in poverty. When they give a portion of their time to service, they have the chance to change the lives of others and be changed in their own hearts. When they claim time for prayer, they open themselves to God and one another. Small decisions matter.

Yet seeking answers to the problems I have addressed in this book is difficult because the details of individual lives are so different. Sometimes we simply will not find specific practices that bind everyone in exactly the same way. The recommendations I have made are flexible and open to adaptation. They may not work for every family all the time. This does not mean, however, that we should give up the process of moral discernment regarding ordinary choices. Living a moral life is not primarily about rules or norms but about striving to become better persons through responding to God's calling. There will be differences among us, but being able to rely on Christian community and tradition for wisdom as we make decisions is a great gift. In this struggle, we are not alone.

Practices of resistance are necessary if Christians want to avoid the very real problems that are pervasive in middle-class American family life. Only intentional practices can enable the majority of Christians who live in families to value both relationships and social change, to connect love and justice, to live up to the best of the Catholic tradition on marriage and its social teachings. Without them it is far too easy to give in. Even with them we will, of course, fall short. Human beings, as Flannery O'Connor so vividly showed us, are limited, but we can remember this and still strive to become better.

Struggling to live well and do what we can to improve the lives of others is what being a Christian is all about. It is, as Mev Puleo said, "the same struggle for life, against death in all its forms."[1] Surely this struggle is worth all the time and energy we have to give it.

Note

1. Mev Puleo, *The Struggle Is One: Voices and Visions of Liberation* (New York: SUNY Press, 1994), 5.

Index